STILL A MOTHER

STILL A MOTHER

Noncustodial Mothers, Gendered
Institutions, and Social Change

Jackie Krasas

CORNELL UNIVERSITY PRESS **ITHACA AND LONDON**

First published 2021 by Cornell University Press

Library of Congress Cataloging-in-Publication Data

Names: Krasas, Jackie, 1965- author.
Title: Still a mother : noncustodial mothers, gendered institutions, and social change / Jackie Krasas.
Description: Ithaca [New York] : Cornell University Press, 2021. | Includes bibliographical references and index.
Identifiers: LCCN 2020021019 (print) | LCCN 2020021020 (ebook) | ISBN 9781501754296 (hardcover) | ISBN 9781501754302 (paperback) | ISBN 9781501754319 (pdf) | ISBN 9781501754326 (epub)
Subjects: LCSH: Absentee mothers—United States. | Motherhood—United States. | Custody of children—Social aspects—United States. | Social institutions—United States.
Classification: LCC HQ759.3 .K73 2021 (print) | LCC HQ759.3 (ebook) | DDC 306.874/3–dc23
LC record available at https://lccn.loc.gov/2020021019
LC ebook record available at https://lccn.loc.gov/2020021020

For the noncustodial mothers who so generously gave
of their time for this book

Contents

Acknowledgments

Research and writing are messy endeavors. There are fits and starts. Life happens. Our plans fall apart. We arrive at a polished manuscript only through the combined efforts of our unseen supporters, who are there through the good, the bad, the ugly, and the utterly ridiculous. I owe a debt of gratitude to my family, my friends, and my feminist communities for keeping me going. Thanks for listening, for encouraging me, and for making me laugh. Only the anxiety of leaving someone out prevents me from attempting to list everyone, but you know who you are. Cecilia, our experiences together helped me to know what to ask and how to listen to and comprehend what participants had to say. Matthew, I appreciate your amiably ignoring the mounds of papers and books forever increasingly encroaching on our living space. The support from both of you, whether a simple dinner, a bad joke, or a family trip, renewed my spirits so I could look on the manuscript with fresh eyes.

In today's academic environment, I am especially fortunate to have a tenured position at a university that afforded me not only a highly manageable teaching load and a sabbatical during which to write but also the access to health care that carried me through a major illness. I had flexibility and job security so I could care for a sick parent. I am indebted to the College of Arts and Sciences at Lehigh University for financial support and to my colleagues there for their unremitting encouragement. Anna Orchard and Colleen Martell provided editorial support for various incarnations of the manuscript. The writing retreats at our Humanities Center led by Suzanne Edwards provided the gentle peer pressure that I needed during the early, ugly writing days to get a move on. Thank you, Suzanne and all of my colleagues who participated in those retreats, for creating such a generative space. Truly, I would need another ninety thousand words to properly thank my colleagues and friends in my department and the Women, Gender, and Sexuality Studies Program at Lehigh University who provided intellectual community, but also brought dinner for my family and me when I was in treatment.

It has been a pleasure working with Cornell University Press again. Thank you, Fran Benson, for connecting me with Jim Lance, who shepherded this book through a downright constructive editorial process and secured insightful feedback from two anonymous reviewers who gave of their time to think alongside me and offer thoughtful critique. Most importantly, I want to acknowledge all of the noncustodial mothers who spoke so candidly with me at length, through laughter and tears, about deeply personal topics. Wendy Reetz, you were there at the beginning. Others opened up to me because they trusted your judgment. Without your initial help and encouragement, I might not have written a paragraph, much less a book.

STILL A MOTHER

A CONTRADICTION IN TERMS

If motherhood is *being there* (E. Boyd 2002), then mothers without custody of their children are nonmothers. They are anti-mothers. Bad mothers. Undeserving mothers. They are suspect, to be reviled, or at the very least a cautionary tale. For the purposes of this book, a noncustodial mother is one who does not have majority physical or legal custody of her child or children in a postdivorce or post-relationship agreement. This is not a book about mothers who have had children removed by the state, nor is it a book about mothers who had their children adopted. Each of these populations is important in its own right, and their stories are not entirely discontinuous with those of the mothers in this book. The population of noncustodial mothers in this book appears to be growing as post-relationship parenting arrangements are changing. What are the challenges of being a mother without primary custody of one's child? Might there be benefits to being a noncustodial mother? What might the growth of noncustodial motherhood signal to us about motherhood more generally?

Since the 1970s, divorce and child custody have become more gender neutral in the eyes of the law. Families increasingly choose or are assigned shared custody of children in the wake of relationship dissolution. Many, but far from all, custody arrangements will have come into contact with the family court system; however, the outcome of each case is determined in a more fluid manner than a simple custody hearing. Some disputed cases are actually resolved before they come before a judge. Some undergo a formal custody evaluation. Others involve round after round of motions and court appearances, charges of contempt, and changes in parenting time.

As of 2010, shared child custody arrangements were more common than sole mother custody after divorce (Meyer, Cancian, and Cook 2017). However, it is difficult to precisely gauge the size of the noncustodial mother population. There is no single data set to count them. Much of the data on custody arrangements is held at the state and local levels. Many custody arrangements are informal, and not all families have child support orders in place. We do know that in 2016, of the 27 percent of children under twenty-one who had a parent who did not reside with them, 19.6 percent had a custodial father. This figure increased from 16 percent in 1994, representing a 22.5 percent increase in father custody in a little more than twenty years (Grall 2018). While it is problematic to assume that a custodial father always implies there is a corresponding noncustodial mother, we can approximate that 5 percent of all children in the United States have a mother who is noncustodial.

This book arose in part out of my own short-lived journey as a mother without primary custody when I took a new job half a state away. I found it excruciatingly frustrating that, as a gender scholar, I was having feelings about being a noncustodial mother that I knew were socially driven. That is, there were times when I was uncomfortable with my status as a noncustodial mother, even as I looked at my situation with a critical, sociological eye, knowing I should know better than to buy into societal prescriptions of motherhood. I decided to dive into the scholarly literature on noncustodial mothers to better understand my own reality. Finding very little, I decided to conduct my own research and analysis, ultimately leading me to write this book.

Early on, I turned to the internet and eventually found several groups of noncustodial mothers discussing, making sense of, and theorizing about their realities. Hesitantly, I joined in and quickly realized that this seemingly invisible group that I was a part of had existed all around me. I was not the only mother without custody of her child. While my noncustodial journey was brief in comparison to that of many of the mothers I met and spoke with, I remained connected to these communities of mothers who gave me much food for thought. I have enjoyed their company and their spirit since 2008, which makes this a long-term participant observation endeavor. I conducted thirty-five formal, in-depth interviews with noncustodial mothers and have had too many informal conversations and interactions to count. I approached the project as an institutional ethnography, which, although it focuses on the experiences of individuals, endeavors to understand the social relations that shape those experiences. Institutional ethnography is more than just qualitative interviewing. It starts where people are to understand their everyday lives but also attends to power relations, or the relations of ruling (D. Smith 2005). Toward that end, institutional ethnography incorporates multiple sources of data that can include things like interviews and participant observation, as well as discursive analyses of texts or documents.

There are some places where my own experiences will resonate with those of the mothers in this book, but there are many places where my experiences differ. My social location as a cisgender, white, heterosexual, middle-class, tenured professor shaped how I experienced my status. For example, I could easily afford transportation and time away from work to travel to see my daughter and to bring her to me. Child support payments did not mean that I struggled to pay my rent. Some noncustodial mothers I interviewed were similar to me in this regard, but many were not. Despite some obvious differences, the fact that I was a mother who had been noncustodial seemed very important to many of the participants and it likely smoothed the way for more candid discussion than would have been possible had I not had that experience.

My research has several aims. First is the desire to make visible and give voice to a highly stigmatized group of women who hold a seemingly contradictory identity in contemporary US culture. In addition, the analysis seeks to examine common trajectories leading to noncustodial status, the common experiences of noncustodial mothers, and concerns where these lived experiences intersect with gendered social institutions. At the same time, I seek to incorporate a range of experiences, as noncustodial mothers come in all shapes and sizes. Some reflect a portion of the negative stereotypes that tell us only mothers who have done something wrong lose custody of their children. Others more closely resemble June Cleaver. Or Roseanne Barr. Or Clair Huxtable.

This book concerns more than just noncustodial mothers, however. Although they are the immediate subject of the book, the analysis of their experiences provides us with a window into the complexities and contradictions of contemporary motherhood overall (Hays 1996), as well as the varied institutions, from psychology and employment to the legal system and popular opinion, that construct, enforce, and shape motherhood. Contemporary motherhood rests firmly on the ideology of intensive motherhood (discussed in depth in chapters 3 and 4), which promotes both the primacy of mothering in a woman's life and the primacy of a mother in the life of a child. Intensive mothering practices require substantial investments of time and money and an adherence to the mothering expertise of the time (Ennis 2014; Hays 1996). Class, race, and other dimensions of social inequality shape women's ability to closely adhere to the tenets of intensive motherhood, which often cannot be accomplished without the unpaid and underpaid labor of less privileged groups of women.

The ideology of intensive motherhood also resonates with principles of neoliberalism (Giles 2014). As understood by sociologists, neoliberalism is a set of political economic relations that rests on principles of market rationality, individualism, and privatization, resulting in a reduction in government support and oversight of social programs and institutions. Social problems become individualized and conceptualized as failures of individual choices. For example, employment relations in the United States and global North have been subject to neoliberal forces since the 1980s resulting in a decline in decent employment that provides a living wage and important employment protections like sick days and paid family leave, supports that working people need. Neoliberalism is organized on a global scale, with much of the reproductive labor in the global care chain undertaken by poor women, women of color, and women from the global South (Hochschild 2000; Parrenas 2015). Intensive motherhood places mothers in the role of the primary source through which individuals learn to make good choices, and in the absence of necessary social supports, the responsibility (and blame) for raising good, productive citizens rests squarely and solely in the hands of mothers. Thus, neoliberalism and intensive motherhood are mutually reinforcing.

We also live in a time that is purportedly postfeminist, and postracial, where critics of movements for social equality contend that they are longer needed because equality has been achieved (Hall and Rodriguez 2003). Similar discourses are emerging with the advent of marriage equality. Although these are cultural myths, post-ism ideologies have had important effects on power dynamics. When it comes to gender inequalities, gendered language is eschewed in favor of gender neutrality. Critics of affirmative action have struggled against the policy on the grounds that it is racially biased because it takes account of race. In this context, pointing out racism or sexism can be cast as racist or sexist. Intensive motherhood, neoliberalism, and post-isms are powerful companions in the social context of contemporary mothers' lives. The experiences of noncustodial mothers are instructive because they bring to the surface the dynamics of these social forces experienced by other mothers, particularly in heterosexual families, that are more easily hidden until child custody is at stake.

Motherhood and the Sociological Imagination

C. Wright Mills (1959) urged us to connect biography and history in order to understand individuals' experiences in their milieu within the larger social context. Motherhood is a social phenomenon that feels like a highly personal space. Romanticization of motherhood and intensive motherhood have urged us to see motherhood as a highly individualized experience. Yet motherhood is not merely personal.

Motherhood is a concept and status engaged by nearly every variety of feminist theory, although there is very little agreement in regard to its meaning, nature, or anything else. Of biological motherhood alone, assessments range from

its being the means of our oppression (Atwood 1986) to its being an epistemo-
logical advantage (Ruddick 1980). A common theme through much feminist
analysis of motherhood is the distinction between the institution of motherhood,
embedded within and intertwined with deeply patriarchal institutions, and the
experience of motherhood. Adrienne Rich (1976) drew our attention to the fact
that, although highly personal, motherhood is also a social institution. Thus, the
experiences of mothers should be understood in sociohistorical context. In other
words, noncustodial mothers' personal troubles should be understood as public
issues (Mills 1959).

Monolithic and romanticized portraits of motherhood have not held up to intersectional interrogation. The experience of motherhood, however, has never
been *the* experience of motherhood, although feminist theories across the spectrum often proceeded with that unspoken assumption. Much of second-wave
feminism's discussions of motherhood rested implicitly on white, middle-class,
cisgender, and heterosexual motherhood. A classic example is Betty Friedan's
(1963) concept of *the problem that has no name*, the alienation and lack of purpose experienced by suburban college-educated stay-at-home mothers. Friedan's
work did not resonate with mothers who had neither the privilege of college education nor the choice to stay at home full time with their children. The work of
Friedan and other second-wave feminists, however, may have unintentionally contributed to the devaluation of motherhood (Rothman 1989).

While mainstream liberal feminist publications like Friedan's *Feminine Mystique*
pointed to a kind of motherhood malaise, cultural feminists celebrated mothers'
special and embodied closeness to children, an approach that relies heavily on gender essentialism. Some radical feminists eschewed childbirth and mothering altogether and saw them as the root of women's oppression. The polar opposite of a
romanticized motherhood is Shulamith Firestone's infamous characterization of
childbirth as "shitting a pumpkin." For more than four decades, feminist literature
was filled with proposals for group parenting, artificial childbearing, and the liberation of children. Socialist feminists went about the task of having mothering
recognized as work that benefited both men and capital. Black feminists, like
Patricia Hill Collins (1991a), note that Black[1] women's mothering does not rest on
the Eurocentric and class-laden *cult of true womanhood* but rather has always incorporated work both inside and outside the home. Black families are less tightly
associated with the strict gender-divided nuclear form, with "othermothers" being
fundamental in the institution of Black motherhood (Collins 1991b). Similarly,
work on transnational mothering shifts our focus to financial caregiving in lieu of
in-person intensive motherhood (Hundley and Hayden 2016).

Contemporary cultural constructs of motherhood can be harrowing and ex-
ceedingly narrow pathways to navigate. It is almost, by definition, impossible to

be a *good mother* given the expansive responsibilities shouldered by many mothers today in an era of decreasing social safety nets. Breastfeeding is a matter of moral imperative, but mothers must be sure not to breastfeed in public. Natural child-birth holds cultural approval even as caesarean rates climb. And we are still playing tug-of-war between Ferberizing and attachment parenting. Employed mothers are seen as neglectful; stay-at-home mothers, indulgent. The balance between work and family is a frustrating mirage for so many mothers who shoulder the bulk of household labor despite having an adult partner in the home. Shaming mothers for being employed is nearly beside the point when the United States has no federal provision for paid maternity leave or even mandated paid sick days. Poor women and women in precarious jobs are unlikely to access such perks even when provided by employers. Our anachronistic minimum wage and high levels of multiple job holding are both a cause and consequence of poverty. Through all of this, mothers remain the objects of intense cultural surveillance.

The 2016 comedic film *Bad Moms* takes on the myriad ways in which mothers, even middle-class, college-educated mothers, continuously feel that they are failing. Rejecting the gluten-free, nut-free, soy-free, egg-free, milk-free, salt-free bake sale instructions from the PTA president, Mila Kunis's character exclaims, "I'm so tired of trying to be this perfect mother. I'm done!" Commiserating, her friends declare, "There's so many fuckin' rules now! Don't punish your kids. Don't say no to your kids." The center of much of the comedic action, these mothers are labeled "bad" for merely pursuing common adult behaviors such as going out with friends and having a cocktail.

Terms such as *tiger mother, single mother, Jewish mother,* and *welfare queen* reveal that, where motherhood is concerned, more than gender is at play. Definitions of *good mother* and *bad mother* are bound up with, among other things, race, class, and religion (Gustafson 2005, 29). Increasingly, motherhood is criminalized through surveillance (Minaker and Hogeveen 2015), also known as maternal profiling, in which mothers "are the scapegoat for community concerns about child welfare" (Park 2013, 50). Poor, Black, and Latinx mothers are particularly vulnerable to policing of motherhood and experience greater surveillance and harsher consequences thanks to laws that criminalize or prosecute mothers for neglect or drug use (Love 2008). For example, a mother whose child fell into the gorilla exhibit at a zoo immediately was the target of calls for her arrest. A mother who let her seven-year-old child walk to the park alone was arrested for felony child neglect, and a mother who could not afford childcare was arrested for allowing her nine-year-old child to play in a park adjacent to her workplace. Another mother left her two small children in the food court so that she could interview for a job in an adjacent shop. She received a sentence of eighteen years' probation.

There is some outrage and resistance to all of this surveillance. However, the cases that seem to draw the most outrage have been those in which middle-class, college-educated, cisgender, heterosexual, white mothers (and fathers) have found themselves the object of surveillance. Free-range parenting is a parenting movement that resists overly close supervision of children in order to promote their independence by allowing them to walk to school or play in the park by themselves. One couple subscribing to this practice made headlines because they were investigated for allowing their children to play independently away from their home. The free-range parents who were investigated were white, and in the end they were not charged with a crime. A quick internet search supports the suspicion that free-range parenting is a parenting movement primarily aimed at whites and wealthy folks (Land 2016).

On the other end of the spectrum from neglect, mothers are criticized for overparenting. Despite the gender-neutral buzzword *helicopter parent*, most of the shaming directed at overparenting is reserved for mothers. Attachment parenting is the controversial cousin to helicopter parenting. Television star Mayim Bialik routinely faces criticism for various facets of her adherence to attachment parenting, including public breastfeeding and co-sleeping. The *Time* magazine cover featuring the question, "Are you mom enough?" caused quite a stir and, predictably, the animus was directed at the mother on the cover, who was breastfeeding her three-year-old son, a practiced labeled as extreme parenting. One thing is for certain. Whatever the practice, mothers are always doing it wrong—too much, too little, the wrong kind.

A History of Custodial Practices in the United States

Noncustodial mothers have always existed. For most of US history through colonial times, with the important exception of slavery, fathers had sole rights to their children, as children were understood to be economic property of their fathers. Fathers determined how, for whom, and under what conditions children labored, and fathers received the proceeds of their children's labor. Fathers alone determined custodial arrangements for their children even after the father's death. In this era, "the natural right is with the father unless the father is somehow unfit" (Mason 1994, 50). Along with the right to one's children came the absolute economic responsibility of providing for the care, religious upbringing, and education of the child in his care (Mason 1994). Unmarried mothers and widows had no recourse to custodial arrangements made by the father, and married women were invisible in legal terms as they were unable to enter into contracts or own property.

Although women gained property rights during the nineteenth century, it was not an appeal to those property rights that secured custody for mothers. Instead, the combination of the cult of domesticity and a best-interests-of-the-child standard shifted practices toward mothers having custody. The cult of domesticity was the dominant gender ideology of the nineteenth-century middle and upper classes, and it prescribed a strict gendered division of labor where women's energies were devoted to home and children. Changing economic arrangements and declining birth rates solidified the worlds of work and home into separate spheres, at least for some groups of women. Women, keepers of the home realm, were seen as uniquely suited for the nurturing of children while men operated in the public sphere of economic and political life. The cult of domesticity elevated mothers to a cultural position of moral superiority.

Our current notions of childhood as a magical time are relatively recent in origin in a historical sense. By the nineteenth century, childhood was romanticized as a special, innocent time, and children were believed to require care and nurturing to grow. Contrary to our belief that the best interests of the child is a contemporary legal standard, this doctrine actually had already emerged in the nineteenth century. Mothers were understood to be inherently nurturing; therefore, the gender ideologies of the time meant that mother custody became synonymous with the best interests of children. It was this combination of the cult of domesticity with romanticized notions of childhood that set the foundation for the tender years doctrine, which held that young children should not be separated from their mothers. It was judicial discretion and the vague notion of the best interests of the child rather than changing legal rights that helped the pendulum to swing toward mothers. Nevertheless, in the nineteenth century there were few divorces and thus few divorce-related custodial disputes. Still, women who did not measure up to the portrait of a nurturing mother were harshly punished with removal of their children. Women who committed adultery or who initiated the dissolution of the marriage risked being punished through the loss of their children (Mason 1994).

In the Progressive Era, from the 1890s to the 1930s, we see the ascendancy of the state in matters of custody and the care of children. The state adopted a principle of keeping poor children with their families, providing state assistance to poor worthy (that is, widowed) mothers, but unwed mothers could lose custody of their children. It is during this time that the state began to seek financial support from absent fathers, and mothers were granted, for the first time, equal—not superior—rights to fathers under the law. Mary Ann Mason (1994) refers to this period, in which fathers were awarded custody in 31 percent of cases (mothers were awarded custody in 41 percent), as the "historical nadir for fathers" (119). The loosely defined best interests of the child, combined with a continued sentimentality for motherhood, underscored a de facto preference for mothers as the custodians of children. But preferences are not rights, and despite the doctrine, mothers did not have equal parental rights under the law. In 1930, nine states still had not recognized equal parental rights for women (Klaff 1982).

Keep in mind that in many cases the custody question is not between a mother and a father but between the mother and the state. Nevertheless, we can frame a preference for mothers emerging during this time, and it is to this preference (emerging before World War II) that contemporary fathers' rights movements refer when they cite a preference for mothers. However, this preference was short-lived and began to erode as early as the 1960s, and most certainly by the 1970s. In 1973, the *Watts v. Watts* case successfully challenged the tender years doctrine on the grounds that mother preference was a violation of equal protection granted by the Fourteenth Amendment (S. Boyd 2003). In the 1970s much of the language of custody had become gender neutral, although the primary caregiver was still likely to be the mother (Chesler 1984). No-fault divorce and a cultural shift toward gender equality led to a cultural waning of the tender years doctrine during this time. Women who were seen as somehow unfit (for example, promiscuous, wage earning, stubborn, or flighty) found themselves losing custody of their children in this era.

By the 1980s, significant custody reforms were well under way, and most states instituted some sort of joint custody provision (Coltrane and Hickman 1992). In the 1970s, mothers and fathers came to hold equal custody rights under the law and much of the language of custody was becoming gender neutral, favoring joint custody and referencing parents rather than mothers or fathers. "The abolition of mother preference coincided with the movement of women out of the home and into the labor market" (Mason 1994, 11). Some even rejected the mother-child bond, as did one New York court, stating, "The simple fact of being a mother does not, by itself, indicate a capacity or willingness to render a quality of care different from that which the father can provide" (123). No-fault divorce and the search for gender equality formed the background against which the tender years doctrine waned and women who worked outside the home lost any special status that motherhood may have conferred in earlier times. During this time, men regained any ground they had temporarily lost during the Progressive Era. Even so, in approximately 85 percent of cases, mothers maintained custody of children, not because courts ruled in their favor but because most child custody decisions are agreed on between the parents. Outcomes, however, were different when men sought custody. In a review of court decisions in 1990, fathers who sought custody won with a slight majority over mothers. In fact, judges had demoted motherhood as a determining factor in custody. Far greater weight had come to be placed on the parent with superior economic stability or who acted as the primary disciplinarian. Although there was a slight preference for fathers in disputed cases in 1990, the vast majority of routine custody arrangements reflected some kind of joint custody. In fact, most legal disputes between parents concerned unpaid support rather than the custody of children, and most custody arrangements were routine and fell outside the judicial process (Mason 1994). To review, what we have seen is a shift from absolute fathers' rights (for some men) to a historically short era of seeming mother preference followed by an officially gender-neutral stance toward child custody.

Today, in disputed custody cases, the best-interests-of-the-child standard prevails in most states. However, the factors considered in the determination of the best interests of the child are variable and wide ranging. Some examples are stability of the household; the mental and physical health of the parents; the wishes of the child; income; lifestyle; conduct; parents' employment; domestic violence; and which parent will better promote the relationship with the noncustodial parent, a standard known as the cooperative or friendly parent. The extent to which a child's preference is considered is also highly variable. In some states, judges will consider the child's wishes at a certain age (also variable) or upon demonstration of sufficient maturity. An exception, Georgia allows children at the age of fourteen to select the parent with whom they will live. Many states explicitly reject any preference for a parent based on gender or primary caregiver role, and states increasingly start with the presumption of joint custody.

Mediation is being used more frequently in the divorce and custody determination process (Emery, Otto, and O'Donohue 2005). In California, for example, mediation is required before divorce and custody disputes head to the courtroom (Heim et al. 2002). While California has required training for custody evaluators, this is not true of all states. In many states, a guardian ad litem, whose job it is to advocate for the child, can be imposed by the court or requested by one of the parties. Custody evaluators, usually mental health professionals, are also used to function as impartial arbiters to help determine the best interests of the child through interviews, home visits, psychological testing, and the gathering of other relevant information. Judges have few constraints on their decision-making in family court and, along with custody evaluators, they enjoy legal protection with regard to their decisions. Psychology and psychologists can weigh heavily in today's child custody determination processes. The American Psychological Association has issued "Guidelines for Child Custody Evaluations in Family Law Proceedings," which is a document containing principles to be applied to the process, including advice to maintain a stance free from biases, to complete evaluations in a timely manner, and to triangulate any data gathered. At just under five pages in length, the utility of the document is unclear.

The term *noncustodial* has a range of meanings. States vary widely in language and practice, but generally custody has two conceptual components, legal and physical. *Legal custody* refers to rights to participate in major decisions affecting a child's life, including schooling, religious, and medical matters. *Physical custody* refers to the right of the parent to spend time with the child. On one end of the spectrum, noncustodial status might mean that there is no legal right to participate in major decisions that affect the child, that the parent has no visitation rights with the child whatsoever, or that any contact time is supervised. On the other end of the spectrum, *noncustodial* could simply mean that one parent has less than half of the parenting time or is considered nonresidential in some way. There might be joint legal custody but a parenting-time split where one parent has the child 25 percent of the time and the other has the child 75 percent of the time. One parent may have no legal say but will have significant contact with the child. A parent may share legal custody but only see the child very rarely.

When some people refer to standard noncustodial parenting time (or visitation), they are likely referring to the every-other-weekend and one-night-a-week pattern that prevailed in the 1970s. Although there has been a marked increase in joint legal and physical custody since that time, most custodial arrangements still do not break the threshold of shared parenting (greater than one hundred overnights per year for the nominally noncustodial parent). Some states defer to the standard parenting arrangement, but others increasingly begin with the presumption of some kind of joint custody rather than the designation of one custodial parent. The reasons for this shift are political in the sense that they are based on assumptions promoted by interest groups and are not necessarily underscored by empirical evidence that shared custody is best for children in an emotional or developmental sense.

A Note on Fathers' Rights

A billboard on my way home from work mysteriously advertises a law firm that is "dedicated to helping men," reminding me that fathers' rights has become a specialization for some divorce attorneys (Chapin 2016). As early as the 1970s, fathers' rights groups arose and were successful in pushing for gender-neutral language in matters of divorce, alimony, and custody by arguing that judges and courts were biased against fathers (Coltrane and Hickman 1992). Canada saw the rise in these groups occur in the 1980s, coinciding with sweeping changes in family law (Bertoia and Drakich 1993), and in California, fathers' rights groups found considerable success advocating for no-fault divorce alongside liberal feminists. The resurgence of fathers' rights groups in the twenty-first century occurred in the wake of increased governmental attention to divorce reforms and support enforcement and the increased punishment of avoiders (Berns 2005; Bertoia and

Drakich 1993) in the United States, Canada, and the United Kingdom. In the United States specifically, the welfare reform of the 1990s spurred a host of changes that were aimed at increasing pressure on fathers who were not complying with child support orders.

The upsurge in the fathers' rights movement and its surrounding publicity have brought to public attention the issues surrounding child custody after divorce (Crowley 2008). Fathers' rights activists' assertions of family court bias frequently cite the statistic that women have primary custody 90 percent of the time (Clatterbaugh 2000). When we consider the fact that the vast majority of custodial arrangements are agreed on outside the court system with fewer than 5 percent of cases contested (J. Kelly 2007), maternal preference *by courts* is unclear. The few studies of court outcomes that exist do not reveal a maternal preference (Bertoia and Drakitch 1993; R. Kelly, Redenbach, and Rinaman 2005).

While this book does not engage these groups or their claims directly, it is important to provide a basic background on their perspective because what we think we know or take for granted about gender and child custody largely reflects the campaigns and concerns of these groups. Fathers' rights groups are the most prominent public voices about issues of child custody, and their perspectives have become incorporated into our commonsense understandings. They participate in public hearings and on task forces on everything from child support to domestic violence. Search the internet for the terms *divorce, child support,* or *custody* and you will find fathers' rights attorneys and fathers' rights groups. As mentioned by nearly all of my participants, there is no parallel mothers' rights movement. In this light, it should not be surprising that much of what we learn from noncustodial mothers may seem strange or unreal, because contemporary cultural discourses of child custody are so firmly shaped by the fathers' rights movement.

While not unitary in perspective, fathers' rights groups share a concern mainly with issues of custody, child support, divorce, and paternity claims. The fathers' rights movement's origins lie in the larger men's movement, a broad movement incorporating a diverse and sometimes contradictory set of beliefs about men and gender. John Fox (2004) outlines three historical strands of the men's movement: profeminist, mythopoetic, and men's rights. Fathers' rights groups are a more tempered offshoot of the men's rights movement, which can be extreme and antiwoman in their discourses (Crowley 2008; Fox 2004). A softer tone that focuses on children by invoking an ethic of care does not render their aims unproblematic (Jordan 2018). Individual men participating in these groups, however, range widely in the extent to which they adhere to some of the more extreme viewpoints (Crowley 2008). Some men in these groups appear to have more in common with noncustodial mothers than with fathers' rights advocates (Clatterbaugh 2000; Crowley 2008; Fox 2004; Jordan 2018).

When I refer to fathers' rights groups in later chapters, it is to contrast the knowledge gained from noncustodial mothers to the culturally dominant discourses that fathers' rights groups have shaped. Noncustodial mothers are keenly aware of fathers' rights discourses. Many sought information and support from these groups online. Some noncustodial mothers felt welcomed by these groups, while others experienced outright sexism. Some came up against fathers' rights attorneys in court, yet others hired them.

Research Methods

The content of this book draws on in-depth interviews and over seven years of participation in online noncustodial mother communities. Originally, I was searching the internet for information about child custody given my own situation. Most information I found resided on fathers' rights groups' websites. I was struck by the gendered nature of not only the location of the information but also the ways in which custody and parents were framed. Other than fathers' rights groups, many of the sites I found were connected to law practices that focused on custody. The presumption of these sites was that the noncustodial parent was the father, which is not surprising given that most noncustodial parents are, in fact, fathers. Thus began my search for mothers without custody. They were hard to find. In the end, I found two online support groups and one informational site geared specifically toward mothers without custody. Over time, these sites have dissipated and much of the discussion has moved to Facebook groups.

I limited the scope of my research to the postdivorce (or postrelationship) context for several reasons. While I am certain that there are shared experiences with mothers whose children are removed by the state, cultural and institutional changes in marriage and divorce constitute a compelling context in which to understand noncustodial mothers. Nowadays, women's labor force participation is not seen as an anomaly in any social class and women's employment patterns have come to more closely resemble men's. Men's participation in household labor has not changed as thoroughly. Women still tackle the bulk of household labor, but men have increased their contributions, particularly around time spent with children. Attitudes about the gender division of labor in the household, if not actual behaviors, are more egalitarian than they have ever been.

Given the stigmatized nature of the noncustodial mother status, participant recruitment was challenging. At first, I relied heavily on volunteers from the communities in which I participated. Involvement in the online support groups skewed toward some level of dissatisfaction with their current parental arrangements, and it was important to expand participation to mothers who were satisfied with their situation or who defined their situation as voluntary rather than imposed.

I spent part of a summer on the road covering thousands of miles to interview my first noncustodial mothers in person. I felt it was important to start with in-person interviews to build trust in the communities. We met in living rooms and diners; among children, pets, and second spouses; and in rural as well as urban areas. I even found myself lost in a soybean field with a plow heading my way thanks to a malfunctioning GPS. Interviews brought tears, anger, and even laughter. When emotions ran high, I checked in with participants frequently during interviews, making sure they wanted to continue. When I was asked about my own experiences with child custody, I freely shared them. Because of the deeply personal nature of these interviews, I felt that, in keeping with feminist methods, it was important to offer some reciprocity of our stories (Oakley 1981). At the end of each interview, I always gave my participants the chance to ask me questions, including personal questions.

After my road trip, I soon learned to use Skype to conduct and record audio interviews with participants. Word of my research spread and some individuals found me. I combed blogs and online news to find still more participants. Participants connected me with more potential participants in the true fashion of snowball sampling. I worked to draw in diverse noncustodial mother experiences—for example, putting out additional calls for participants who would characterize their situation as voluntary.

Some mothers have had additional children with a new partner and thus straddle both custodial and noncustodial statuses. Some mothers are also stepmothers with male spouses who mostly have secondary, but sometimes primary, custody of their biological children. Some mothers share some custody with their ex-partners, while others rarely or never see their children. A few have regained custody of one or more of their children. While the group of interview participants represents a good deal of economic diversity, racial/ethnic and sexual orientation diversity was harder to come by. I have no way to know for sure why that is; however, in-depth interviews on such a personal subject require an initial leap of faith on behalf of the participant. It may be that white women felt more comfortable reaching out to me than women of color. It may also be that traditions of othermothers in Black communities do not position children as property (Collins 1991a), and labels of *custodial* and *noncustodial* are less salient. When I began gathering data, *Obergefell v. Hodges* (marriage equality) had not been decided, so nonbiological LGBTQ parents largely had no legal standing to seek custody. These and other unknown factors certainly shaped participation.

Participant observation, however, provided me with greater exposure to diversity in race/ethnicity and sexual orientation. Although difficult to tease out in depth here, there is something about whiteness and heterosexuality that strongly structures the experiences of noncustodial mothers. We do know that custodial fathers are more likely to be white than custodial mothers (43.7 percent of custodial mothers are white, while 59.2 percent of custodial fathers are white) and less likely to be Black (29.3 percent of custodial mothers are Black, while 15.8 percent of custodial fathers are Black). Custodial mothers are more likely to have never married (42.6 percent) than to declare any other marital status, while custodial fathers are more likely to be divorced (32.9 percent) than to declare any other marital status (Grall 2016). Nonhomonormative LGBTQ parents, those whose families do not closely approximate heterosexual families, face an uphill battle when it comes to child custody (Pearson 2012). Whiteness and heteronormativity are themselves important aspects of a critical analysis of custodial practices. For that reason, I use heteronormative language (for example, *husband*) where it echoes the words of the participants because I do not want to obscure the analytical point that many noncustodial mothers' experiences are embedded in the problematic institution of heterosexual marriage. When not drawing on participants' language, I use the word *partner* to refer to married or unmarried partners regardless of gender identity or sexual orientation.

In total, I have interviewed thirty-five noncustodial mothers. The majority are white, with the exception of three Black, three Latinx, and two Asian American participants. Their ages ranged from twenty-eight to fifty-two, and their financial situations ranged from below poverty level to upper-middle class and were spread evenly across income ranges. Interviews lasted between one and three hours and were recorded while I jotted some notes. The recorded interviews were transcribed verbatim while removing identifying information. All interview participants will be referred to by a pseudonym and details of their cases may have been modified for the purposes of maintaining confidentiality. Confidentiality was a significant concern for many research participants, some of whom were still in custody litigation at the time of their interview. Other participants expressed concerns about confidentiality because their ex-partner was abusive to them. Therefore, I err on the side of protecting confidentiality by minimizing identifying information accompanying the presentation of interview data and not systematically presenting all characteristics of interview participants in a way that would aid people who know them in identifying them. Minimizing identifying information also helps to keep the focus on the social and institutional processes rather than individual participants.

Respondents were asked to describe their current custodial status and then to provide a retrospective history of their custody status from its initial determination. I also asked questions about topics ranging from their household divisions of labor, child support, current care arrangements for their children, and their relationships with their children, co-parents, and new partners of their ex-partner, to their feelings and openness about their noncustodial mother status; their conceptualizations of motherhood, fatherhood, and gender; and their assessment of the processes of custody determination. To be true to the words and feelings of noncustodial mothers who participated, I use sometimes long, verbatim quotes from their interviews.

Online Support

Online support groups are increasingly common (Barak, Boniel-Nissim, and Suler 2008), and many people turn to them for support and information on medical questions, social problems, and relationship issues. I have participated in online discussion and support groups across a diverse set of interests: noncustodial mothers, breast cancer survivors, and caregivers of parents with dementia, to name a few. There are commonalities of etiquette among these groups, such as not sharing posts outside the group and using language like "newbies" and "OP" (original poster). Yet each group takes on its own dynamic or focus. For example, I belonged to several breast cancer survivor groups and eventually narrowed my participation to two. One was oriented toward emotional support of survivors, and the other was more oriented to the politics and science surrounding breast cancer.

When it came to noncustodial mothers, support groups were difficult to find, particularly in the first decade of the twenty-first century. Most groups had sporadic activity, but there were a few that offered continuous, robust, and wide-ranging discussion. When I first joined the noncustodial mother support groups—after becoming involved in custody litigation when I moved for a new job—I learned that many members had first tried participating in forums for divorced fathers since these seemed to provide more information on navigating custody. While they found some good information there, the groups were primarily informational, and it was not uncommon for them to cite a lack of emotional support as a reason for leaving. In addition, mothers cited outright misogyny as a reason for leaving some of those groups.

Much of the information shared on the sites was very practical. One common refrain was that it was better to document and not use information for one's case than to not document it and need it. Other practical information included advising noncustodial mothers to keep their court orders and all paperwork handy at all times. Many mothers kept these documents in their cars. There was an emphasis on communicating via email and in a businesslike manner, whether it be to their ex-partner or to their child's teachers. One group had a practice of encouraging mothers to post drafts of emails to their ex-partners so that the group could help them rewrite it to be more effective and less emotional. Sometimes this took a humorous turn even though the content was serious. For example, a group member known as an expert letter writer would interject with a salutation like, "Dear ActYourAgeNotYourShoeSize" or sign off with something like, "Best regards, IHaveYourNumber." Also on the lighter side, mothers shared pictures of their children, themselves, their pets, and their hobbies.

Venting was a significant part of the interaction in the noncustodial mother support groups, but mothers also discussed their experiences with attorneys, courts, custody evaluators, guardians ad litem, mediators, ex-partners, schools, physicians, therapists, friends, and family. Problems ranged from minor irritations to physical abuse. One thing that surprised me was the vast knowledge of legal processes and strategies, case law, and even state-specific laws and practices that mothers brought to the site. One site had an extensive set of resources available to members. There were a few attorneys and paralegals in the groups, but most legal knowledge came from mothers' own research and experiences. For instance, a noncustodial mother might share a lot of very practical information about working better with one's attorney. An important theme was maintaining documentation on everything, particularly things like having parenting time cut short or denied. Mothers would also share emotional problems and discuss the holidays, a particularly tricky time for divorced and noncustodial parents.

Stigma, examined extensively in chapter 3, was a frequent source of discussion in the support communities. As Dee Dee shared, "I had no idea there were others like me until I found this site. I don't talk about it and I usually don't even mention that I have kids. You feel like you're one of a kind and it really sucks. People don't really get it unless they've been through it. And you feel like they're sitting there thinking you must've done something, you know, because mothers always get custody." Stigma and the importance of connecting with others who understand was often one of the first issues a newbie would bring up.

Finally, one very common but controversial topic of discussion was parental alienation syndrome (PAS). PAS is a term used to describe a nonvalidated psychological phenomenon wherein children are brainwashed to hate a parent, usually a noncustodial father. Participants generally embraced the concept of parental alienation, and there were even women in my sample and in the online support groups who were in situations that seemed to reflect commonsense understandings of PAS. A much deeper discussion of PAS will be taken up in chapter 7 in the context of gender violence.

My participation in the online communities served two purposes. The first is that it yielded a tremendous volume of field notes. I did not keep screenshots or verbatim details of online discussions. Doing so would have posed a problem for obtaining informed consent because of the sheer volume of participants and their often transitory connection to the groups. I did keep notes, however, on the themes that emerged and the range of opinions on the issues noncustodial mothers identified. These notes provide me with a very well-rounded and thorough understanding of the range of issues noncustodial mothers face. For the purposes of presentation in the book, I rely heavily on interviews to best represent the actual words and thoughts of noncustodial mothers, supplemented by my knowledge and notes from participation in these two groups. Second, participant observation helped me to know the extent to which any experience is shared and to proceed with more purposeful, theoretical sampling. I cannot say with any certainty that my interview sample is representative of all noncustodial mothers. I suspect that online communities skew toward individuals who are in some way unsatisfied with their situation. Using snowball and purposeful sampling, I sought out mothers who labeled themselves as voluntarily noncustodial mothers.

Any interpretive scholarship, particularly feminist scholarship, is scrutinized for potential bias. Research is never value-free. The view from nowhere (Nagel 1986) perpetuates a false notion of objectivity. Feminist methods direct us to be explicit about our values. How can one prove, for example, that gender has something to do with noncustodial mothers' experiences? We can never know without having been there through the whole process and having access to the mind of the judge or other decision makers. Even then, we can never know for sure. However, feminist method places women's own voices at the center of knowledge production and starts from the perspective that women are reliable narrators of their own lives. A feminist approach gives voice and authority to participants who often occupy a marginal status by working to understand and situate the lived experiences of participants. While the experiences here may not be exhaustive, the analysis provided does contribute to our understanding of social processes, interactions with institutions, and the meanings of contemporary motherhood in which the experiences of noncustodial mothers are embedded.

This work in no way infers anything about noncustodial fathers. The normative nature of fathers' withdrawal from children's lives postdivorce and society's more casual and accepting disposition toward noncustodial fathers are important issues in their own right. They, too, speak to gendered experiences of parenting. The focus on noncustodial mothers in this book does not imply that fathers without custody do not miss their children in ways similar to noncustodial mothers, but noncustodial mothers form an important group because their position defies cultural expectations. Noncustodial mothers' experiences are filtered through society's gendered expectations of women who parent in nontraditional ways.

Finally, this book is not intended to be the definitive book on noncustodial mothers. Rather than being the last word, the book is intended to invite further

discussion and scholarship about gender, parenthood, caregiving, and child custody. Noncustodial mothers are a heterogeneous group but nearly uniformly invisible. Their stories and the patterns that emerge should generate a larger discussion about what it is to mother, who does it, who can do it, and under what
circumstances. Are we ready to move to embrace the actual practice of gender-
neutral parenting rather than just the language? What would that entail, and what
social conditions would be needed to support such a shift?

THE MOTHERS

When people learn that a mother does not have custody, the first question is always "Why?" We know that, postdivorce, if children live with one parent, it is most likely the mother. In the vast majority of cases, a child's primary residence is with their mother even if they spend significant overnight time at their father's house (Cancian et al. 2014; Kelly 2007; Meyer, Cancian, and Cook 2017). Because there has been a dramatic increase in shared residential custody, sole mother custody has declined in recent decades from 76 percent in 1989 to 42 percent in 2010. Thus, despite social changes in children's living arrangements postdivorce, a single or divorced mother without her children, even in the twenty-first century, presents somewhat of an anomaly. So we will start with trying to understand how these mothers became noncustodial mothers postdivorce. Why these mothers? What can we learn from their stories? One of the most interesting findings from this research is that there are so few characteristics that are emblematic of noncustodial mothers.

Certainly, as a sociologist, I could hypothesize that some mothers would be more likely to lose custody, although not all mothers in the study would need to lose custody by official determination such as a court order. Some understand their status as, at least to some degree, voluntary. But the concept of choice is a funny thing, where agency and constraint are mingled in ways that only become clear upon a more detailed telling of one's story. The following brief portraits represent just a part of the very wide range of experiences of noncustodial mothers in the United States, from completely involuntarily noncustodial to happily, voluntarily noncustodial. Following the portraits, the sections are more analytically focused on some of the themes that permeated the interviews and online support communities. Some of the themes briefly identified here in the overview of the participants are analyzed in greater detail in subsequent chapters.

Chris, Angela, and Virginia are three mothers who vary greatly in terms of how voluntary they would describe their custodial status.

Chris was a stay-at-home mother to two young children. She had a background in early childhood education but had quit her job during a difficult first pregnancy. Her youngest was less than a year old when her husband was awarded sole legal and physical custody. Despite the label, her children spend roughly 40 percent of their time with her. At the time custody was turned over to her husband, he had never put the kids down to sleep and did not know the bedtime routine. At trial, she was labeled histrionic and threatened with contempt for crying in court. In the end, the judge did not feel that Chris would promote a healthy relationship between her children and their father if she had custody.

Angela found herself working long hours, shouldering the bulk of doctor appointments, teacher meetings, and cleaning while she was married to her husband. When they divorced, they agreed that she would have her two boys at least every weekend because her work entailed long hours during the week, while his job was less intense and more flexible. After six years of this informal and flexible arrangement, the court reduced her parenting time by nearly half when it ruled that Angela would only get the standard of every other weekend and one evening a week for dinner.

Virginia and her son's father were never married and never lived together. In fact, they were old friends who decided to have a child together and have cooperated since he was born to find the best situation for him. Given his special needs, the availability and cost of schooling and medical care have always been significant factors. Sometimes this meant residing with his mother and sometimes with his father as situations changed or a parent moved for work. They worked out child support on their own with each change in custody. As her son has gotten older, Virginia has observed that he needs more time around his friends, so she does not insist on the same schedule they had when he was younger. Primary residence is with her son's father and they share legal custody. Virginia stays involved remotely through phone calls and by keeping track of his school progress online.

Given the strong influence of the ideology of intensive motherhood, I felt certain that primary caregiving, stay-at-home mothers would be a rare find among noncustodial mothers. I assumed that these mothers' very status as "100 percent mother" should immunize them against losing custody. They had the moral high ground. Yet it was not difficult to find former stay-at-home mothers who had lost custody to their ex-partner.

Amy is a forty-five-year-old mother of two who describes herself as a "twenty-four-hour-a-day mom." She was a stay-at-home mother with two children and also babysat other children as part of a small, unlicensed daycare operation. Her first child from a prior relationship was older and beyond custody determination when Amy became the noncustodial mother of her eighteen-month-old daughter. Amy had visitation (or parenting time, as it is often called) every other weekend during the school year, several weeks of consecutive time over the summer, and some holiday time. Amy's married life had revolved around her family and her church, while her husband was only peripherally involved in the household life. When her husband kicked her out of the house, he changed the locks and prevented Amy from seeing their daughter. With no money, no job, and no family, Amy had to move in with a friend who lived a few hours' drive away while she and her husband attempted reconciliation and mediation. She was able to find low-wage work for a few hours a day in order to pay the child support order that took about two-thirds of her after-tax paycheck.

Emily, at her husband's insistence, gave up her part-time job to become a stay-at-home mother when their son was born. Her husband's highly variable work schedule made it difficult for him to participate in parenting, but it also made it challenging for Emily, who was charged with keeping her son quiet during the day so that her husband could sleep when he was on nightshift. During what Emily thought was a temporary separation from her husband, she and her infant son stayed with her parents. When her husband asked for a divorce, Emily ended up representing herself during the divorce and custody motions because neither she nor her parents had the money for an attorney. Despite living less than a dozen miles away from her ex-husband, she sees her son only every other weekend, with some additional time during the summer months at her ex-husband's discretion.

The following stories come from employed noncustodial mothers who could afford good legal representation. My assumption was that, although their professional status might make their case vulnerable on gendered ideological grounds, their financial status would leave them with more bargaining power in the process. On the other hand, I knew from my previous research that the status as a working mother still held negative connotations in our society and may affect decisions regarding child custody.

Maggie worked full time while her ex-husband worked sporadically and had long bouts of unemployment. Although Maggie was the primary breadwinner in the relationship, she still took on the lion's share of the household chores and childcare. At first, Maggie was only granted time with the children, ages four and six, on the weekends because she was employed during the week. Eventually, she went back to court and was able to get time with them on Wednesday evenings. When I met Maggie, she had been working with this same arrangement for over seven years. Although she had parenting time that was traditionally allotted to men, she was still doing the majority of caregiving for her children through managing their sports, school, and medical needs even when they were not in her physical custody.

Sandra, a registered nurse, was set to move with her children back to her home state. Before the move, Sandra had custody of her children during the week, while her ex-husband had them on the weekends when she worked very long shifts. There was a signed legal agreement that she would initially move with her preschool-age daughter and that her son, an elementary school student, would join them at the end of the school year. Court proceedings took longer than expected, and Sandra's new, irregular work schedule meant that she would temporarily have difficulty finding childcare. She and her ex-husband agreed to push the children's move back by six months to accommodate her work schedule, which was set to regularize after a few months. During that time, Sandra traveled back to see her children as frequently as she could. When the time came for the children to move, her ex-husband would not honor their agreement and filed for a change in their custodial agreement. It was incumbent on Sandra to return to the state of jurisdiction (over a thousand miles away) each time there was a motion or a hearing in the case. Ultimately, the court decided that the six-month delay in moving the children was enough to refuse to enforce the original mutual agreement that placed the children primarily with Sandra. Sandra sees her children for several weeks each summer, but very little at other times of the year.

While plenty of financially strapped mothers have custody of their children, the following mothers found themselves without custody primarily because of their difficult financial position.

Married at seventeen, Jeanne never finished high school. When she got divorced, she signed the document her ex-husband's attorney drew up because she could not afford legal consultation. She did not understand the legalese that gave her ex-husband primary physical and legal custody. In the months and years that followed, any time a dispute arose that involved court, Jeanne had to take time off from her jobs (mostly in fast food and retail) and spend money to stay in a hotel room because jurisdiction over the case was several hours away. The disputes were often over child support. Jeanne was unable to afford an attorney to address either the custody or the child support arrangements, so she had to represent herself. Occasionally, Jeanne lost a job because of the time off she needed to travel. Jeanne's child support payments ranged from $500 to $1,000 a month, sometimes nearly half of her gross pay, for her two children over the years that she was a noncustodial mother.

Carla's ex-husband, arguing that she had kidnapped her children, filed for emergency custody while Carla and her daughters were visiting her family out of town. She and her husband were still married at the time. Carla scraped together some money to fight for custody of their daughters. When Carla's ex-husband decided to move to another state shortly after their divorce was settled, she had no money left to fight the children's being moved. Carla also felt that she could not counter the argument that her husband could better provide for the kids because of his high income and family money. One December, Carla and her new husband saved enough to visit the girls over the holidays, only to find out that her ex-husband had moved far enough away that travel to see them was too costly. After eight months of not seeing her daughters, Carla heard from child protective services that her current husband had been accused of sexual contact with the two girls. Although Carla's husband was eventually cleared of any wrongdoing, she had no money to fight her ex-husband's motion to change her to supervised visitation. Supervised visits would require her to pay the additional expense of an approved supervisor for each visit with her daughters.

Diversity and Commonality

What became apparent during my interviews was that there seemed to be no discernable pattern among the mothers who did not have custody.[1] Often, the mothers would recount how they were cast as unstable, because of their jobs, their romantic relationships, or a known diagnosis of depression or anxiety, but there were also mothers who were known to be devoutly religious, community volunteers, and tenured professors. Some lived within a mile of their children, while others lived clear across the country. The age and gender of the children did not seem to matter. Some mothers had remarried, and others remained single. Some went on to have additional children, and others did not.

In terms of the demographics of this group, every socioeconomic category was represented. Online, race was hard to judge since not all mothers included photos of themselves or their children in their profiles. Different historical trajectories and levels of paternal involvement would certainly shape how gender and child custody intersect. There were several out lesbian mothers who regularly participated in the online support groups. At the time these data were collected, nonbiological same-sex parents had little recourse and were treated as legal strangers to the children they had been raising with their ex-partners.

These varied situations indicate that, at least for some mothers, there was no benefit from the now-defunct tender years doctrine, which held that very small children, if at all possible, should be kept with their mothers. Among the mothers I spoke to, the youngest children were under a year old and still breastfeeding when primary custody was granted to their father. Older children were occasionally heard from in custody proceedings, but, with very few exceptions, they had no decision-making power. In most states, children's wishes can be heard but have no legal bearing on the outcome.

Finding noncustodial mothers who were noncustodial purely by choice was a challenge. One such mother ran a blog for mothers like her, though she estimated that 70 percent of mothers on her blog were only "kind of" by choice. "Kind of by choice" mothers also included those who had health issues that precipitated a change in custody, as well as mothers who were doing poorly in court and made the change rather than continue in what they saw as a losing battle.

Financial Strain

The costs involved in a custody dispute are thoroughly and fairly criticized by fathers' rights activists and others. For noncustodial mothers, gender inequalities in earning power were an important factor. Even though stay-at-home mothers were at a particular financial disadvantage, every noncustodial mother who entered the family court system struggled with the cost of litigation and the hiring of experts, from custody evaluators to visitation supervisors. For many mothers, cobbling together $2,000–$5,000 for a lawyer's retainer was extremely difficult, if not impossible. Like many others, Pam found that the costs of custody litigation resulted in the accumulation of significant personal debt. She noted, "There needs to be equality of representation. I've been able to afford an attorney, but only because I've taken everything out of my savings. I spend nothing on anything other than necessities and have gone into debt $30,000. He and his wife are making over $500,000 a year. It's a drop in the bucket for them and I can't compete with that. And it's almost whoever has the most money wins."

One working-class mother, who had never had any experience with lawyers, was surprised to find that her retainer dwindled so swiftly, in part because she was charged for "every phone call and email" to her attorney. A few mothers reported spending well over $100,000 in legal and other costs related to a custody dispute. As a result of the steep costs, some mothers represented themselves, with varying degrees of success. In one of the support groups, there were several women who had done well pro se, and whole discussion threads were devoted to providing others with resources that would help them do the same. Many who represented themselves in court reported facing hostility from judges, as well as the opposing attorney.

Despite the few mothers who spent very large sums of money fighting for custody, it was more typical to find that an ex-partner's resources overpowered the mother's ability to participate in litigation. They could not enter into litigation, so they turned over custody. Sometimes mothers got started with litigation but ran out of money to continue to fight for custody. Regardless of their own financial position, most noncustodial mothers thought that affluence was a real factor in the custody decision itself whether the determination was by a court, through the involvement of a mediator or custody evaluator, or by attrition.

Fiona decided to turn over custody to her ex-husband because she felt that her children would be better off in his household since he had greater financial means. She said, "Over the course of the mediation sessions, and I was still in school and working part time, I just started thinking. You know, he can provide for the kids better than I can right now. And you know, I'm in school, my schedule changes a lot, I don't have much money, I live in a tiny apartment. I thought, rather than going through a trial, I would get as much as I could out of the mediation, more visitation time."

Maggie ceded custody to her ex-husband because she was concerned about her children suffering during the custody battle and because she could not afford to continue the legal proceedings. She explained, "My kids were four and six at the time. They're still babies and they're in the middle. And he's pulling some nasty shit on my kids, you know. Trying to, you know, 'love dad, hate mom.' And they were already in such bad shape from being stuck in the middle for all this time. I said, my god, I can't keep doing this to them. And then my attorney says, 'by the way if we go to trial, I'll need $12,000 up front.' Oh well, let me just bend over and shit that out!"

Not all ex-partners with custody had high-paying jobs. In fact, mothers who made more than their ex-partners felt that their higher status was used against them and the custody decision was perhaps a form of masculinity compensation. The father's status of unemployed or underemployed led to the assumption that he must be the primary caregiver rather than the mother. One mother's ex-partner was routinely unemployed and rarely held a job for an entire year. The court informed her that, since she had greater earning power, the children would reside with her ex-husband and she must work full time to support them. Nurses had a particularly hard time, as their irregular hours worked against them in the custody decision; they were cast as unstable. However, mothers would also lose custody to fathers with demanding jobs or jobs with fluctuating schedules like those in construction.

Household Division of Labor

With very few exceptions, the mothers with male ex-partners in the study had done the bulk of the household labor before their divorce or separation from their partners. This was irrespective of the employment status of either partner. This echoes national data on the unremittingly stubborn gendered nature of the household division of labor (Lachance-Grzela and Bouchard 2010). The relationship between work, gender, and household labor will be taken up in greater detail in chapter 5.

Noncustodial mothers report frustrations and concerns that the father did not know some of the basic information or routines for their child. This is not surprising given that "partnered fathers spend only about 8 percent of their time parenting solo" (Palladino 2014, 291). Like many noncustodial mothers, Sandra was the parent who did the bulk of the day-to-day parenting of her children. She explained,

> I was parenting and he was babysitting. He was fun-time dad. I was the one that made them brush their teeth and eat their vegetables. You know, do the important nonfun things. And he kind of went to work and came home late and ate his dinner and got on the computer. And I was, you know, being a mom. That's pretty much how it still is. I mean, he does the basics now, [but] no discipline. There's no consequences. So it's very difficult when they come here because it's like I have to erase ten months of them not having any responsibilities, no chores, no consequences, just running wild and then I have to pull the reins in for two or three months.

While fathers have increased their involvement in childcare over the last few decades, patterns of even the most involved fathers' care tend to revolve around "bouts of heavy weekend involvement" and "concerted cultivation," hallmarks of intensive fatherhood, a corollary to intensive motherhood (Palladino 2014, 287). This practice, however, renders invisible mothers' steady, routine parenting and household labor, without which fathers would be unable to accomplish involved fathering. None of the mothers I spoke with lost a custody dispute to stay-at-home or highly involved fathers. It was the mothers who voluntarily ceded custody who had ex-partners who had participated more fully equally in childcare and other household labor during the relationship. These mothers spoke well of their ex-partner's parenting skills. Olive said, "He wanted to be the primary caregiver, said that he would take care of everything and that I just had to help him sometimes. And when the marriage fell apart, I didn't want to be a single mom. And he did."

These more voluntary noncustodial mothers discussed the ways in which their ex-partners participated in the minutiae of childcare and household labor, including the mental effort needed to keep track of sport schedules, favorite foods, routine medical care, and even whether there was toilet paper in the house. Virginia explained, "Dad was basically stepping in and becoming mom. You have to have a dad who understands, whether you're remarried or in a relationship, that they're the primary caregiver, so they're getting up [when the children are sick]. You need to realize that you need Motrin in the house and Pepto, and your child might need chewable Pepto. All the little things that you figure out as a mom, Dad has to be willing to figure that out."

A lesson here might be that mothers feel better about more equally shared, postdivorce parenting when it represents a closer continuation or approximation of the predivorce household division of labor. One main concern of fathers' rights groups is that fathers receive too little parenting time after a divorce. This research suggests that families with more equal sharing of household labor during the marriage may make more time available for fathers' parenting time on their own after divorce. The larger pattern holds because a larger cultural shift in the gender division of labor and parenting is required. Only when we move away from the token nature of fatherhood (Rich 1976) to a more equally shared household division of labor that includes, but is not limited to, childcare will there be more voluntary, truly shared parenting postdivorce.

Guilt and Pain

A common refrain among noncustodial mothers is the pain they feel in missing their children. Most mothers, but particularly those who had the standard every-other-weekend parenting time, or less, struggled with issues of guilt and pain. As Sandra said,

> It's so painful being away from your kids and being denied the opportunity to do the right thing. It's painful not being able to go to their school functions, be there on their birthday or on Christmas. Not ever seeing their face when they come down to see the Christmas tree. It's an amazing pain. An amazing guilt that I feel because if I'd only done this or only done that or decided something else, they wouldn't be in the situation they're in. They don't have their mom ten months out of the year. All their friends have their moms, you know, and what do they say when they ask where their mom is?

Christine observed, "It's like a scab that never heals. Every week the scab gets pulled off and it's kind of healing by Wednesday and then Thursday they are back again and we go through the same thing until Sunday it gets pulled right back off when they leave again." Like Christine, Dee Dee felt that the loss of her children was a pain that never got better: "It's like in these situations, you get a divorce and you have a healing period, but you heal. You're allowed to heal. But everything else, it's not been allowed to heal. We've not been able to go forward."

Friday elation and Sunday-night blues were routine for many noncustodial mothers. For mothers who lived at a distance from their children, the car ride home was often long and difficult. Bonnie told me, "I cried all the way home. I still do. Every time." Even mothers who characterized their custody arrangements as highly voluntary struggled with a sense of loss when their children left. Fiona said, "It's difficult. It really is. Because you carry them, you bore them, you've been there through all of their hurts and their pains and to have that taken away feels like part of your heart's been ripped out."

The mothers who did not seem to suffer had the best and most communicative relationships with the father, lived very close by, or had parenting time approaching 40–50 percent. Virginia felt that trust between ex-partners was the most important factor in her peace of mind: "Maybe it has to do with the parents trusting each other. There has to be that connection between the parents, trust. You have to know he's in the best hands. And, for me, there was no question." Nevertheless, some mothers felt that they learned a deep appreciation for the time spent with their children that full-time mothers could not understand.

In the online support groups, the amount of time mothers had with their children was a source of some tension within the groups. Mothers regularly tempered their expressions of loss by recognizing that they at least had some access to their child. Emilyanne explained,

> It's a chronic pain. There's no way to heal. You can't get that time back and you just can't. My problem is just how long it is. And the helplessness of not being able to help my kids. But I come to appreciate a lot of things you may come to take for granted otherwise. Just moments. You grab every moment you can if you're given that. I know some of the moms don't have that. It just fine tunes everything and you don't take 'em for granted. Whereas a lot of moms have 'em every day. There's no way they can understand, no way they can fathom that pain.

The noncustodial mothers had various means of coping with the pain. Some fought depression ranging from mild to severe. Many mothers had been prescribed antidepressants after their loss of custody. Sandra, like a number of other mothers, described herself as having a double life: "I'm trying so hard to be a good mom. I'm trying so hard to do everything I need to do for them in that little time I have and I'm trying so hard not to be depressed and keep up with everything." Amy copes by removing all signs of her daughter when she is not around: "It's not like I broke a fingernail. I have to send my little girl away. I have to turn a switch off that says you're not a mom right now. I shut her door and I wash all her clothes because I can't run across a pair of underwear and a pair of socks and all the pretties she's done for me. They're all put away in one room so that I can't see them." Mothers also described taking up new interests, getting back to old interests, and going back to school as efforts that helped them to cope with their child's absence.

Co-parenting

One of the most frequent complaints from noncustodial mothers was a lack of co-parenting from their ex-partner. Christine said, "I would say he wasn't co-parenting. It might look that way on the outside. But he signs them up for all sorts of things that happen on my time. I take them because, of course, I will." For Janet, a lack of co-parenting by her ex-partner means she does not receive information on her daughter's serious medical condition: "[The doctors] changed her medications. She was recently in the hospital when she was with me. But anytime this happens to her, I never know about it. The only way I find out about it is if one of her school friends texts me and tells me." Another of the most common concerns raised by all but a few mothers was that there was very little communication coming from the ex-partner. The noncustodial mothers lacked basic information about things like school progress, health care, and sports or other activities. They often had to work very hard to obtain that information. These are things that they were used to handling before their separation, and many found it jarring to have so little input in their child's life. As Katie told me, "I still don't know if she's gone to the dentist. I don't know about her daily life. I don't know anything about school. I got a report card, sort of, and her school picture in December. I tried to talk to the teacher. I thought we were going to have a conference together. He said he didn't want me there, he wanted it private, and that I couldn't be there and had to schedule a different time." Sometimes the situation was made worse when a new girlfriend or wife came along, though occasionally this change precipitated an increase in communication with the noncustodial mother.

Damned If You Do, Damned If You Don't

For every discernable reason a mother gave for not having custody, another mother recounted just the opposite. Taken together, there is a kind of crazy-making, nonsensical quality to the data. There was a clear pattern of gender asymmetry in the experiences of many mothers who were in heterosexual relationships. For example, where both parties had had affairs, the mother found that it affected the outcome to her disadvantage. When both had a history of drug use, mothers faced the greater penalty. Another couple had tried swinging at the husband's insistence, and this was then successfully used to discredit the mother but seemed to have no bearing on the court's opinion of the father.

When it came to household arrangements, noncustodial mothers were at a disadvantage whether or not they remarried or lived alone. Living alone often put them at financial risk, and the prospect of single motherhood carried a negative connotation that did not seem to apply to single fatherhood. The detriment here concerned the ability to provide for the children, as well as the ingrained belief that single mothers are inherently unstable. At the same time, mothers who relied on their family for any form of support were deemed too reliant.

Sexuality was especially fraught terrain for mothers who started new relationships. A number of participants found that their postdivorce relationships were scrutinized in a way that their male ex-partners' were not. Mothers with new male partners felt that their relationship put them at a disadvantage in the custody process. This effect was exacerbated if the mother had been the one to leave the relationship. Boyfriends were also cast as a sexual threat in their own right. Being remarried was not a sure path to custody for women either. Even if a new husband provided stability or financial resources, he was sometimes characterized as a potential threat to the child's well-being.

When fathers relied on extended family or a new partner for childcare, it was seen as a positive by judges, courts, or evaluators. Much like the fatherhood bonus at work, a new family bestowed on fathers the quality of stability and having a family life. Whether it was the child's grandmother, a new wife, or even a girlfriend, the presence of another woman in the father's household worked against the noncustodial mother. Some of the mothers I spoke with referred to this phenomenon as "custody by stepmother" or "custody by grandmother." Angela voiced her frustration with this dynamic in this way: "I think what often happens is that other ladies move in. You know, they become the maternal influence and then everything's fine. Well, then you have a mom who's fuckin' shut out. That's not cool, either." Fathers' new partners were not problematized in custody proceedings in the same way that the noncustodial mothers' new partners were. In nearly all of the cases of the women I interviewed, the father had a wife, a girlfriend, or his mother residing in the household at the time he was granted custody.

Similarly, physical disabilities were construed as liabilities for mothers but as assets for fathers because disabled fathers with limited employment could be seen as having time to be with their children. In contrast, mothers with disabilities were understood as incapable of providing care. This kind of overrecognition of fathers' caregiving, discussed in greater depth in chapter 5, meant that fathers who had any involvement at all were able to successfully claim that they were the primary caregiver. When both parents had similarly demanding jobs, mothers reported that their job, but not their ex-partner's, was a significant factor in the custody decision.

Veronica lost custody because her ex-husband was employed full time and she was employed only part time. The opposing counsel successfully portrayed her as unable to properly provide for her child. Stay-at-home mothers' abundant time for focusing on the children was, however, not seen as an asset. Even a mother who homeschooled her children based on religious beliefs and held fast to the ideals of intensive mothering found that her homeschooling was seen as a detriment to the children.

When it came to finances, mothers with high earnings were seen as better able to provide the child support needed, and mothers with low earnings found themselves scolded for being lazy and unable to provide. This characterization is similar to the ways in which poor fathers, in particular poor fathers of color, are portrayed in society. Contemporary discourses about gender, custody, and child support would have us believe that only fathers pay child support; however, unless arrangements were made outside the court system, every noncustodial mother had a child support obligation. Amy paid $84 each week out of her $116 paycheck. At the height of her child support obligation, Christine paid $3,500 every month, approximately half of her gross salary, for her two children. Former stay-at-home mothers found that they were imputed an unrealistic income by the courts in order to calculate child support. One mother, a master's-level educator from another state, had been out of the labor market for several years. She found it impossible to make inroads into the teaching profession in her current location because her teaching credentials were not transferable from her former state. Nevertheless, her child support obligation was imputed based on the income of an educator in that state with a master's degree. Her job working in a nursery school paid only a fraction of the amount of income imputed to her.

In the end, when custody is contested, mothers only need be disqualified by something. By anything. One way to make sense of these disparate experiences is that the cultural contradictions of motherhood that occur at the intersections of intensive mothering, postfeminist ideologies, and neoliberalism have intensified such that mothers can lose custody for not pursuing financial gain, while we still cast stay-at-home mothers as selfish (Hays 1996). The neoliberal model requires that mothers be employed in order to diminish reliance on the state at the same time it eschews mothers' employment for anything other than utilitarian reasons (Ennis 2014; Giles 2014). Mothers should have *jobs* rather than fulfilling careers, but neither are they permitted to be unemployed. This idea will be pursued in greater detail in chapter 5.

From the Mundane to the Ridiculous

Some of the mothers' experiences when it came to custody were extreme.[2] While not representative of all noncustodial mothers, these cases are illustrative of what some noncustodial mothers face in the current institutional and cultural context of motherhood. What struck me most about these cases was the sheer lack of recourse for the noncustodial mothers. If an ex-partner decided to prohibit contact or reduce parenting time, court was an expensive and imperfect undertaking. Certainly the lack of efficacy in the system is a problem for noncustodial fathers as well; however, the most problematic situations that arose implicated and exacerbated existing gender inequalities.

One of the broader discourses around gender and custody characterizes custodial mothers as likely to take children away from their fathers. On more than one occasion, my participants noted that fathers raised the specter of maternal kidnapping when custody was being disputed. These accusations are especially likely in highly contentious cases—for example, those involving abuse. There is ample documentation of the problems that mothers face when they bring up abuse, sexual or otherwise, in the context of divorce. Because courts see mothers who allege abuse as trying to work the system, men with long records of abuse end up with custody of their children (Chesler 2011; Neustein and Lesher 2005).

Daisy's ex-husband, for example, had been to jail on domestic violence charges. He was well known to the police, as he had also been arrested for public intoxication and driving on a suspended license. During the custody dispute her ex-husband demanded that she be tested for marijuana use (they had both routinely smoked marijuana). Testing positive for marijuana resulted in her losing custody. In another case, it took a second marriage to reveal abuse the courts had previously ignored. The court did not believe Carla's original accounts of domestic violence. Only when it was revealed that the stepmother had surreptitiously recorded a violent clash on her cell phone were Carla's former claims of abuse given any credence. By the time her children were returned to Carla, they had not seen her for a few years.

It was not unusual for the mothers I spoke with who had no history of abuse and no criminal record to find themselves with supervised visitation. Ruth struggled with postpartum depression, and her husband left her when she checked into a psychiatric hospital after a subsequent bout of depression. She received treatment and was released. Nevertheless, her ex-husband was able to use the hospital stay to have the courts require supervised visitation even though Ruth had never harmed her child. Emilyanne had bipolar disorder and had been successfully in treatment and in compliance with that treatment for seven years but found that she could not get the supervision lifted without going back to court, something that she could not afford.

Finally, many courts fail to recognize financial abuse and, in some cases, even seem to reward it. Ingrid originally had custody of her three children in the marital home. When her ex-husband stopped paying child support and cleared out the bank accounts, the former stay-at-home mother made so little money at her part-time job that she could not pay the heating bill while her complaint against him made its way through the child support system. Because child support enforcement is handled separately from custody determinations, she had no recourse. Her ex-husband alerted child protective services to the fact that three children were living in a home without heating and, even though she explained the situation, she was told she was at risk of having the children removed. She borrowed money from family and friends to keep the heat on, but eventually, her lack of money precipitated a change in custody. Without access to marital assets, she could not fight for custody. Her ex-husband ended up with the house and with custody of the children.

In summary, noncustodial mothers are not a unitary group. They are former stay-at-home mothers, sales clerks, fast-food workers, nurses, accountants, business executives, and veterinarians. They are high school dropouts and advanced degree holders. Their reasons for being noncustodial vary. Some have chosen this unconventional path, while others were shocked to find themselves in their current situation. Some have good working relationships with their children's other parent while others may have a restraining order against them. Voluntarily noncustodial mothers have the most confidence and trust in their ex-partners when it comes to their children's care and well-being. Many others are shocked that custody was decided in favor of an ex-partner who was marginally involved in a child's life. Regardless of the situation, noncustodial mothers struggle with many aspects of their unconventional social location. Most salient among these struggles is the stigma they feel from not having primary custody of their children.

SHE MUST HAVE DONE SOMETHING

Noncustodial mothers, whether voluntarily so or not, often experience some form of stigma in relation to their status as mothers without primary custody of their children. Stigma is a robust subject of sociological and psychological inquiry. Sociological literature is replete with studies of stigma, including stigma and mental health (Pescosolido 2013), sexual orientation (Herek, Widaman, and Capitanio 2005), teenage pregnancy (Mantovani and Thomas 2014), fat stigma (Monaghan 2017), and smoking while pregnant (Wigginton and Lafrance 2016). Bernice Pescosolido and Jack Martin (2015) provide an extensive review of the theoretical developments and widening scope of the application of the concept of stigma, such as to singlehood, gambling, and stripping. These studies rest on the classic work by Erving Goffman (1963), who offers a useful framing of and nomenclature for these experiences.

Noncustodial mothers experience a spoiled identity, a "blemish of individual character" (Goffman 1963, 4). Spoiled identities operate such that they confer a whole host of additional negative traits to the stigmatized person as we search for a reason to explain the blemish. The stigmatized person "is reduced in our minds from a whole, usual one to a tainted, discounted one" (3). Rather than identifying stigma as a purely psychological state, Goffman conceptualizes it as something that is both relational and contextual. Stigma always occurs against what is usual or normative. Our interactions and our social institutions shape the experiences, and even the life chances, of the stigmatized. In addition, the stigmatizing attribute may surface or recede in one context versus another, and depending on one's social location, stigma may be more or less salient. Stigma is also a place where

intersectional identities play out. For example, noncustodial mothers with disabilities can face additional challenges. Until recently, nonbiological same-sex
parents had no legal standing to bring a custody suit, but nonhomonormative
LGBTQ parents still face considerable additional discrimination (Pearson 2012).
In communities with greater routine paternal involvement in daily care, stigma
for noncustodial mothers may be less considerable. For example, despite stereotypes, Black nonresidential fathers maintain greater contact with their very young
children than other groups (Edin, Tach, and Mincy 2009).

Those who experience stigma must also then manage that stigma. Noncustodial mothers are, in Goffman's terms, discreditable. Unlike the discredited whose
stigma is more visible, the noncustodial mother's stigma is not immediately apparent. It remains concealable. Stigma management, then, takes a variety of forms
that relate directly to the concealed nature of their stigma. The noncustodial
mothers I spoke with had a range of means for navigating their discreditable status. At other times and in other contexts, when their noncustodial status is
known, noncustodial mothers find themselves among the discredited, which requires more active managing of potentially outright hostile interactions. This
chapter is devoted to exploring and understanding the stigma noncustodial
mothers face, tracing the sources and origins of that stigma, understanding the
ways in which they attempt to navigate it, and laying out the implications of the
interplay of these processes.

The most common thread of noncustodial mothers' experiences of stigma is
when people assume that they have done something wrong to lose custody of their
child. For mothers, just having custody of a child *contested* is enough to invoke
the stigma (Chesler 2011). Rhonda said, "I can't tell people. I cannot tell people
that I don't have custody of my son. It's horrible. People look at you like something's wrong with you. And I'm ashamed. Not only do I not have custody, I lost
custody of him. And there's such a generalization out there that once you have custody of children that you can't lose it unless you're in jail. And I did. So I just
don't talk about it." Noncustodial mothers report having people assume that they
were alcoholics or drug addicts, that they were promiscuous, that they had abandoned or abused their child, that they were too mentally ill to care for their child,
that they were a criminal of some sort, or that they were just irredeemably selfish. Olive noted, "The huge message from the people in my life and the people in
the greater world and the greater culture is that I was selfish and I was a bad person and that I was a bad mother."

Even though Christine had not lost custody for any nefarious reason, she felt
intensely stigmatized. In the years since she first lost custody, not much had
changed for her: "I've never gotten over it. I have never been able to not be hor-
rified or ashamed. I've never been accepted at the kids' school." Other noncusto-

dial mothers talk about a sense of unease when they disclose their custodial situation. Cassie said, "When he wasn't with us and I would say to people, 'Oh, I have a son,' they would be, like, looking around for him. And I would just get looks [that said], 'You awful person, how could you do that?' I would hear, women would say to me, 'I could never do that.' I would think in my head, well I hope you never have to make that choice, but I would just kind of clam up."

For many noncustodial mothers, budding friendships were made more difficult, or even derailed, by stigma if they chose to disclose their status. Christine remembered, "She invited me over to a Super Bowl party. I said the kids had two homes and she goes, 'Oh my gosh, what happened?' So I told her the whole story, and the more I told her the straighter her back was getting and her head was turning the other way. And by the end, she had taken back her invitation, and she hasn't spoken to me since." Like Christine, Cassie felt that she had to overcome others' judgments of her before she could form new friendships: "There was always that initial, you know, reaction. It was like I had to prove myself as a mom to them before we could become friends. And I don't know what it was that I did, but then we were friendly."

Running into old friends and acquaintances came with the potential for stigmatization. Esther did not usually experience stigma in this way since she did not live near her ex-partner or children. However, with social media, she found herself exposed to criticism: "I found some friends from high school on Facebook and this one said, "Oh hey, how are you doing? I heard [through] the grapevine that you got divorced and like lost your kids." I was mortified! I can't imagine how it would feel if he lived in the same town. If you're in the same town, like down the street, why the hell can't the mother have custody? But I don't feel that because my circumstances are a little different."

Other noncustodial mothers found that long-term friendships succumbed under the weight of the stigma. Losing a friend was a common theme of discussion threads in the support communities. Sometimes, noncustodial mothers reported losing the support of family members as well. Pam said, "I lost everybody including the vast majority of my own family. I actually moved out of that town because I was more notorious than Britney Spears."

Monica lost custody when she relocated to another town for a promotion. Afterward, she lost her best friend as well: "This was someone that I went through thick and thin with. I was there for her divorce. The abuse she had to get out of. I never judged her. Now I needed her. I just hurt so badly and she turned and looked at me and told me that I was a terrible mother. Yes, those words. It felt like a slap. And she told me all the things that I should have done differently. She would never move for work if she had a child. It was my fault. P.S. she had no kids." It was not unusual for particularly strong negative reactions to be aimed at noncustodial mothers who became noncustodial because of a move related to their career. Cassie remembered, "He said, 'If that was my child, I'd scrub toilets at Wal-Mart instead of looking at my career.'" Interestingly, mothers who moved to remarry rather than for an employment opportunity did not seem to report the move as inciting additional stigma beyond their noncustodial status.

Stigma is felt in direct and indirect ways. Noncustodial mothers report that their experiences include very direct social sanctions, sometimes from acquaintances or strangers. These ranged from subtle to outright nasty. Take the case of Rahna Reiko Rizzuto, the author of *Hiroshima in the Morning*, who has been vilified (including on television) and threatened with violence because she gave her ex-husband physical custody of their children. Despite the fact that she lived down the street from her children, was involved in every aspect of their lives, and had a good co-parenting relationship with her ex-husband, she was repeatedly accused of being selfish and abandoning her children. The following quote is from Rahna, who agreed to allow her name to be used in the book. Here she summarizes the criticism she has faced, including from her appearance on *The View*:

> One of the things people keep saying to me is, "You think your kids are great, but you don't know the kind of abandonment issues they're going to have when they're older. You don't know the kind of emotional havoc that you're wreaking," and Barbara Walters [saying], "How can you go back to kids who know you don't love them?" The idea that you are not there means that you don't love them. I think that my kids are old enough that we can talk about this a lot. They feel very secure and they feel very loved, and I really do think that they're having some really interesting and eye-opening experiences about what happens when adults are complicated and fallible, and trying their best and trying to change their world. [They say], "My mother is different but she's a good mom." What does that mean about motherhood in general? And isn't it ok to change your life to suit yourself as long as everybody is cared for. I think it's a hugely important lesson and a very interesting one, and again, people don't see it that way.

The kind of hyperbolic vitriol Rahna has experienced is the stuff of nightmares for the noncustodial mothers I met. While most of them would never have an encounter with Barbara Walters on television, fear of similar feedback was a constant companion. Poor public treatment of noncustodial mothers was something talked about in the support communities. In person, particular kinds of situations provided greater opportunity to be judged publicly. For those mothers who are able to be involved in school-related events, sporting events and parent-teacher conferences were a source of anxiety. Diane experienced difficult interactions with other parents at her children's sporting events: "You can tell by the facial expression, reactions, the way they talk. You can just sense it. Some of it may be in my mind but I'd say more times that it isn't. The automatic reaction is probably, 'What did you do?' 'What's wrong with you?'" Rahna echoed the experience of negative reactions from other parents who seemed to ostracize her: "When I dropped the kids off or something like that, other parents I knew wouldn't talk to me. They wouldn't look at me. They were just like, "Who are you and what are you doing here? I'm really angry at you." People get angry at me as if my kids were going to be in jail."

Parents of their children's friends were another source of anxiety, as were teachers and school parent-teacher associations. Angela's experience with her daughter's school highlighted a common theme in online discussions.

> There was a school receptionist, and it was in the middle of our court case. You've got all seven sets of documents that you've got to give these people. Listen, all I want to do is see my kids' grades. All I want to do is make an appointment. All I want to do is talk to her teacher. But you have to convince them that you have every right to do this. She says, "You're not a real parent," and I was like (gasps), I recall very vividly how I felt. I don't recall what I said to her but it was a good five-minute dissertation.

Like Angela, Virginia found herself disqualified as a parent because of her noncustodial status.

> I joined a meet-up group for moms and you have to give a description of your family life, why you want to join. And the leader of the group replied back to me and said, "So I'm not really understanding what is your motivation behind wanting to join this group if you're not a full-time mom." I thought it was not a very cool email. I'm a mom. If your child was in college, would I tell you that you're not a mom? What's my motivation? I wanted to connect with more moms regardless of where my son is. I'm still a mom, period.

The stigma of being a noncustodial mother can make its way into the courts. Angela, who voluntarily became the noncustodial parent after her divorce, felt some hostility coming from the judge when she had to go to court to enforce her custody agreement: "I was a noncustodial mother in court so I didn't look good. I looked like some sort of degenerate who just took off. [That] was the first time I realized truly how society viewed me. I mean, there were people at work, but it wasn't as oppressive a feeling of, "Oh my gosh, they think I'm bad!" And that was pretty eye opening when I realized this guy in the black robe in front of me would decide my entire future and it's already predetermined what I was. And that was not cool."

The effects of stigma spill over onto the children when they are treated differently from other children or excluded in some way. Goffman (1963) and others have referred to this as courtesy stigma, a kind of guilt by association. Christine expressed a similar sentiment: "They judge our children. They discriminate against our family. They are not empathetic about your going a day or two or eleven without seeing your children. There are some children that are no longer able to associate with my children. I tried for four years to be active in the PTA or be the class mom and I never got chosen. In third grade they needed someone in my son's class. Instead of letting me do it, they begged and pleaded with another mother in the class who worked full-time and couldn't even come to most of the stuff." Even ex-partners experienced courtesy stigma as part of a divorced family with a noncustodial mother. Tabitha observed, "When someone finds out that he's a single dad and they ask him, 'What did she do?' you know and he's like, 'Nothing. Nothing bad. And she still comes and gets them and does what she needs to do.' 'Did she not want them?'"

Overall, stigma is one of the most common experiences noncustodial mothers share. In 2012 I authored a blog post about stigma and noncustodial mothers for a women's news website. As this book goes to press, that post has garnered almost seven hundred comments. The comments precisely echo the data from my interviews and online support group participation and include everything from, "I feel like there must be something wrong with me," to, "It's refreshing to know that I'm not alone."

Stigma Management

Noncustodial mothers engage in many kinds of stigma management, including passing as custodial mothers, attempting to control information, and concealing stigma symbols, the things that reveal their stigmatized status (Goffman 1963). The deep shame and fear of a stigmatized identity leads many noncustodial mothers to remain silent and even to hide their status as mothers. Many noncustodial mothers specifically mentioned being very careful about telling someone that they do not have custody. This included potential friends and romantic partners, as well as coworkers, neighbors, and casual acquaintances. A lot of thought goes into determining what information to reveal and whom to reveal it to. Some noncustodial mothers avoided friendships specifically with those who had children at home. When asked why they do not let others know about their situation, the most common answer is fear of judgment. Noncustodial mothers often mention their shared history of being on guard and managing strange looks, insensitive comments, and harsh judgments from friends, family, new acquaintances, part-ners, and school personnel.

Information control was something that was very much on the minds of non-custodial mothers when they talked to me about stigma. Of information control, Goffman (1963, 42) writes, "To display or not to display; to tell or not to tell; to let on or not to let on; to lie or not to lie; and in each case, to whom, how, when, and where." Many noncustodial mothers I spoke with practice stigma avoidance through information control by keeping their family life separate from their work life. Pam explained, "It's a place where exactly two people know about my per-sonal life. That's pretty much the way it always is. I don't really feel like I can share that part of myself. It's just, you know, way too much."

Another shared tactic was limiting their contacts and friendships, though this self-imposed isolation led to its own set of difficulties. Some augmented their strategy by befriending only single women, which accomplished the dual purpose of enabling them to avoid stigma while also allowing them not to focus on miss-ing their children. Nina explained, "Who do you socialize with? I've always had problems having friends with kids because I can't join the conversations. I can socialize with people who don't have kids. That's usually been easier. It puts the women in a place, especially if you don't remarry and have more kids or some-thing, it puts you in a strange category, social-wise." Like Nina, Bonnie finds it easier to have friends without children so that she does not have to talk about her situation: "My friends don't have children because I really couldn't be around other children without hurting so bad and wanting my own children. My friends don't have children so I never talked about it with anybody." For mothers who disclosed that they had children, one strategy was to simply say that the children were "at their dad's house" without reference to the custodial situation at all. This strategy was effective only in transitory contacts and interactions; strategies of in-formation control were different for more sustained relationships. Thus, stigma management was more difficult at home, where neighbors could observe the pres-ence (and absence) of children. For example, some mothers talked about avoid-ing neighbors, who could more easily figure out the custodial situation by seeing their children around on the weekends but not during the school week. Esther, whose children lived in Europe, had a slightly different approach: "I kind of make it sound like the kids are doing something more important, you know. I say, 'Well, my daughter's in art school in Europe, and my son is studying 3 languages next year!' [They say], 'Oh how wonderful!' So I can kind of hide behind that." Non-custodial mothers who choose to manage stigma by passing prefer to render their children invisible to outsiders as a way to pass as a woman without children. The workplace was a common arena where noncustodial mothers were especially careful about exposing themselves. They actively avoided coworkers with children or remained silent in conversations about children. In an effort to manage the stigma, noncustodial mothers concealed stigma symbols, avoiding adding personal touches like school pictures or Mother's Day cards in their offices or workspaces. Beyond the emotional effects of stigma, some had the practical concern that they might lose their jobs if anyone were to find out their noncustodial status. Bonnie explained, "I don't tell anyone I'm noncustodial. It's none of their business. Especially at work. I don't want to have to explain the whole thing and get the look." Jeanne felt that her wage garnishment for child support gave her away to her employer, leading to her losing her job:

> I would go get a job and with the wage garnishment, I just can't keep it. I've been brought in and told, "This doesn't support the company's values." They don't know where I've been. They're certain I've cleaned up my life now, but for this to be going on, they don't want any part of it. They can see my credit and that I pay my child support. I have never missed a payment regardless of how sick I was, unemployed, anything. I was a person who paid child support. They see my child support and just know I'm a horrible mother.

Most employment in US states is at-will, meaning that a person can be fired for no reason or any reason, as long as it is not an illegal reason. It is unlikely that noncustodial parental status can be construed as part of any protected category, and although there is legal protection from being fired for having a wage garnishment, like other forms of discrimination, it is nearly impossible to prove.

In the support groups, mothers shared additional stigma avoidance strategies. These were a topic of much discussion and debate, particularly since the participants were straining to "feel like a mom" even as they removed tangible signs of their children from view. Some noncustodial mothers were adamant about not denying they had children. Fernanda said, "I can't do that. I mean, they're local and my kids live close to me. I do see them often. I mean, if someone out and out asked me, 'Are you a mom?' I would say 'Yeah.'" Some hid their motherhood status at home as well as at work. They were quick to add, however, that they kept cherished pictures and drawings their children had made, but that it was too risky and too painful to surround themselves with these reminders that could invite internalized self-stigma or stigma from visitors. Noncustodial mothers often felt conflicted about these kinds of stigma avoidance strategies, particularly when they rendered their children invisible to the outside world. However, sometimes the path of least resistance was welcomed.

Noncustodial mothers who have other children who are custodial—often from a newer relationship—did practice information control. Their information control was different because their custodial children served as a kind of disidenti-

fier. Disidentifiers can disrupt the interaction enough that the mothers successfully avoid stigma. Val noted," I don't think I've experienced the stigma as much
as some of the other noncustodial moms I know. I don't know if it's just that when
people ask, I'm really matter of fact about it. Or, I'm like, I have 3 kids. Two live
with their dad and one lives with me. And it's not a big deal to me."

For noncustodial mothers, stigma, stigma management, and stigma avoidance
were constant unwelcome companions that rendered normally routine relationships and interactions problematic. Fernanda observed, "There are good days and
there are bad days for everyone. I imagine that if people knew I was noncustodial
they could look at me on one of those bad days and go, 'Oh, maybe that's why,'
you know. 'Maybe she acts that way with her own kids.' I don't want to go there."
Daisy worries that she will cry in public when she sees other people enjoying their
children: "It's hard to see anybody with their kids. I just don't have a lot of friends.
[The stigma] makes me cry a lot. I'm just at home a lot."

The main effect of the stigma, however, was a profound sense of isolation for
the noncustodial mothers, often because of others' judgments or their fears of
judgment. They expressed having difficulty trusting new friends or work acquaintances, and often changed their behavior or plans in anticipation of stigma.
Stigma management was ever present.

Being the Good Mother

A common method of stigma management was being the "good mother." Finding ways to enact "good motherhood" was important in resisting stigmatization.
Despite the constant need to manage and avoid stigma, most of the noncustodial
mothers I interviewed did not internalize stigma. Even though they spent considerable time enacting stigma management, contrary to Lynne Clumpus's (1996)
findings, they did not blame themselves, nor did they accept the label of "bad
mother." They clearly articulated that they had not done anything deserving of
losing custody. Also unexpected was the low degree of othering aimed at other
noncustodial mothers. Most noncustodial mothers steered clear of reifying the
good mother–bad mother binary by comparing themselves with mothers who
they thought deserved to lose custody. Instead, they contended that any mother
could lose custody. Yet even as they recognized this, on occasion, noncustodial
mothers reinvigorated the stereotypes that plagued them. Christine said, "I could
have been Mother Theresa. In fact, I was darn near close. They had nothing on
me. I wasn't an alcoholic, drug-dealing, prostitute."

Although not explicitly stated by participants, race and class are implicated,
as they always are, in definitions of good motherhood. At these moments, the

narrative around noncustodial motherhood does not challenge the stigma but rather reinforces hierarchies among women.[1] On the other hand, in the context of discourses of responsible fatherhood aimed at communities of color, broader definitions of motherhood that incorporate nonbiological and othermothering may alleviate the need for some mothers to manage stigma quite so closely. It remains an empirical question whether or to what extent stigma is shaped by parents' racial and other identities.

Despite the centrality of stigma to their identity, noncustodial mothers do have a keen sense of the broader context in which their status arose and they work hard to "be a good mom" under the circumstances. Even if they were long-distance noncustodial mothers, most found ways to be a good mother given their current status. Indeed, finding ways to be a good mother and sharing those with the support group was another common means of managing the stigma. For example, noncustodial mothers often shared information about ways to impart their values or deal with discipline in the space of a weekend. They made suggestions for how to interact well with the other parent or maintain contact with teachers. Some of the most heartfelt exchanges involved suggestions for how to help with homework over the phone and to stay close to children over long distances.

There were many creative and impressive ways noncustodial mothers found to enact their definition of a good mother. So how exactly did noncustodial mothers work toward good motherhood in their stigmatized status? For some, being a good mother meant ending the custody conflict, but for others it meant that they "never stop fighting." Very frequently, noncustodial mothers mentioned not bad-mouthing the other parent as an important component of being a good mother. The experience of being bad-mouthed, however, was a recurrent theme in the online support communities. Avoiding bad-mouthing was difficult to do in high-conflict relationships, particularly if it was evident that they were being disparaged in the custodial parent's household. Tabitha said, "If they tell me things aren't going the way they want at home, I try not to do anything in front of them that says I don't support their father because that would be very, very bad. He usually makes pretty good decisions. It's hard." Some noncustodial mothers emphasized the importance of managing their demeanor in front of their children, especially when interacting with their ex-partners or their children's stepparents and in public settings like recitals, graduations, and school events. Angela urged, "Always take the high road. No matter what occurs or happens in front of you. That's ultimately what's gonna be what serves your children best. You're gonna provide an example. These things are so lengthy. It's years after it starts. So if you can spend that period doing something, keeping your mouth shut, not saying what you think, just taking the high road, it really does make a difference."

Those few who internalized stigma were hesitant to be more involved in their children's lives. The mothers who most internalized the stigma often had some form of supervised visitation, which designated them as discredited rather than just discreditable. Supervised visitation, while not necessarily more visible in all situations, does mark the mother's status as extreme because she is unable to see her child without third-party supervision. None of the mothers on supervised visitation that I spoke with had a pattern of violence toward or neglect of their children. One mother had a history of mental illness that had been controlled well for several years. Two other mothers had supervised visitations because they were seen as at risk for kidnapping their children because of a highly contentious custody battle. Supervised visitation also carries an extra cost since the supervisor is often paid unless a family member can be agreed on by both parties to act as supervisor.

Even mothers who were not under supervised visitation found it difficult not to engage in defensive cowering (Goffman 1963, 17), a way of making oneself inconspicuous by sitting in the back of the auditorium or watching sports from afar. Sometimes, defensive cowering was a means to avoid conflict, which they understood as part of their efforts to be a good mother. Others disagreed with this strategy and felt that it was in resisting their marginalization of themselves that they were being good mothers. These mothers made a point of not appearing ashamed in public by sitting in the front row and asserting themselves in social contexts like religious ceremonies, birthday parties, and school plays.

The mothers with the most fraught co-parenting relationships or with supervised visits found it hardest to find ways to be a good mother. For example, having an ex-partner who interfered with parenting time made it difficult for participants to feel like a mother at all. There were participants in my sample and in the online support communities who had not seen their child in months or, in some cases, years. At those times, participants in the online support groups often brought up this idea of mothering as something that does not end when your child reaches age eighteen. Even though they may be missing the early childhood years, noncustodial mothers remind themselves to take the long view of parenting as a way to resist internalizing stigma. Val explained, "I'm focusing more on what I'm going to be able to do for them when they're grown. You know, when they graduate high school and they move out of Dad's house, how am I going to be able to help them find their way in this world? So, when I get frustrated, I just remind myself of that. I know we're going to have a really good relationship when they're adults. I'm the one who can show them how to budget, how to make decisions about what they want. I can help them be grownups."

A prominent theme that arose was the importance of doing the mundane things that mothers do, such as tucking kids in at bedtime, doing laundry, cooking meals, talking with teachers, and taking kids to the dentist. Many specifically juxtaposed their own style of doing these mundane activities with that of the Disneyland dad. Angela said, "One of the things I don't want to be is the Disneyland parent. I don't want that. I hated it. I saw it so many times with other families around me and I did not want to be that. So my big thing is that we do normal household stuff on the weekends. We wake up. We make breakfast. We work in the yard. We do laundry. We may bowl later or something. We may go to a movie. But it wasn't a constant stream of entertainment. It was all about creating those routines in our home." Similarly, Nina explained, "I love washing their clothes, and making them dinner. And everything you do exemplifies [being a mother], at least for me, you know, I don't get to do it very often."

Similarly, noncustodial mothers were proud when they were seen as the go-to adult when children had important decisions to make or difficult topics to discuss. For example, talking about sexuality (having the talk) and dating with one's children is not necessarily something that is easy to do when limited to two weekends a month, but mothers who experienced these moments were able to cast off, even temporarily, the shameful shroud of noncustodial motherhood. As Val shared, "Sometimes I get little parenting moments. My son last year talked to me about sex. And he brought it up, you know. And that was amazing. I mean, I have to make myself remember that when he's being a brat. He talked to me about something really important. He trusted me. So, you still get to parent for some things." Some seemed surprised that even though they did not have extensive contact with their children, they were still an important source of emotional support for them. They may not be able to perform the day-to-day tasks they did when they lived with their children, but they could take on the emotional labor, as Fiona observed: "They would call me when they were with their dad to talk about important stuff, to help 'em make decisions." Similarly, Daisy said, "I had been all along telling her, look you can tell me anything. And I'm like, I won't get mad, which is hard, so she'll feel comfortable telling me things. And so [my daughter] told me about my son getting thrown across the room by a roommate."

Taken together, the picture of noncustodial mothers is of a group of women who, despite stigma, distance, and sometimes very little parenting time, manage to enact motherhood in important and meaningful ways. One mother said it was important for her to "keep [her] mom identity," and another characterized it as "keeping a foot in the door." Cassie drove eight hours every other week to see her son, even when she was pregnant with her second child. These mothers' stories match data that show that noncustodial mothers largely do not step out of children's lives postdivorce (S. Stewart 1999).

Reproducing and Resisting Intensive Motherhood

The noncustodial mothers I interacted with made impressive efforts to remain meaningfully involved in their children's lives, in spite of the logistical and emotional difficulties. In their efforts to manage stigma and to feel like a mother, it was common for noncustodial mothers to continue to try to meet the standards of intensive mothering regardless of time and distance. The noncustodial mothers whose efforts most closely mirrored intensive mothering offered that it was a means to help them feel like a mother. For example, Christine stated, "I'm at all of their school events. I'm at all of their sporting events. I'm at every single thing that I could possibly be, not that their father wants me there." Maggie similarly voiced,

> I don't hesitate to call the schools. I keep in touch with the teachers. Now I participate at the Karate studio. Football games, I was always at them. I coached their other sports. And then it was "you need to take them to practices, you need to do this," because I signed them up. So yeah, I've done basically everything for those kids and driven myself into poverty.
>
> [*Husband interjects:*] For two years straight she worked, left, went to sports Monday, came home, ate, went to sleep, got up, went to work, left work, went to sports, came home, ate. Wednesday, went to work, picked them up and brought them home, and had to take them back to Dad's. Then, Thursday was sports again. Saturday was sports again. It went on for two years where she didn't miss a game. The first game she missed [her ex-husband told her son], "Your mom doesn't love you."

Noncustodial mothers whose children were old enough and whose contact their ex-partners did not block made use of technology like cell phones and social media as a way to mother from afar. Helping with homework on the phone was not uncommon. Fernanda, who used to homeschool her children, continued to offer them intensive academic help when they were with her: "I still have homeschooling materials and I still use them with the kids to help them with stuff they're struggling with at school or to provide them extras, enrichment opportunities type of thing." Attending sporting events, meeting with teachers, helping with homework, and driving them to activities were responsibilities that the mothers had when their children had lived with them full time. They continued to perform many of these tasks via phone, Facebook, Snapchat, and email.

Those whose access to their children was curtailed still found ways to use technology to connect with them. Janet's teenagers were forbidden from using the computer in their father's home without close supervision explicitly because he wanted to limit contact with their mother. In contrast, when they were at her home they were allowed to be on the computer. She and her children wrote emails to each other that at least she could read when they were not there. Some mothers used social media to get a sense of what was going on in their children's lives. One common experience of noncustodial mothers was the inability to get routine information about how the children were doing socially. These mothers felt that it was an important part of mothering to monitor their children's social media for any problematic activity, and they would address that with their children.

For those who lived more than an hour away from their child, enacting motherhood was especially difficult; however, there were many examples in interviews and in the online support groups of mothers who would drive great distances, sometimes several times a week, to see their children's sports. For example, Pam routinely got up at four o'clock in the morning to drive over three hours to her son's Saturday soccer games, which started at eight o'clock.

Birthdays posed a special problem for noncustodial mothers. Even when the co-parenting relationship was good, many mothers felt that planning birthday parties should be their responsibility as a mother. For those with poor co-parenting relationships or those who lived at quite a distance, birthdays could be an exercise in frustration. It was difficult to connect with friends or classmates. Often they did not have access to that information. Suggestions to hold a second birthday party were appreciated but difficult to execute.

Another frequent discussion in the support groups was children's clothing. It was not unusual for the noncustodial mother to purchase most, if not all, of her child's clothing (Chalabi 2015), sometimes to her own financial detriment. The expectation of child support payments is that they would cover a substantial portion of a child's necessities like clothing, but often the mothers found that this was not the case. Hannah explained, "I could not just let him have ripped socks or pants that were two sizes too small. It didn't matter to him. How could I let him have these dirty clothes? I was broke, but I made sure that he looked presentable. Of course, the next month, he'd come with something else that was a mess." Noncustodial mothers ended up purchasing clothing for reasons connected to their own ideals of mothering. Even though noncustodial mothers were not physically present in the same way as when they were full-time mothers, they felt they would still be judged for their child's poor appearance. Their child's cleanliness was a source of anxiety for them. Monica said, "Oh my god. He smelled. It was heartbreaking. They were just dirty people and he smelled when he got here. So I would throw him in the tub immediately. And I would tell him to remember to take a bath at his dad's house. I would remind him so he wouldn't smell. I couldn't let him go to school like that."

Lastly, it was not unusual for noncustodial mothers to arrange for routine medical care for their children. These mothers knew all of their child's medical providers and kept track of when they were due for dental cleanings and eye exams and would keep detailed records even after losing custody. Pam explained, "I keep journals of who their friends are, who their teachers are, what they're doing for homework. I always try to make sure that I have accurate and up to date knowledge of what was actually happening in their lives. I would have to, very forcefully sometimes, integrate myself into their school life. I made sure that their teachers knew I existed; I was part of their life. I wanted to be copied on all teacher notes. This takes some work."

Taken together, these examples show that many noncustodial mothers were still taking on the management part of mothering even when living at a distance. The invisible labor of managing children's lives is almost always mothers' labor (Walzer 1996). Mothers' responsibility for every aspect of their children's lives is integral to the operation of intensive mothering. Mothers who could not accomplish intensive mothering often felt that they were failing, as Christine explained: "I'm just beating myself in the head because I'm teaching my babies things that are important in the three or four days that I have them. Slouching at the table, wearing matching socks, washing her hair every day. I've taken her to the doctor. But I don't know how to be a [noncustodial] mom. I don't know because I don't have a model. There's no one I can ask. I just try to do as much as I can in the days that I have them."

A subgroup of noncustodial mothers, especially those who had their children for large blocks of time over the summer, really struggled with the seasonal shift to intensive mothering. Sandra observed,

> It's so hard to understand going from not being a mom for 10 months then all of a sudden being a mom 24/7 for the two or three months that I have them. And don't get me wrong, I am so grateful for the time that I have and glad to have them here, but it's really hard to flip that switch. All of a sudden, you're a mom. It's very jarring. You know, I go from doing whatever all day long and then all of a sudden my entire focus is the kids. [People] think you should just be so grateful that they're here, you know, and you're not with them all the time. And once they get past the "why don't you have your kids all the time," they think you must have done something really bad not to have custody because "moms always get custody."

Not being able to uphold intensive mothering made many noncustodial mothers feel guilty, a finding that is not surprising given the gender guilt gap (Hays 1996). Nevertheless, they continue to try to meet the standards of intensive motherhood. As a result of these stigma management strategies, noncustodial mothers unintentionally reproduce and reinforce the cultural power of intensive motherhood.

All of these actions around mothering children from afar can be understood as doing gender, a term that will be discussed in greater depth in the next chapter.

Briefly, *doing gender* is a term that highlights the ways in which gender is not something that is static or something that we have but rather something that is interactional and that is accomplished by what we do and how we do it (West and Zimmerman 1987). Noncustodial mothers enacted motherhood in a way that was important to their understanding of this gendered identity. At times, they subscribed to intensive motherhood, an ideology that contends that good mothers must be "child centered, expert-guided, emotionally absorbing, labor-intensive, and financially expensive" (Hays 1996, 54). Not surprisingly, doing gender often reproduces larger social relations of power.

Nevertheless, noncustodial mothers often did resist stigma in a variety of ways, despite the cultural power of intensive motherhood, and the lack of role models. Sometimes their resistance lay in explicitly rejecting the stigma of noncustodial motherhood as something they deserved, as Nina did: "The old stigma that's around, you know. Well, bad things do happen to good people. Hello!" Some noncustodial mothers like Angela were more assertive than others: "You see it in people's faces. It's just there. I had to get to a place where I just say, 'they live in another state with their dad, it's not my choice.' I just spit it out. I still talk about 'em as my girls and things like that but oh yeah. People draw really quick judgments on it but since I've been doing it for so long, I haven't broken down and slapped any of 'em yet. I'd like to!" Other noncustodial mothers pushed back against friends, family, teachers, or others whom they felt stigmatized them. Olive explained, "They weren't supportive of the idea that there might be a different kind of motherhood. I was really flying blind. I was internalizing all this kind of stuff. It took a long time I think for me to feel good about what I was trying to do and able to claim it as 'No, this is a different kind of motherhood but I am still here.'" Although not initially someone who pushed back, Carla eventually came to resist feelings of shame: "Being a mom, not having your kids, you're ashamed. You don't want to tell anybody. You just claim not to have kids. It used to be the better way to do it. It's not anymore because I know I don't have anything to be ashamed of now."

Noncustodial mothers often found expectations placed on them by their ex-partners. Noncustodial mothers like Sandra resisted by putting the onus of daily oversight back onto the custodial household: "I can't tell you how many incidents this year he's forgetting his homework, not doing his work, lying about it and all kinds of really bad school stuff. So he puts them on the phone for me to talk to them. I'm like, you know I can talk to them and reason with them but I can't set up consequences from here. I can't walk behind [my son] and make sure he's doing what he's supposed to do."

In other cases, noncustodial mothers like Val had to directly address their children's expectations of them as a mother: "Sometimes they try to use their stepmom to stab me in the heart. When they say [their stepmom] is a better mom than you are or whatever. You know, that kind of hurts, but I just tell them that I'm a different kind of mom than she is."

There were mothers like Maggie who clearly articulated a resistance to societal judgments of them both in terms of stigma and in terms of what is expected of mothers and asserted their motherhood status: "I take my role as mom very seriously. It's my priority. And it doesn't matter what title society gives me. I'm still a mom. It doesn't change."

Some mothers spoke directly to the social construct of motherhood, decoupling the quotidian or the emotional labor from being a good mother. As Olive observed,

> If the mother is the person who has to take care of stuff, the mother is the person who is always monitoring things, always putting the kids to bed and stuff like that. I have been told that if I'm not the one putting the kids to bed than I'm missing out and I'm not a mother. But I don't feel like I have to be part of every single moment of their lives. Or that if I didn't tuck them into bed, it means that I didn't have all the other things I needed to be close. I think in our society that women, especially mothers, are seen as responsible for somebody else's happiness.

As mentioned earlier, most noncustodial mothers did not participate in the kind of othering that reinscribes a good mother–bad mother dichotomy. Although many worked hard to uphold the dictates of intensive motherhood, some challenged those norms, potentially undoing gender (Deutsch 2007).[2] Neither did they, on the whole, unbecome mothers as described by Diana Gustafson (2005), who notes the difficult social process encountered by mothers who come to live apart from a biological child. These noncustodial mothers, however, very much asserted their status as mothers and attempted to remain connected and meaningfully involved in their children's lives while sometimes reproducing and other times challenging the tenets of intensive motherhood.

It's about Gender

The stigma that noncustodial mothers feel is related to the ways in which they fall short of normative motherhood, a stigma that is decisively gendered. The new momism and its impossible expectations, monomaternalism, and neoliberalism all contribute to the stigma that labels noncustodial mothers as deficient, defective, or shameful. In dominant cultural discourses in the contemporary United States, the terrain between good mother and bad mother under any circumstances is short and steep. It is easy to slip from good mother to bad mother because there is an "extraordinary elasticity of the 'bad' mother label" (Ladd-Taylor and Umansky 1998, 2), indicating a vast array of ways in which mothers can come to be labeled bad. This flexibility of the "bad mother" label is demonstrated in the following list of historical reasons why children have been removed from their mothers by the state: "because for example the woman in question was disabled, a political activist, too young, unmarried, comatose, divorced and had sex, too old, the wrong race, an atheist, a Native American, deaf, mentally ill, retarded, seeking an abortion, lesbian, reported to speak Spanish to her child, enrolled in full-time college, a drug user, poor" (Solinger 1998, 383). This list echoes the vast, variable, and often contradictory list of reasons for losing custody given by the noncustodial mothers I interviewed and interacted with. Furthermore, the label "bad mother" stretches and contracts to fit any situation in ways that implicate other dimensions of identity and social inequality, such as sexuality, race, and class. For example, expectations placed on white, middle-class mothers mean that dropping out of the workplace can be framed as securing social approval, while for poor mothers or mothers of color, social expectations and institutional constraints make the same action of dropping out difficult, if not catastrophic. When poor women and women of color drop out of the workforce, they are at the very least confronted with the labels "lazy" and "bad mother."

The new momism (Douglas and Michaels 2004; Ennis 2014; Hays 1996; McHenry and Schultz 2014) consists of "standards of success [that] are impossible to meet" (Douglas and Michaels, 4). The imperatives brought by the new momism are mandatory motherhood, primary mother care, and full mental and physical devotion to one's children. No matter what else you are, you must demonstrate, repeatedly, your good motherhood and "first prove that you are a doting, totally involved mother before proceeding" (Douglas and Michaels, 22) (1). Mothers only need one strike to be disqualified.

Recall that the reasons women gave for their noncustodial mother status included everything from lengthy court proceedings and not having enough money to moving for work or voluntarily giving custody to the father. Regardless of the reason for their noncustodial status, every mother in the study experienced some degree of stigma relating to that status. At times, the stigma they felt was intense. Certainly stigma has an impact on the psychological level, but it is also embedded in our social relations and institutions. Noncustodial parenting produces identities for women in a way that it does not for men. Even mothers who do not feel psychological effects of their noncustodial status are subject to highly stigmatized identities that do not exist for noncustodial fathers. While noncustodial fathers may dislike their situation or miss their children, their status as noncustodial does not as swiftly confer on them a societal judgment about their gender, nor does it require them to manage their identity as a father without custody. The exception is for poor fathers, especially poor men of color, who are often judged as deadbeats. The label of "deadbeat dad," however, relates to the financial imperatives of fatherhood more so than to daily caregiving. Noncustodial fathers may also be socially rewarded for any amount of caregiving participation with the label of "involved dad" so long as the financial requirement has been met.

The normative nature of the low expectations placed on the noncustodial father is problematic in its own right. Here, however, that normativity is part of the relationality of the stigma that noncustodial mothers face. Our low expectations of fathers are intertwined with our high (and impossible) expectations of mothers. This makes noncustodial mothers gender transgressors. By definition, these mothers fail to do gender properly by virtue of their distance from the status of primary caregiver. The sharpness of the stigma aimed at noncustodial mothers is a form of gender policing, a social sanction for violating the tenets of intensive motherhood. Noncustodial mothers like Carla are quite aware of this gender dynamic: "With a noncustodial dad you say that to somebody and they're like, "oh, ok, poor thing. I'm sorry you don't get to see your kids." Nobody questions what they did to become that way. Nobody ever questions that. You say you're a noncustodial mother and people start filing through the list of offenses that you must have done to become that. You must be a drug user, you must have been neglectful, you must have been an abuser, you must have just up and left 'em." Noncustodial mothers fail immediately on one key dimension of motherhood in contemporary US culture: being there. Stay-at-home mothers identify the necessity to be there for their children as an important principle for their not being in the labor force. Even though they are not with their children every minute of the day, they understand their location outside the labor force as making them more available to their children, just in case—in case of sickness, for homework help, or anything else. Employed mothers, however, feel the need to explain the ways in which they are there despite their location in the labor market. If employed mothers struggle with maternal legitimacy because they are seen as absentee mothers, then noncustodial mothers may experience this even more so because their absence is not limited to work time. Dominant discourses and media portrayals of motherhood reinforce that motherhood is still defined in large part by being there in terms of both quantity time and emotional support (E. Boyd 2002). Cassie shared her frustration in this way:

> I was getting so frustrated too because all the books about the dads in my position celebrated what a good dad he would be if he had the child one night a week and every other weekend. But people were looking at me like what a horrible mother I was because I only had him one night

a week and every other weekend. So on the one hand, I'd be reading these books talking about how heroic the dad would be and when I was doing the same thing, it was like way less. For the moms, somehow, we've failed. Somehow we've failed. We haven't sacrificed enough for our kids because if we did, they'd be with us.

Today's attachment-parenting movement hyperbolizes the tenets of being there and intensive motherhood, dictating that mothers must be omnipresent and, preferably, wearing their babies. Attachment parenting promotes a kind of oneness between mother and child, a practice that is critiqued for denying mothers their own needs (Vissing 2014, 116). Mothers must embrace every aspect of motherhood without expressing ambivalence, much less displeasure. White, upper-middle-class women are most likely to subscribe to intensive mothering; and therefore race and class are implicated in the stigma that noncustodial mothers feel about their status. Whiteness and middle-class status shield some women from the worst of mother blame that poor women and women of color bear the brunt of in the form of social policies. Middle-class, white women have the privilege of not experiencing the material effects of mother blame until they lose custody (Ladd-Taylor and Umansky 1998). While not all white noncustodial mothers come from privileged backgrounds, their experiences are shaped by expectations not unrelated to race and class privilege. Those most jarred by their experiences either came closer to the ideals of intensive mothering (that is, stay-at-home mothers) or have class or race privilege that made their previous experience of motherhood relatively free from social and state surveillance until they entered the family court system.

Monomaternalism

Also at the root of much of the stigma that noncustodial mothers experience is what Shelley Park (2013) calls monomaternalism. Monomaternalism is the notion that there is only one real mother for a child, with the real being equated with the good. In addition, "part of what's at stake in claims about real mothers is white privilege and class privilege as these intersect with norms of femininity" (4). Biocentric,[3] heteronormative motherhood erases nonbiological mothers, such as birth and adoptive mothers, lesbian co-mothers, othermothers, stepmothers, or anyone else who mothers.

There are a number of models of families that do not follow monomaternalism. Some kinds of queer families may practice polymaternalism yet still bump up against institutions that press them to identify *the real mother*, typically the biological mother. Despite negative stereotypes, stepfamilies can sometimes incorporate more collaborative mothering; however, monomaternalism discourages the practice. When children are not cared for primarily by their biological mothers, the biological mothers are considered demoted from their status as real/good (Park 2013). Historically, Black families have been more accepting of nonhegemonic forms of family, including blended, step-, and multigenerational families (Butler 2014). Othermother figures, such as aunts, neighbors, friends, and sisters, are a vital component of Black motherhood and mothering (Collins 1991b). Specifically with regard to stepmothers, "African American scholarship has normalized stepmothers as an element of fictive kin relations" (Butler 2014, 78), potentially opening up room for nonstigmatized space. Park (2013) includes all non-monomaternal families under the rubric of queer families, a term that at one time would have been considered an oxymoron.

Thus, it is monomaternalism that frames to a great extent the stigmatized experiences of noncustodial mothers. Noncustodial mothers occupy a queer space. Families "become queer (whether it is their conscious intention or not) because of the ways in which they live outside of normative familial time and space" (Park 2013, 12). In her book, Park's focus is on the ways in which adoptive and blended families are discounted as ersatz families with ersatz mothers. With regard to noncustodial mothers, the stigma of this queer location is most acutely felt by noncustodial mothers who were previously stay-at-home mothers and most closely resembled the socially desirable *real mother*. Many contemporary understandings of genuine motherhood remain based on biology, but also on maternal proximity and the quotidian, hallmarks of intensive motherhood that connect intensive motherhood and heteronormative monomaternalism.

The existence of stigma reveals that something in the social order is at stake and relations of power are structuring the experiences of noncustodial mothers. The new momism carries some hefty cultural currency. Because of neoliberal imperatives for mothers' employment, today's mothers experience less stigma regarding their employment than those a few short decades ago. However, the pressure to participate in intensive motherhood regardless of one's employment conditions is one of the many reasons that work and family balance is elusive even among the most privileged mothers in the workforce. Whole segments of the population, however, historically had no access to the breadwinner-homemaker family model and constructed very different understandings of what motherhood entailed. For example, for Black mothers (Collins 1991a) and transnational mothers (Gustafson 2005; Hondagneu-Sotelo and Avila 1997), economically providing for one's child is a normative and integral part of being a good mother. While cultural tolerance of maternal absence for employment has expanded under neoliberalism, that tolerance does not seem to extend to accommodate the type of absence experienced by noncustodial mothers, and the experience of stigma forms a central part of the lives of many mothers without custody.

Stigma is an important, but not the only, gendered dimension of noncustodial motherhood. The next chapter explores how noncustodial mothers saw the relationship between custody and gender and how this shaped their experiences. Noncustodial mothers enter their status with ideas about gender and motherhood ranging from essentialist to very unconventional, but they all navigate their uncertain terrain both doing and undoing gender.

STILL A MOTHER

Noncustodial mothers' experiences of stigma are gendered, as we saw in chapter 3, but how do mothers themselves understand the larger terrain of gender at work in their custody experiences? What role, if any, do they feel that gender played in their path to becoming a noncustodial mother? How does gender shape their experiences of noncustodial motherhood, and how are their ideas about gender shaped by being a noncustodial mother? This chapter builds on my analysis of the meanings of motherhood in the context of the social stigma attached to the noncustodial mother status by taking a broader and deeper look at the range of understandings of motherhood held by the noncustodial mothers who were interviewed or who participated in online support communities. I do so by engaging noncustodial mothers on the gendered nature of their experiences, specifically asking them to reflect on whether and how gender should matter in determining child custody.

Most participants spoke about gender unprompted during the interview just in the course of our conversation about their experiences. The interviews were designed with a few questions toward the end specifically related to gender. I saved these questions for the end of the interview for two reasons. First, both questions are more general in nature when compared with the bulk of the interview, which asked about their own experiences as a noncustodial mother. Second, I did not want to shape their other answers by framing any questions around gender. I wanted the participants to talk about their experiences in gendered ways of their own volition. The first direct question about gender was whether they thought being a noncustodial mother and being a noncustodial father were similar. Because the voices of fathers' rights groups seem to be among the most audible today, the second question focused on their awareness and perceptions of these groups and their issues. I asked them specifically about some of the central claims of fathers' rights groups, including the idea that fathers have a more difficult time gaining custody than mothers. It turned out that all participants had some level of awareness of fathers' rights groups, and many participants sought information on custody and divorce from fathers' rights websites or attorneys. A few even participated in online or community-based groups.

Gender Traditionalists or Gender Rebels?

As a group, noncustodial mothers have quite a varied and complex understanding of gender and motherhood. We might expect voluntarily noncustodial mothers to have the most nontraditional views of gender and motherhood, and we might expect those most unhappy with their unconventional status to have the most traditional or essentialist views of gender. The data reveal much more complexity. Those who were most unhappy about being a noncustodial mother did not simply embrace traditional family arrangements and did not believe that only mothers could care for children. Nor were the most radical gender resisters confined to the group of voluntarily noncustodial mothers. Mothers in households with a highly gendered division of labor before not having custody did not necessarily believe that their arrangement was superior to others. They did not uniformly have highly gendered ideas about families. Many spoke explicitly about the importance of parents of other genders and felt that many family configurations were possible and acceptable for raising children. Mothers who were voluntarily noncustodial were more explicit about degendering mothering and advocating for different kinds of families, but they too struggled with ideas about identity, mothering, and gender. Some noncustodial mothers significantly changed their ideas about both gender and motherhood as a result of their uncommon social location. They rethought the relationship between gender and motherhood, as well as their understanding of what it meant to be a good mother.

The range of approaches to mothering included those of stay-at-home mothers who advocated for intensive mothering and those of employed mothers who actively resisted the demands of contemporary motherhood. Many mothers embodied aspects of more than one approach, both embracing and resisting traditional and unconventional views of motherhood. Within these groups, mothers navigated contemporary motherhood in ways that sometimes reinforced and sometimes challenged intensive mothering. A mother might, for example, embrace intensive motherhood by going to extremes to watch all of their child's sporting events even as they actively attempted to redefine what constitutes a good mother by rejecting the notion that motherhood means self-sacrifice.

Some noncustodial mothers' conceptualizations of motherhood were closer to what we call a gender essentialist position, meaning that motherhood is understood as something biologically linked or more natural than it is a product of social arrangements. Others spoke in gender-neutral terms of parenthood even as they vocalized that caregiving remains primarily women's responsibility in heterosexual families. These mothers envisioned a future in which men and women might participate equally in raising children. A third group, which I term the gender undoers, was focused on actively disconnecting acts of mothering from biological women. They offered a well-thought-out and more expansive view of mothering that incorporated mothers of all genders and in many kinds of families. While I conceptually categorize noncustodial mothers into groups of traditional, gender neutral, and gender undoers, most noncustodial mothers navigated territory that incorporated more than one perspective. Many mothers, even those with more traditional understandings of motherhood, unexpectedly and unintentionally participated in undoing gender. I think of this kind of noncustodial mother as an accidental maverick. These moments of undoing gender often prompted mothers to rethink some aspect of their experiences of and thoughts on motherhood.

Many noncustodial mothers who described identity struggles around feeling like a mother sometimes resolved those struggles, particularly when driven by stigma, by finding ways to enact intensive motherhood. Intensive mothering requires that mothers be child centered and absorbed in the minutiae of their child's life (Ennis 2014; Hays 1996). Intensive mothers defer to child-rearing experts, keeping abreast of the latest developments in mothering practices. Intensive mothering is labor and time intensive. Some participants wholly embraced these mothering tenets. They tended to be stay-at-home mothers but were not exclusively so. Many mothers who were employed also attempted to meet the demands of intensive mothering. Those who embraced intensive mothering the most expressed the greatest disruption in their sense of identity when they became noncustodial. These mothers often referenced natural or biological reasons that mothers should have custody, as Nina did: "Just by the nature of men versus women. I mean moms are the nurturers and I'm not saying there aren't men that nurture but it's the instinct and men don't have it." However, very few mothers articulated any strong preference for mother custody. Patrice was unusual in calling for the custody default to rest with the mother: "I believe kids need their dad. He's still your dad and you need your dad. There are good things that dads can do. But kids need their moms. Moms are moms and you know, at the risk of not sounding politically correct, I think in most cases if kids have to go with one or the other, it ought to be the mom unless you can prove some extreme, verifiable, documentable neglect or abuse." Even as she articulated a preference for mothers, Patrice made room for fathers in children's lives in ways that represented a kind of gender complementary—mothers are good at some things, while fathers are good at others. She believes that a mother should have primary custody unless she is dangerous to her children.

Abby linked biology and primary caregiving, focusing on the tender years as a time when mothers should have custody: "I think there are social norms that make this hard and then there's a biological connection to your child. You carried the child and breastfed the child. Especially if you are the primary caregiver in the child's early years. Those things aside, if a couple adopted a child together and then split up, I think the hardest part would be the stigma, but with the biological component, it's compounded. The difficulty is compounded by the fact that you carried the child, you took care of the child in the early years."

Fernanda was the breadwinner as well as the primary caregiver in her marriage. She almost apologetically incorporates a biological understanding of motherhood to explain what made being noncustodial so difficult for her, but then distinguishes between being a father and being a mother based on who provides primary care for the children and how each parent responds emotionally to being noncustodial:

> At the risk of sounding sexist or something, you know, I carried these kids inside my body for 9 months. I feel like there's generally a different kind of closeness with a mom and with a dad. And without trying to put too much of my own situation in it, if I had a cooperative custodial dad who was communicating with me and keeping me informed and allowing the kids to call at bedtime, the experience would be kind of different. Just like being a parent is being a parent but being a mom is different from being a dad. I think being a noncustodial mom is different from being a non-custodial dad. I think my heart is ripped out a little further than a non-custodial dad's would be. It seems to me that being a dad is a different experience to being a mom. All those years where I was the primary caregiver and having that taken away has been . . . Maybe it would be different if a stay-at-home dad lost custody. I was so wrapped up in their lives, their preschool, their parties. I'd go help with field trips. I was involved. And now I can't be.

Fernanda feels that her being noncustodial would be a better experience for her and the children if her ex-partner were more cooperative and communicative.

Like Fernanda, Rhonda uses the term *primary caregiver* as a gender-neutral expression of mothering. Even though she identifies the pattern of actual mothering practices as gendered, she allows for the possibility of fathers being similarly situated to noncustodial mothers by virtue of caregiving:

> Sometimes I've seen marriages where dad is the primary caregiver. It's unusual but it happens. It's usually the mom that takes care of everything. Sometimes it's 50/50. I've seen that too. It seems like there's always one doing more of the grunt work. I think whoever is primary stays that way. I think if the person who was primary becomes noncustodial, then I think that's a very hard process whether that's a mother or a father. Because you're the one who does everything for those kids and if the parent helped out even during the marriage, what's the difference after? But if there was no help during the marriage and the child was taken away, the parent, the child, everyone suffers.

Rhonda references the unequal division of household labor to explain why being noncustodial would cause suffering for the primary caregiver as well as the children. For Ruth, nurturing irrespective of primary caregiving is what matters more than the day-to-day care of children. She likens her noncustodial experience to that of her current husband, who was in a marriage where he was the breadwinner with a stay-at-home wife who took care of the day-to-day household labor and childcare: "If you have a dad like my current husband who was the nurturer, he took care of the kids and she was [emotionally] distant. So for him to be noncustodial probably feels like it does for me. But at the same time, moms just have, I don't know, it's hard to describe. I think my husband is an exception for dads. Most dads are the opposite. They love their kids but don't necessarily have the same connection, really. So I think it depends on the type of parent that you have." In her eyes, it was Ruth's husband's emotional labor rather than daily caregiving that made him more like a mother such that he could identify with her noncustodial experience.

Virginia, a voluntarily noncustodial mother, is what I call a gender undoer. Gender undoers intentionally resist traditional ideas about motherhood, explicitly reject any biological basis to motherhood, and articulate alternative ways of understanding child custody. As she said, "Just because you have a vagina doesn't make you a better mom. So that's what I kind of say. 100 percent just what was best for the child. And in many cases, the child asked to go and that could be for something. It could be because where daddy lives, I have more friends. Or it could be that the child wants to go, especially with boys, at a certain point, I want to stay with dad. As hard as it may be, and it is hard, it's what's best." Virginia focuses on practical aspects of children's lives that have nothing to do with day-to-day caregiving. She and her child's father live in different states and have made custody changes over the years for a variety of reasons, including changing school districts or finding quality medical care for their son.

Cassie echoed Virginia's call for focusing on factors other than caregiving, including a child's opinion of what custody arrangement would be best: "I think if the child is old enough the child's opinion should matter. Things like education and safety should matter. Quality of life issues are important, but not necessarily just monetary. I think all of those things should matter, but when all of those things are equal, I have no idea how court or anyone can make the decision. If you have two responsible parents who both want the child, I don't think it should automatically be one or the other, that moms get the right just because they're the mom. Dads can be amazing parents too." Without gender, caregiving, or nurturing as a basis for decision-making, Cassie believes that impartial determination of custody is a daunting task when there are two good parents.

"Kids need both parents" was a common and unprompted refrain among noncustodial mothers. Nearly all participants expressed the idea that having two involved parents[1] was ideal regardless of the custodial arrangement. As Carla articulated it,

> I'm not one of those people who think that the kids have to be with mom. I think that if you could have a situation where they're with mom and dad and they can cooperate, that's gonna come out better for the kids. It's always gonna be better for the kids if mom and dad can cooperate. If that takes going to counseling or whatever, do it because it's going to make your life better and more importantly it's going to make your kids' lives better. If you can get out of the situation where they have to choose between loving mom or loving dad, you know then it's the better way to go. They should never have to make that choice.

As a group, noncustodial mothers strongly advocated for joint custody and involvement of fathers in children's lives postdivorce regardless of their level of involvement in the former relationship. Their sense of what joint physical custody means is varied, ranging from any amount of regular, meaningful contact to a default of fifty-fifty, which few thought was practical. Sandra, like some other mothers, was asked by a judge whether she would keep the children from their father:

> You're the bad guy because "you're moving away and trying to disrupt things and keep them from me." And the judge actually looked at me and said, "You're not intending to try to keep the kids from him, are you?" I said, "Of course not. That's their father. I would never do that because they need their father." I mean, to me, it never entered my imagination whatsoever because they need both their parents. And I never wanted to do anything to alienate him or anything to disrupt their lives. I just wanted to be able to provide the best I could for them and I couldn't do it there.

The words of mothers like Sandra mirror widespread discourses of fathers' importance in children's lives. These discourses are echoed in the language of state custody laws, the National Fatherhood Initiative, welfare reform policies, child development literature, fathers' rights groups, popular culture, and some feminist perspectives.

A common theme among noncustodial mothers was that fathers were rewarded simply for asking for custody, as Lydia observed: "They used to be deadbeat dads, but now it's 'Oh, you're doing so good because you want your children.'" As Lydia's comment suggests, many understood mothers' losing custody as reflective of larger social changes promoting fatherhood. This is a kind of overrecognition of men's caregiving, which is a larger theme in chapter 5. I raise it here to connect noncustodial mothers' experiences to social processes that strongly promote father involvement and may shape how arbiters in the custody process view and value men's requests for primary custody.

The friendly parent[2] is another discourse that shaped participants' understandings of child custody determinations. In the friendly parent standard, courts embrace the idea that children should be in the primary custody of the parent who best promotes a good relationship with the other parent. Some mothers more than others were more aware of the friendly parent standard, but even those who did not mention the term knew that it was important for them to talk positively and inclusively of their child's father as they went through the custody determination process. They felt that not doing so would place them at a disadvantage. So strong was the notion that fathers are important that even mothers who had been abused by their ex-husbands advocated for their involvement in raising their children unless they had been violent specifically to the child.

When I pressed participants to elaborate on the specifics of the importance of fathers, their answers were often vague. Mothers who had a highly gendered division of labor in the house with a husband who worked long hours and participated very little upheld the idea that fathers were important in general and that their ex-husband had been a benefit to their child even if they could not clearly articulate what it was. Voluntarily noncustodial mothers held the most expansive views of fathers' involvement, often extending to others outside the nuclear family. Olive, for example, spoke about the need to spread around caregiving responsibilities. She had not enjoyed being the primary caregiver to her children:

> I don't think that I would have had the fears that I had. I don't think there would have been the struggles that I had if there was some place in society that said, "You don't have to do it all. Nobody is going to expect you to do it all. The father can do it all or some of it and the aunties can do some of it." You know? That there would be systems in place and the

expectations are not so enormous and focused all on you. It may have been that if I had the expectation of more support to begin with, none of it would have happened.

Fathers' rights discourses helped to shape noncustodial mothers' understandings and experiences of gender and noncustodial parenting. Most participants had substantial knowledge about fathers' rights groups and their goals. It was common for participants and those in the online support communities to indicate that they had used these sites for information about custody because of the dearth of information geared specifically toward mothers. Not unexpectedly, noncustodial mothers held a range of opinions about these organizations. Some felt that fathers' rights groups were sexist or anti-mother. Angela felt that the groups prioritized fathers over mothers:

> I have some thoughts on them. Some of them have really good points and having been a noncustodial parent, I understand their perspective. I do. I understand. But there's a point where you become venomous in your views. When it's no longer about the kids, it's about your rights as a father. And then you have to ask yourself, what about the rights of the mother? And then the rights of the kid? The concept of fathers' rights is putting the rights of the mother and the rights of the child in a lower place. You're saying the rights of the father are more.

Abby referred to the sites as sources of propaganda: "There's propaganda on their site that says something like, 'They think women are so important but they're denying children the contact with important women such as stepmothers, their father's girlfriends, their father's mothers, etc.' It just all comes back to women again. It's really weird. Parental alienation syndrome is a huge one. I've seen websites where the advocates are saying, 'Have you been accused of domestic violence? Well, your ex-wife might have mean mom syndrome or parental alienation.' You get all kinds of stuff like that." Patrice characterized the groups as more about power but sees fathers and mothers without custody as similarly situated.

> The father's rights movement and all of this b.s. about them being mistreated, to me it's just a bunch of bunk. I think it's a power trip. I think in some instances, either parent could be very guilty of trying to alienate the other one. I have met plenty of women who don't know when to shut up. I have tried to be a good friend and say, "You can't be talking like that about your ex-husband in front of the kids." So everybody can be guilty of it, but why does there need to be this group for rights for people who have all along in history had all the rights? I don't understand. I don't get it.

Most noncustodial mothers felt that fathers' rights groups and their websites could serve as a source of some useful information about custody for mothers as well as fathers. Tabitha was representative of a very practical orientation that many noncustodial mothers had toward fathers' rights groups: "My thoughts are that the fathers' rights groups are good. I bet more mothers are using the resources than the fathers." Others found the sites particularly useful to get a sense of what strategies their ex-spouses might employ, particularly if they were using a self-identified fathers' rights attorney. Patrice's ex-husband used to email her articles that he found on fathers' rights websites: "That's where he was getting a lot of his information. He told me. He was sending me articles saying 'This father's rights article says that you can't do this or can't do that.' I remember reading things that he would say to me verbatim and I'm like, 'Oh he's been looking at this website.'" Fernanda disliked and avoided fathers' rights groups but became familiar with them because her ex-spouse had hired a fathers' rights attorney.

> Fathers' rights sites kind of tick me off. I don't use them. But I did learn after the fact that my ex's lawyer is a fathers' rights attorney. That's kind of how she touts herself, you know, getting custody for dads. That's like her specialty. I don't spend much time looking at fathers' rights stuff because they just irritate me. It was incredible to find this group because it was the only one I found. It seems like there's a lot of support for noncustodial dads and I don't see a lot of that support out there for noncustodial moms.

Some noncustodial mothers felt more positively toward the groups and their aims. Maggie feels the claim that mothers sometimes push fathers out is valid and firmly believes that both parents are important: "Do I think fathers have rights to their kids? Absolutely. I believe in two fit parents in the child's life. Our specific situation is that we don't have another fit parent to work with. I know fit dads who get pushed out of their kids' lives. A friend of ours has an ex-wife that is forever trying to turn the kid against him." Even among those who felt they had more in common with fathers' rights groups, many like Janet were turned off by the ones they encountered.

> Fathers' rights groups speak to the things we talk about that affect us but I think that it's more geared to hating the mom, especially if they're in the custodial position. I think sometimes they go a bit overboard because they're more toward making it out to be it's always the women who get custody, it's always the moms who get custody and the fathers are put out to pasture. They don't understand that there are moms out there that are treated the same way. I think that if we could come together as a

united front and fight this fight together, then you know it wouldn't be so bad and noncustodial fathers making us all look bad.

Pam actually went to a local meetup of fathers that was affiliated with a fathers' rights group:

> I went to a noncustodial parenting support group through a local church group and when I talked to the people they said, "Oh yeah, we have women come." And I went into the meeting and there were thirteen very angry men and one crackhead prostitute and I was like, "Oh ok. Alright." I stayed for the first hour and a half and got up and walked out. I never went back. It was too hard. For every single one of them it was the case of their wives having custody and then it seemed primarily about money. And they would say stupid things like "I bought her this house and she wanted a BMW and she wasn't happy because I had to work all the time to pay for it."

To recount, noncustodial mothers have a diverse set of beliefs concerning gender, motherhood, parenting, and custody. In general, they did not feel that biological mothers were the only acceptable caregivers for children. Even those who had been stay-at-home mothers felt that fathers *could be* primary caregivers. While a few embrace more traditional formulations of mother custody, most have moved toward a more gender-neutral stance with no preference for mothers. Fathers' rights groups were sometimes useful to noncustodial mothers, who often did find some commonality of experience with noncustodial fathers; however, they often also found the groups highly problematic.

Many noncustodial mothers supported the idea that primary caregiving should be an important criterion in determining custody, but they also explicitly decoupled the idea of primary caregiving from gender. They felt that the primary caregiver, regardless of gender, should be the custodial parent and were mystified that their caregiving status did not sway the decision in their favor. At the same time, many noncustodial mothers acknowledged that most caregiving remains women's work, and they felt that the custody arrangements should reflect that work. To the extent that men participate fully in this work, custody arrangements would follow. They felt that fathers were important, especially if they were like mothers. Finally, gender undoers focused much less on caregiving and more on practical aspects of children's lives. These noncustodial mothers were not all voluntarily noncustodial and did not uniformly have ex-partners who were involved fathers. However, noncustodial mothers who felt the best about their arrangements had not gone through court or a custody evaluation and described their child's father as hands-on, a good father (or even as a good mother), inclusive, flexible, and communicative.

Undoing Gender

While some noncustodial mothers set out to undo gender, many others participated in a variety of practices that arose out of having to navigate their contradictory position of being a mother without custody. As a group, participants understood their position as atypical in the contemporary United States. As discussed at length in chapter 3, even voluntarily noncustodial mothers experienced some measure of stigma from their status. In addition, noncustodial mothers found it difficult to know what was normative because they lacked role models or peer support. Christine regularly struggles to figure out "how to be a mom like this" because she lacks examples of motherhood that reflect her new experiences:

> I've learned that as horrible as my situation is it can be ten thousand times worse with these poor mommies that never ever ever see their children. And here I have not appreciated the eight years that I've had that I really do have such a strong influence on both of their lives. I'm at all of their school events, all of their sporting events. I'm at every single thing that I could possibly be. Not that their father wants me there. I speak to them for many minutes every single night, rarely missing a night. I'm active in their homework and active in their daily events. I'm just not there to do for them all day, every day. It's kind of like being an aunt, but then when they're here, I can't just relax. I haven't found myself yet. You know it's been eight years and I'm trying my best. I don't even know how to raise myself right now, so I don't know how to be a mom like this. I'm sometimes so lovey-dovey, but the anxiety, and other times I'm raging like a lunatic. I don't know, maybe it's because I don't have a model. There's no one I can ask.

Online support groups were peppered with comments about noncustodial mothers finally finding others like themselves. A common theme in the groups concerned determining what behaviors are within the normal range versus indicators that something is wrong with a child. Nina consulted a close friend because she thought her children seemed distant on recent visits:

> It's real hard. I can't look at their pictures from the younger days when I had 'em. It's hard to feel like a mom. Now especially that they're teenagers there's that natural pulling away. I talked to them every night before. They wanted me to call them and they were excited to see me. Now it's like "mom, who?" My girlfriend tells me, she's got two girls herself, and when I said my kids won't talk with me, she says, "you know. I live

with them and they won't talk to me!" Well, maybe it's kind of normal. It's hard to know.

Most noncustodial mothers have never met another noncustodial mother in person, at least not one that they were aware is noncustodial. This is not surprising because stigma hinders disclosure to new acquaintances. Because discourses around motherhood today still rest on the imperatives of post–World War II white, middle-class, heterosexual, nuclear, breadwinner-caregiver families, many noncustodial mothers described feeling adrift or, as Pam says, like "a blank canvas":[3] "Becoming a mom was one of the things that I had always planned for my life. It's what I knew that I was meant to do. And then to have the experience of being a mom to these beautiful healthy wonderful girls and then to suddenly not, I lost all sense of who I was at all. I mean, I was just a complete blank canvas. How do you explain to someone what it's like to wake up and you're a stranger in your own body. I was lost. I was devastated."

Many noncustodial mothers framed their experience of being noncustodial in terms of a process of social change resembling a pendulum that has swung to favor fathers. Maggie explained, "I think the pendulum in our society is always swinging. And I really truly do believe this is some sort of twisted payback for all of the moms who shoved all the dads out of their lives and just went after them for their money. Because how many judges in this country are male? How many are divorced? How many pay child support?"

Pam and others felt that judges wanted to avoid appearing biased in favor of mothers. They understood the social change as more of a backlash to social changes around gender equality. Pam observed, "So then you wonder is a judge taking his entire three minutes that he's going to think about this and saying, 'Oh I can't be biased against men because it's not popular to be biased against men now.' You know they obviously have rights as a father." Their gender consciousness did not necessarily mean that they embraced feminism, even if they recognized that women remained disadvantaged in many contexts. As Carla explained, "I'm not a feminist or anything, but my honest thoughts are that judges don't want to appear gender-biased anymore. They're trying to get away from the stigma of being for the mom you know. Maybe the lady judges like in my case, she's trying to prove something. That she's not for moms. I think that's probably been part of it. They don't want to look gender biased anymore. Because it's supposed to be equal, men and women. And it's not always that way. I mean women are still getting paid less than their male counterparts in most places." Others like Val felt that mothers' not having custody of their children was part of the price of admission to feminism:

> Women fought for years for equality and this is one of the things that comes with it. I think if you buy into the social part, the mom's role, that

it would be harder for women. But for me, it's like I don't know, maybe I'm like an overly liberal woman or whatever, but I think it's about what situation works best for the kids and what works for the parents. Mom or dad, it doesn't matter. I'll say though that when he says in his court affidavit he was the primary caregiver since they were born, it's kind of. . . . I've always wondered how his breasts produced milk because I breastfed my son for 13 months and my daughter for 10. So that kind of makes me go, hum, how did that work?

Wherever they stood in terms of feminism or fathers' rights, noncustodial mothers saw their status as some way reflecting broader social changes around gender that might represent an undoing of gender. Noncustodial mothers participated in undoing gender by redefining motherhood, engaging and changing social institutions, and breaking motherhood taboos. Some were very intentional about attempting to disrupt the gender order, while others were not.

Redefining Motherhood

Participants spoke about redefining what it means to be a good mother. They did this for themselves and for those in their immediate social circles, but some also shared these strategies with others in the online support groups. Speaking of the many unsolicited emails she received after being on a television talk show, Rahna saw her position as one that potentially prompted women to rethink motherhood and gender: "I get a lot of bashing emails but I did get a lot of women who are like 'You're so brave. You make me think of my situation. You make me think there's hope.' There's a lot of people who think 'Wouldn't it be great if this could change? If women had more flexibility? If they weren't judged? If the situation were a little bit different?'"

Virginia, like other voluntarily noncustodial mothers, was highly vocal about the ways in which her custody arrangement contributed to redefining and resisting contemporary constructions of motherhood:

> Well kindergarteners now come home with homework that is way too much for kindergarten and requires mommy to do it. And they send home like 5 sheets a night. I was a stressed out mom. I'll never forget one day the homework sheet. They had to name the articles of clothing. And it was a hat. And the teacher said it was wrong. And I questioned it and wrote the teacher a note, why is this wrong? She said it's a bonnet. I said really? Really? She said yes, a bonnet has flowers on top. I said are you kidding me? I was so done. And one day after that she sent a

homework sheet and I said "Mommy has a headache tonight" and that's what I wrote across it! So that's why I said I'll be a better mom for it.

Virginia specifically resisted intensive motherhood by explicitly rejecting, in writing, the homework that was assigned to her son as a kindergartener. Importantly, Virginia felt that by refusing to complete homework that she saw as unnecessary and stressful, she became a better mother.

Some mothers did not set out with the intention to redefine motherhood or the social order but, as Pam articulates, found themselves doing so out of necessity: "Being a mom is a very social experience. You're around other moms for games or birthday parties, that kind of thing. One minute you're part of that group and the next you're completely ostracized. So suddenly you have to redefine what you think of as being a mother. Suddenly you're a stranger in a strange land. You don't speak the language. You're not allowed to speak the language. You're not welcome. It really just makes you feel as if you've been piloted to another world and everything you think you know about the world no longer exists." Several participants made the point that if they were fathers, what they did as a noncustodial parent would be celebrated. Cassie observed,

> When I first started going through all of this I tried to find lots of resources. I tried to find books, research. Everything I found was on the dad being the one. And I was getting so frustrated too because all the books about the dad in my position celebrated what a good dad he would be if he had the child one night a week and every other weekend and was involved. But I was a horrible mother because I only had him one night a week and every other weekend. So on the one hand, I'd be reading these books talking about the heroic dad and when I was doing the same thing, it wasn't.

Several voluntarily and involuntarily noncustodial mothers commented that they made "excellent divorced dads" because they were knowledgeable about and involved with their children's lives. Monica felt that her involvement with her child would be praised rather than stigmatized if she were a father: "The noncustodial dads who are as involved in everything that I was, that's seen as the sign of a great man, a great father. For the moms, somehow, we've failed." Olive adds two additional dimensions to her rejection of intensive motherhood. She does not believe that mothers should be responsible for carrying out emotional labor in the family, and she rejects the idea that children are helpless:

> There's a lot of ideas in our society that women in general and mothers in particular are responsible for somebody else's happiness. Somehow we have the idea that children are young and fragile and can't take care of themselves. Therefore this person who had them, not the father, but

the mother, has to be the one who comes in and fills in for them and takes care of them emotionally and in every other way. People feel in our society like they need that so much that they can't imagine if the mother decides that it's not her only role, or her only priority, then that's wrong.

Some noncustodial mothers like Pam redefined motherhood as something similar to being an aunt or a doting relative: "At a dance recital when the other moms were stage moms and they call them to go backstage and help everybody get dressed. I would sit out in the audience and I would be the person that would just clap when the show was over and hand them their flowers and take them out to dinner and drive home. So you become like a doting relative who's not part of their everyday world. You just get to watch it." Tabitha felt that being an aunt was sometimes more like being a mother than being a noncustodial mother was: "I feel like a displaced mom. I don't think in their mind that anything will every replace me, but I feel more like a mom when my nieces are here and I get to do their hair and play with them. But of course, they're just my nieces. I get to take 'em back to mom."

A common theme among interview participants that also arose in online discussions was resistance to the idea that motherhood meant sacrifice. Tabitha struggled with the idea that being OK without her children meant that she was a bad mother: "Others seem to take it harder than I have and I don't know why or how. I wonder whether sometimes if I have the same capacity to love my kids as they do theirs. Maybe that's what I've learned is that you don't have to be miserable to love your kids and want what's best for them. And realize it may be that they're better off with their dad." Olive echoed the idea that mothers could be OK apart from their children and that it did not mean that she had abandoned them. She added that mothers who prioritize their own needs still love their children: "Sometimes your priorities are for yourself. And sometimes your priorities are for your work. And sometimes your priorities are for your kids. And it doesn't mean that you don't love them if you have to work today or it doesn't mean that you abandoned them if you went away for three months in the summer. Can you imagine? I went away for three months for my job and I left my children. You send your kids away to camp for three months or to boarding school. Nobody said you don't love them." Because Olive has been very open about her noncustodial status, she has been told directly that because her children live primarily with their father (within walking distance), she does not love them.

> I do think that, you know, with motherhood and with women we really end up finding a certain amount of value and worth with sacrifice. Sacrifice never feels that good and if you can at least feel like you're giving it for somebody who will be ok, you can feel better about yourself. People

get really angry at me as if my kids were going to be in jail. The stuff that people have said is just phenomenal. Absolutely no basis in truth, absolutely no understanding of the relationship, absolutely no sense of a family that's founded on love as opposed to a family that's founded on familiar structure.

Virginia experienced some initial resistance from her family when her child went to live with his father. After seeing how things worked out, they came to appreciate her choices.

I think we're programmed to believe that women are the nurturers. It's not until after you have the child that you get all that's involved. We always talk about this bond. Oh, the bond when the baby was born. For some people that happens, absolutely. For some, it doesn't. It doesn't mean you don't love your child. It might be that we're told we'll have it so we say we did. I don't think we come into ourselves until we're 30 or 40. You may have thought your life was going one way and it's going another. Or all of a sudden you want something else but you can't because you have an eight-year-old. So we give up ourselves. And I think if there's the opportunity where the other parent can take on that role, you can still be who you are and have a healthy life. But we put that aside because we're the mom and we could never do that. What would people think? It really comes down to what will people say. And that goes for family. Family is sometimes the worst.

Some noncustodial mothers gained a sense of freedom or relief from the unceasing demands and devaluation of contemporary motherhood. Tabitha felt that she "needed a break from being a full-time mom." Mothers who acknowledged a sense of relief also often mentioned that the experience of not having primary custody made them "a better mother for it." For example, Sandra felt that the time apart from her children, although very difficult, provided her with the distance to rethink how she cared for herself and for her children.

If I had known what was going to happen, I wouldn't have moved in the first place. But I don't know that that would have been the best thing. I may never have gotten to a healing point for myself had I not moved away. And I might be a really bad mom right now. I don't think I was a really good mom when I was in the thick of it because I was so destructive to myself. I know I wasn't the kind of mom that I needed to be. But I'm a much better mom now that I'm healthier and with them. In concrete ways, I'm a much better mom. I don't know if I had stayed would I still be on that path.

Monica felt that being noncustodial improved her ability to be a mother: "I would never wish losing custody on anyone, but I did get something out of it. I think it forced me to think carefully about things that we just do on autopilot when we're stuck in the day-in, day-out merry-go-round. Knowing that I only had so much time with him before he went back to his dad's, I had better focus, more patience. I learned to be the mom I wished I had." Echoing Monica's sentiments, Virginia mentioned a relative who envies her position as noncustodial in a cooperative partnership with her son's father: "People in my family probably think I'm a better mother for it, but that they could never do it. I have a relative who said she wishes her daughter had a father she could make that choice with because there are times when she wonders whether she's even a good mother. And she's tired." Val, who had been out of the workforce, felt that being noncustodial gave her the opportunity to explore other parts of herself.

> So I didn't know myself really well. You really don't know yourself when you're only 20. I never had an outlet that was just me. If I did leave the house or go out besides running errands, it was just something for the kids. Or I was out with my husband and nothing was just me. What am I good at? What's my contribution to the world outside of my family? And when I started going to school, I realized you know, that I have a brain. I have talent. I have goals outside of my family and I don't see that as a bad thing, but he sure as heck did.

Angela described herself as semivoluntarily a noncustodial mother. She came to embrace certain aspects of not being the primary caregiver.

> I thought I did a really good job as a noncustodial mom. I gotta tell ya. I thought I did a really good job and it was hard for me, like my emotions. I guess I really never thought about that as something bad, just as part of the deal. You got divorced, dummy me, it was coming to you. I talked to the kids on a regular basis but I also lived my own life. I had been with my ex since high school and I hadn't grown into a person. And you know, you got a lot of free time and you start discovering things that you enjoy. You know, you start building a life around them. So I enjoyed my time as a noncustodial mom. I did. Other than the emotional turmoil that takes place. I was hell bent on building a new world around myself. I bought a big house in the middle of nowhere. Start over and there's no one here to tell me that I couldn't do something. So for me, I had no problem with it. I thought it was a great arrangement. I was able to continue with my job, my career, I saw the kids every weekend. I talked to them on the phone regularly. All the regular stuff I used to do. I just didn't have that guy telling me that I'm a big loser.

Pam's most recent job change led her to a position that included regular travel and being in charge of others. She felt that this positive development for her was also positive for her daughters.

> I remember someone I worked with at a daycare center one time said to a mother that babies only know their life. They only know their own reality, not what you think their life is supposed to be. And I thought over the years, about incredibly wise that is. She gets all the guilt we keep on ourselves as mothers and all your children know is that you're their mom. My girls will tell me sometimes when they bring friends over and they're like, "Your mom is so cool. She's lived these places and gone these places and she takes you there with her." I of course envy their mothers so much just for the joy of getting to watch their children every day. The girls are like "Yeah, she's cool." And I think I guess they're teenagers and still speaking to me so that's a good sign!

Similarly, Olive felt that her children benefited from the care and attention of more adults but still understood her as their mother even if she was different from what society expected her to be.

> I feel like my children benefit from having many people around them who are interested in them and committed to them and love them and support them. They feel they are enriched by the fact that they have so many different people around them, the sets of parents and parent stand-ins and the parents' friends and all the different things that the people in their lives do. At the same time, I think that my kids feel very strongly that I am their mom. My mother is different but she's a good mom. What does that mean about motherhood in general. Isn't it ok to change your life to suit yourself as long as everybody is cared for? I think it's a hugely important lesson.

It is tempting to romanticize the sort of freedom from constraint that some noncustodial mothers felt, particularly if they were voluntarily noncustodial. Despite intentionally or unintentionally redefining motherhood, noncustodial mothers like Val still struggled with feeling torn between enjoying aspects of being noncustodial and feeling guilty for enjoying those things.

> I would say maybe it wouldn't be so bad for them to stay with their dad, and my mom would just go off, but you're the mother and they're supposed to be with you because you're the mom, you know, and that's what society just tells us anyway. So that was a struggle because part of me was saying, "I'm the mom, I'm supposed to want to fight for them with every-

thing I have and to have them with me all the time." And then another part of me was saying, "I really am enjoying school and want to pursue my career and I kind of like the nights that they're not here." So it was really kind of a struggle between two different viewpoints that I was having.

Cassie felt that although she had a good working relationship with her ex-partner, being noncustodial and remaining involved took a toll on her.

> I very much struggled with feeling like a mom before I had the second baby. We suddenly went from being adults without children to suddenly we're full time parents. There was a lot of adjustment and I would feel guilty that there was so much adjustment. I felt like I should be thankful that I had this time. And we can do stuff together like we'll all go to the parent teacher night and there's like four of us. He seems ok with that. So I feel very good about it. If we had to be divorced, I feel really good about the way we've worked it out, not having him pay the consequences. Why am I stressed? Because now I don't have time to do my work. Professionally, it has killed me. I'm exhausted all the time because I commute so much and I wonder if it's really professionally affected me. I wound up putting him in daycare one summer so I could get writing done and I felt incredibly guilty about that. It's like, oh I'm such a bad mom because I only have summers with him and I'm putting him in daycare. I feel like I don't do either one good enough. Like I'm not a good enough mom because I'm not with them all the time. And I'm not a good enough academic because I split my time between here and there. Think of all the work I could have done in those three hours a day.

Her struggles with the guilt some mothers have with using childcare are exacerbated by her being noncustodial. The commuting time required to remain fully involved in her son's life puts a strain on her, and she feels as if she is supposed to make the most of every minute with her son because she is not with him full time.

Even as noncustodial mothers struggled with feeling like a good mother they often worked to redefine motherhood, pushing back against narratives of maternal sacrifice or omnipresence. While some had set out to do something against the grain, others found themselves accidentally participating in undoing gender.

Changing the System

Most noncustodial mothers can tell you a story about a time when they had a problem with a school, a teacher, a coach, or a physician's office because of their

noncustodial status. Sometimes institutional gatekeeping was fostered by an un-
cooperative or hostile ex-partner, but often these experiences were an outgrowth
of gendered institutional practices built on middle-class, white, heterosexual, nuclear families with primary caregiving mothers. In other words, our social institutions are not designed to include noncustodial mothers, and this manifests in
ways that interact with their stigmatized status.

School and medical forms were a common cause of frustration because they
were most often designed for two-parent, married, heterosexual households.
Sometimes, forms simply did not have enough space, but other times, forms designated one spot for a mother and one for a father only. Some schools had a
practice of issuing only one copy of a report card, which a noncustodial mother
had to obtain from her ex-partner. If their relationship was cooperative and they
lived locally, this was less of a problem, but for mothers who lost custody to an
abusive ex-partner, it was a daunting prospect. Online parent access generally
made staying abreast of a child's progress easier unless someone at the school took
on a gatekeeping role.[4] One noncustodial mother told me that her child's school
only permitted one online access account per family. While this could be problematic for any noncustodial parent, noncustodial mothers felt that much of the
resistance to their requests was due to their noncustodial *mother* status.

Noncustodial mothers employed a variety of strategies to work with institutions and institutional gatekeepers. Virginia and her son's father had a strong
co-parenting relationship and were proactive about making sure that they were
both recognized by the school and included in school communications: "They
know who is going to be calling. Every form that we fill out says "parent," so we
always add lines because he has to be able to contact his dad, his step dad, his
step mom, and me." They even went beyond making sure that both of them were
included and added their new partners to the list of parents for school purposes.

Even more problematic than inadequate forms and communications were the
difficulties some noncustodial mothers had with school or medical office staff.
These mothers have legal and physical custody rights to their children but are not
the primary residential parents. Mothers who ran into this problem found that the
school interpreted their nonresidential status to mean that they had no parental
rights, a situation that they did not believe was as common to fathers. It was not
uncommon for a noncustodial mother to relay a story about showing up to pick
up her child from school only to find the school refusing to allow the child to leave
with her. If the relationship with the child's father is poor, the mother cannot count
on his active assistance in rectifying the situation. Even a supportive ex-partner
was no guarantee that the situation would be resolved quickly and smoothly.

Because these challenges were common, noncustodial mothers were often proactive about providing the school copies of custody agreements. This was no guar-

antee that the school would reference the agreement or even honor it. One piece of advice regularly handed out in the online support groups was for noncustodial mothers to keep a copy of their custody agreement on them or in their car at all times. Sometimes this would resolve any confusion. Mothers with the economic means could have an attorney intervene on their behalf with the school district.

Dee Dee shared custody of her daughter with her ex-husband. When he remarried, he changed their daughter's school.

> There was no reason to move her. He never discussed it with me. I live within walking distance to her school, but it's inconvenient for him. She was hysterical telling me that she won't see her friends anymore. She's been there since forever and doesn't want to go to the school all the way across town. I'm wondering how on earth this can happen? How can he do this?! We have joint legal custody. The school can't act on his word alone. I made an appointment with the principals and the superintendent to get to the bottom of things. It turns out that he and his new wife made the request. Since his new wife has his last name, no one batted an eye. I guess it shouldn't surprise me. Her school has a copy of our custody agreement, but they can't manage to get important information to me. I have to push my way in over and over. Hi, remember me? I'm the mom.

In the face of gendered stigma, noncustodial mothers commonly report skepticism or outright difficulty communicating with their children's teachers. In addition to the assumption that they might be unfit parents, noncustodial mothers find that teachers can assume that they are not and do not want to be involved in their children's education. Online support groups were replete with advice on ways to navigate the difficult waters of interacting with teachers or other gatekeepers who may be predisposed to judge noncustodial mothers. If distance and schedules permitted, attending school events like parent conferences together with the other parent can help disrupt prejudgments of noncustodial mothers. Another common piece of advice was for noncustodial mothers to write an introductory email to their children's teachers at the beginning of each school year. Generally, participants advised omitting any mention of tension in the co-parenting relationship unless it was absolutely necessary.

These interactions with teachers can pose a challenge even when the relationship between the parents is congenial; however, when that relationship is tense or when the ex-partner is actively undermining, noncustodial mothers like Ruth find themselves in an uphill battle:

> When she went back to school and it came out that there were more assignments that weren't completed, it reflected badly on me. So I emailed

the teacher and I said please explain this to me I don't understand what was going on. At first she was like, I could tell the tone of her email was you know, "Dad does a great job, dad is very involved, dad, dad, dad." You know it was kind of like hold on here. I don't know about any of this. I didn't know she was behind in her reading. This didn't get communicated to me so that's when she softened. She was like, "Oh ok, I get it now." So it was that first contact because she's hearing from dad that mom didn't do this and this over break, but when I explained the situation, she softened.

Reports from participants and online support groups indicate that schools largely remain organized around the idea that one and only one parent will be responsible for overseeing a child's day-to-day educational matters. These schools appear to be operating under a cultural lag that fails to recognize the range of parenting and familial arrangements that children may have today. Noncustodial fathers wanting to be more involved in their children's schooling may indeed find these barriers, but they also may be rewarded with assistance and easier access at this cultural moment when we embrace the involved father. Some noncustodial mothers were remarried to men who were noncustodial fathers but did not experience the same difficulties with schools. Schools expect to encounter fathers without primary custody and may be welcoming of a demonstrated interest in a child's education.

Several noncustodial mothers reported conflicts with schools and physicians' offices about problematic policies and procedures. Sometimes it involved individual actions, such as insisting that a doctor's office review the documentation they have on file when they refuse to give out information. Monica ran into this problem with her son's pediatrician: "I'm sitting there telling them to look at their own records and see that I brought this child to every bloody appointment from the time he was born. Her dad brings him once, changes the home address, and you've decided I have no rights to my child's medical information. We don't have the same address but I'm still the mom." Others took aim at making broader changes in their schools or school districts. Noncustodial mothers extensively researched state statutes and education department regulations for information about their rights. Angela was successful in persuading her school to change its policy that excluded noncustodial parents from full participation in their children's school.

Up to that point at the school, only the custodial parent had the right to do things in school. That was like an unwritten rule, not the state law. That was their day-to-day operating procedures. It boiled down to they shouldn't just take the custodial parent's word. He told them I didn't have any rights, no parental rights whatsoever. You can't just listen to the custodial parent all the time. There has to be proof. You have to prove that the noncustodial parent doesn't have any rights. And up until that point, they didn't have to do that. So I was pretty proud of that. It was really important.

Angela's efforts resulted in the school recognizing the importance of having accurate custody and parenting-time information on hand and placed the onus on the custodial parent to provide proof if they contended that a noncustodial parent had no right to their children's information.

Taboo Breaking

In the online support groups, "cherish every moment" is a common refrain that many noncustodial mothers resisted with several forms of taboo breaking. Those who voluntarily took on a noncustodial role were most vocal about aspects of motherhood that they did not enjoy or even found oppressive. Virginia acknowledged how frustrating it was for her when her son had colic:

> There is a thin line between mothers who do a good job and mothers that don't. He had colic for 9 months and I remember one day I took him to the pediatrician and I said keep him. He will not stop. You told me this would end in 6 weeks. This had not ended. It was just noise. It did something to my ears. You know what would soothe him? Driving in the car? No. The sound machine with the waves and the rain? No. I had to lay by his crib and hold a blow dryer or run the vacuum cleaner. That was the only thing that would soothe him.

She thinks that if mothers would be honest with each other about the less savory aspects of motherhood, they would be better prepared: "I tell women who are pregnant, the first time your child moves, you think it's the best thing. But by month 8, you want to sleep and you are like will you tell that child to roll over. It's not cute anymore. They don't tell us this. I think if moms would be honest with each other about all that's involved, we'd have better decision-making and be more prepared." Rhonda acknowledged with humor that when her children are particularly difficult, she feels as if she wants to leave them with their father: "It's so hard. Sometimes I've wanted to take them over to his house and shove them out of the car and go as far away as I can, but that's not gonna be good for them either. Children need two parents present in their lives. They need the good and the bad that goes along with those parents." Sandra has a difficult time when her children are with her in the summer. She experiences the change in schedule as jarring and the sudden full-time responsibility of two small children as overwhelming. She challenges the idea that mothers should cherish every minute and be grateful, particularly if they are noncustodial: "I find it almost as tough when they're here as when they're not here. But for the opposite reason because I'm trying so hard to be a good mom, I'm trying so hard to do everything I need to do for them in that little time I have, and trying so hard not to be depressed. I'm trying so hard to keep up with everything that it's really tough for me. People don't really understand that. They think you should just be so grateful that they're here, you know, 'cause you're not with them all the time." Katie has only supervised time with her children. Although she says she misses her children a great deal, she appreciates having the additional help: "I'm glad to have the supervision because children are tiresome, especially a three year old and a five year old. They have a lot of energy. So it does help to have the supervision. I can't complain about the supervision especially because it's my parents, you know. My parents know me and it's comfortable."

There was a tension among mothers in the online support groups around whether it was OK to be OK without their children. Most of the taboo breaking in this area came out in the in-depth interviews rather than in the online support groups. Christine was unsure whether she wanted to regain primary custody of her children: "It completely destroyed my life for as long as I let it and despite the fact that he got custody of them, it didn't seem to change his life in the least. I don't know that I want custody now. I don't know what that would mean. It's taken me this long to get in this groove. I don't know what I don't know." Tabitha questions whether mothers can be happy without their children but learned that she did not have to be miserable away from her children to prove that she loved them. In fact, she finds she can accomplish more household and other work when they are not with her: "Some days it's real easy to be without them. I can get more done in a day with work and then come home and do laundry and things, but I miss them." Angela, like others, went further and talked about how she enjoyed her time away from her children: "As far as I'm concerned, I have my kids when I have them, which was every five days. But then I had this other time in the middle that I could do literally whatever I wanted and that was refreshing." Angela had not been a stay-at-home mother but was the primary caregiver of her two children while holding down a full-time job in a male-dominated field. She appreciated the ability to have free time. In contrast, Val had been a stay-at-home mother but went back to nursing school after her divorce. In addition to talking about enjoying her independence, Val disclosed that she did not enjoy being a mother: "There was a counselor that I worked with who kind of helped me see that I just didn't really like being a mom that much. You know, I mean especially the stay at home mom stuff I hated. And I really was out and out experiencing this freedom and independence and I was thriving. And so the counselor really helped me let go of some of that guilt that I'm the mom, I'm supposed to have them. And helped me see that it would be okay to let go." Olive had never envisioned herself as a mother. When she got divorced and became the noncustodial parent, she saw the arrangement as consonant with her desires.

> I didn't want to have children. It wasn't my sort of worldview that I wanted to be a mother and that I wanted to take on that kind of traditional mother role. We got together when I was 17. By the time I was 30, it was a real big issue for him that he really wanted to have children. We talked about it and went to therapy about it. He wanted to be the primary caregiver, said that he would take care of everything and that I just had to help sometimes. So I had the children and it was fine really. It was a very different life in retrospect than I had intended and I did become exactly that thing that I had been worried about, but didn't feel bad at the time. Then when the marriage fell apart, I just, I didn't want to, it was very clear to me that I didn't want to be a single mom. I didn't even want to be a married mom. And he did. It made sense to put the kids in one place instead of having them come back and forth.

Whether voluntarily or involuntarily noncustodial, these mothers engaged in breaking motherhood taboos. Sometimes they set out to do so, but at other times, it was their noncustodial experiences that led them to new ideas about motherhood.

Redoing Gender

Even as noncustodial mothers resisted and redefined motherhood, broke taboos, and worked to effect change in the system, many experienced identity struggles that rested on and replicated the gender order. One way this occurred was in the call to keep fighting, which was a common form of encouragement in online support groups. Ruth connected being a good mother with persisting in her goal to regain primary custody of her daughter:

> There was a time when I didn't have all this time with her. So the fact that I've come so far helps a lot. Just talking to her during the week, trying to stay involved and focusing on the fact that I have to keep fighting. That kind of keeps me going, knowing that I'm doing this for her. If you know your child wants more time with you, then never stop fighting for that. Stay as involved as you can. And that's hard. I know it's a

lot harder for some moms than others. And it's hard because it's almost like you're battling with yourself too. It's easy to want to give up and say, "it is what it is. I can't ever change it." And then to retreat. Especially if you have a history of depression or low self-esteem. You're battling your ex and the system and you're battling yourself. It's easy to want to give up, so you have to find ways to just reinforce that you're a good mom. Never give up, just keep going.

Carla feels that fighting for her children made her stronger and gave her a greater appreciation for them: "I learned to grow a spine. I didn't used to have one but I look at ladies there who are strong ladies and are able to put up with this and still keep going for the good of your kids. I learned that you have to do that. You either fold under it or pick it up and move it to the side. I think I also appreciate my kids more than a mom who's never had her kids taken from her. Because I know how easily it can happen. No rhyme or reason." Like Carla, Tabitha felt a renewed sense of appreciation for her children. She went so far as to scold a stranger in public: "I see a lot of people acting like their kids are a burden. And there's one time when I went up to someone I didn't know and saw how they were just seething at their kid and I said, 'I used to do that and now I don't have mine.' That's all I said. And they just looked like a deer in the headlights." Pam encounters friends and family who she thinks are too flippant about feeling overburdened by the second shift.

You know, one of the things that I deal with is having friends and family members who are incredibly busy moms. Working moms. And they're so overwhelmed all the time by all that's in their life, they sort of lose perspective on how precious those things are in life. My sister will say to me, "I would give anything to have fifteen minutes just in the shower by myself." And I think "I would sell my soul to have fifteen more minutes of being with my children." But for me, I have to put every ounce of my focus into being with them when I am with them. And when I'm not with them, I am making sure they always know that I am aware of what's going on in their lives.

If being noncustodial makes it difficult to enact contemporary ideals about motherhood, focusing all of one's attention and resources on regaining custody is another means to reinforce one's status as a good mother. In other words, good mothers are not OK with being noncustodial. Tensions around this idea sometimes arose in online support groups. Rhonda felt that voluntarily noncustodial mothers did a disservice to those like her who could not continue to fight for custody:

That's great that you gave up custody of your children and you follow your dreams but don't glorify the rest of us who did not choose to give up custody of our children. I think there's a difference. There's women who gave up custody as a choice and those who did not. And it's a fine line because you can look at me and say well, you gave him up in mediation. You agreed to it. You weren't in the room when they're telling me if you don't agree they're going to take her away from you because they won't split up the children. So no, I don't think I had a choice.

The call to renewed appreciation invokes intensive motherhood. The imperative to keep fighting reproduces ideas about motherly sacrifice. One voluntarily noncustodial mother told me that she felt unwelcome in most support groups she encountered because of comments like those that Rhonda made. As a result, she started her own support group for voluntarily noncustodial mothers.

Noncustodial mothers came to the experience with differing ideas about gender and motherhood. Even those who held closer to gender essentialist views of motherhood did not advocate for a default to mothers having custody. They did advocate, however, for recognition of the importance of primary caregiving in the custody determination process. Through their experiences with being noncustodial, many of these mothers found ways to redefine motherhood that moved away from monomaternalism and intensive motherhood. They pressed those around them to rethink assumptions about families embedded in the institutional practices of schools, sports, and medical offices. While some set out to break taboos about motherhood, others surprised themselves with what they learned. Their efforts to redefine or resist aspects of contemporary motherhood are not made with ease. Many struggle with ideas about what it means to be a good mother. Some ways of overcoming those struggles acted to bolster ideas about motherhood as requiring sacrifice and making every moment count.

FATHER OF THE YEAR

As we saw in chapter 4, mothers do, undo, and redo gender while navigating their noncustodial status, but their experiences are also shaped by very gendered social institutions. Work and employment, psychotherapy, and the law are discursively gender-neutral social institutions that rest on and reproduce existing gender hierarchies, shaping noncustodial mothers' experiences. In the next three chapters, I will explore how each of these institutions shapes the custody process and experiences of noncustodial mothers. For example, what gendered understandings and assumptions about work and employment or home inform mothers' understandings of child custody and custody-determination processes? What role does the therapeutic orientation of much of the custody process play in mothers' losing custody? What role does our handling of domestic violence play in the custody process?

Some of the issues that arise are not unique to noncustodial mothers. Indeed, there are many times when critiques of institutional arrangements will resonate with parents of any gender who do not have custody even as these remain gendered phenomena. In addition, while much of the discussion here will center on mothers who are noncustodial on an involuntary basis, there are important commonalities with, as well as dissimilarities to, voluntarily noncustodial mothers. The goal in this chapter, therefore, is to demonstrate the manner in which gender matters in child custody determination because, regardless of the actual genders of parents, our concept of parenting is deeply gendered.

In the end, the interplay of these social institutions and the individuals operating therein generates significant continuity with old patterns of fathers' ownership of children, erasing women's caregiving work and contributing to these mothers' experiences of losing custody, for example, to ex-partners who had little role in their child's care before the dissolution of their relationship. Institutional claims to gender neutrality obfuscate the continued existence of gender as a central organizing dimension of social life despite societal desires to be postfeminist.

Child Support as a Gendered Institution

Before looking at employment, we should first address the matter of child support, one arena where parents, regardless of their gender, have much in common. Child support systems are a prominent subject of complaint from fathers' rights advocates, and many noncustodial mothers in fact echo these groups' criticisms of the system. Because of occupational segregation and persistent wage inequalities, child support too is a gendered phenomenon.

Although popular discourses around child support would have us believe otherwise, only approximately half of custodial parents have either a legal or an informal agreement for child support. Parents who have these agreements in place are more likely to have been married and to have higher incomes and educational levels. Of those parents due child support, less than half received the full amount due, and approximately three-quarters received some of the child support due to them. There was, however, no statistically significant gender difference either in the percentage of parents receiving the full amount of support or in the percentage of support they received (Grall 2016). Yet we often talk about child support as though it is something that affects fathers but not mothers (Cozzolino and Williams 2017). Despite myths that women do not pay child support, most of the noncustodial mothers I spoke with did.

Child support is certainly one of the predominant themes on fathers' rights groups' webpages, but it was also something that noncustodial mothers spoke about. The struggles of noncustodial mothers seemed to echo those I found on fathers' rights websites. Concerns included the amount of child support, what it was spent on, and the penalties for getting behind in payments. Val had custody of one daughter from her first marriage and was noncustodial to the two children from her second marriage. Her child support payment was about $900 a month, and she received about $400 a month from her first husband. She was frustrated with the vastly different standards of living she observed between households: "He's got a wife with a full time income and she gets child support for her kids. So they have two child support checks and two full time incomes coming in. You know, and I'm a single mom supporting one child that lives with me and sending him all this money. And then the kids get mad. They want me to buy a house and it's like I can't. I'm paying for your dad's."

The noncustodial mothers I interviewed who had agreements in place paid anywhere from $100 to $3,500 per month for child support, but most paid between $300 and $500 per month. Many had formal agreements, but others worked out more informal arrangements. Lydia was at the lower end, paying approximately $250 a month out of her disability checks, while at one point Angela paid $3,500 per month for her two children. Other expenses, such as braces and travel costs, were not considered child support. Most noncustodial mothers contributed financially to those items.

Voluntarily noncustodial mothers were more likely to have less formal arrangements that operated collaboratively such that the agreements could vary over time according to the needs of both parents and the child. For example, when Virginia and her child's father made jointly determined changes in their son's living arrangements from time to time, they also adjusted the financial contributions of each to his care. They did not have a formal custody or child support agreement because they had never been married and did not want to go to court. When their son lived with Virginia in a big city, he attended private school, for which his father helped cover the cost. Later, her son moved to live with his father in an area with a much lower cost of living.

> We came up with what made sense. I never wanted to leave his dad hungry and we just kind of came up with it. I got $600 a month in child support and day care at the time was $875, so all the child support went to that and I paid the rest. And as he got older, when he first went to his dad, I paid $450 a month. It's gone down because the care is only after school. Right now we owe for braces. Our insurance is $1500 and his dad's is $1500. So there's about $2000 more that has to be paid and we'll split that.

Olive, too, worked out a mutually agreed on plan outside the court system:

> We started to talk to mediators, they wanted me to pay child support but he makes like ten times the amount of money that I do. They were doing these calculations that would end up taking all of my money and giving it to him. So I didn't take alimony and we did that all outside of the system. It just basically came down to what I thought was fair and what he thought he could live with. We really did try and consolidate the resources around the kids for the benefit of the kids so we don't spend our money doubling things up. And the money that we spend to tear each other down is money that [the kids] could use.

Their process was unusual among the noncustodial mothers I spoke with and is virtually the antithesis of what people imagine when they think of child support arrangements. Virginia felt that their arrangement worked well for them because it was fluid and collaborative. Similarly, although Cassie did not describe herself as voluntarily noncustodial, she and her ex-partner worked out parenting time and financial issues outside the legal system. They had what Cassie described as a good working relationship: "He was gonna ask me for child support, which cracks me up because I make like one-quarter of what he makes. I was like, 'Really? If I pay you child support, I can't come see him. That would be any money I had for airfare.' And fortunately, he backed off." While we do not know to what extent these collaborative approaches are reflected across the larger population, we do know that even when parents do not have an official child support agreement, there is often some kind of noncash support given and that mothers are more likely than fathers to provide these kinds of support, which include gifts, clothing, food, and payment of extracurricular, childcare, or medical costs (Grall 2016).

Indeed, it was common for noncustodial mothers to provide numerous kinds of noncash support to their children. One particularly interesting pattern is the provision of clothing and other personal items by noncustodial mothers. Items such as school clothes, coats, shoes, and toiletries are considered to be chief among the expenses that child support is to pay for, yet these were items commonly provided by noncustodial mothers in nontrivial amounts. Pam, like some other noncustodial mothers, reported buying all of her children's clothes even though she paid child support: "I pay him the $400 a month, but I buy all the girls' clothing. I buy all of their shoes, their makeup, shampoo. I buy all of their extracurricular activities including dance, soccer, that kind of thing. I paid for their braces. I pay for everything they have. Occasionally he'll buy a t-shirt for them or something, but he will in a second call me and say, 'When the girls come up this weekend, they really need bras and they said they need toiletries.' And I kid you not, I buy it. Every single thing."

Similarly, in Abby's case, she was not required to pay child support because of the care requirements of her infant from her new marriage. However, she continued to pay for clothing, health insurance, and all extracurricular activities for her son: "He does their laundry, washes their sheets about once a month. But when they come here of course, all they have is ratty clothes so I have to go out and buy them clothes and get them the stuff they need. I think he does that on purpose because he knows I'll feel obligated to do it because I don't want them walking around in ratty clothes and ripped up shoes and stuff."

This pattern of mothers providing greater noncash support reflects our still very gendered modes of parenting, as well as the very gendered way we judge parents' behavior. Much like doing homework on the phone or staying on top of medical issues, buying children new clothes is a form of doing gender (West and Zimmerman 1987). Terry paid approximately $800 per month in child support for her daughter. She also split the cost of after-school care and paid for all summer camps. Despite these financial arrangements, she felt compelled to make additional purchases. She reflected,

> I know I'm being screwed. I mean, in a way. But I mean it's for my daughter. She comes here with gross underwear, holes in her shoes, boots that are too small, stains on her clothes. What's up with that? Every new piece of clothing I buy and send back, I never see again. I end up buying her tons of clothes, school supplies, and everything else and then I never see any of that stuff when she comes back. Are they eating it? So I know I'm being screwed, but what kind of a mother would I be to let her go back like that?

When it comes to child support, gendered jobs and labor markets matter. Women earn on average 80 percent of what men do, and for women of color, the gender wage gap is even greater (American Association of University Women 2018). White women and women and men of color are much more likely to have part-time or contingent work—that is, irregular or temporary employment that lacks job security and any kind of benefits, including vacation, sick time, and health care (Tilly 1990). Poverty rates among women are higher than men's at every age, and women often experience downward mobility after divorce, particularly if they were not employed while married (Bradbury and Katz 2002). It is not surprising, then, that the household income for custodial fathers is much higher than that of custodial mothers. Timothy Grall (2016) puts these figures at approximately $70,000 and $44,000, respectively. When it comes to single-parent households, custodial fathers are half as likely as custodial mothers to be living in poverty (Grall 2016), and custodial fathers and custodial mothers who do not receive the support they are owed are in very different situations. Mona Chalabi (2015) reports, "Custodial dads who don't receive the child support they're due have an average household income that is $9,749 *higher* than dads who do get child support. For custodial moms, it's a completely different story: Those who don't receive the child support they've been awarded have a household income that's $4,132 *lower* than moms who do. That's not all. The average household income of a dad who doesn't get the child support money he's due is $51,791. For moms, that figure is $26,231." In other words, fathers with greater incomes are the ones who do not receive support that they are due, while mothers with lower incomes are the ones who do not receive that support. Low-income fathers' struggles with paying child support are well documented and have implications for employment and mental health, as well as contact with their children (Turner and Waller 2017).

Inability to pay child support is a concern that many noncustodial mothers share with poor and working-class fathers of any race. The likelihood of child support and associated nonpayment penalties impoverishing parents in these groups is greater than if we are considering upper-middle-class white men and women.

Official child support payment calculations vary by state, with variability in the amount of discretion each case provides the judge involved in determining any deviations from the formulas. Some states incorporate joint physical custody arrangements into their child support calculations by adjusting for the percentage of time or the number of overnight stays with each parent. The guidelines and calculations are explicitly gender neutral and take one of several forms depending on the state in which the order is issued. States use a percentage-of-income model, an income shares model, the hybrid Melson model, or some variation on these approaches. Each state may take other factors into account, such as additional expenses like childcare or health insurance or the proportion of overnights a child has with each parent. Some parents might find that rather than have their actual income used in the calculation, their income is imputed based on an amount that they are perceived to be capable of earning if the judge perceives them to be voluntarily underemployed.

Some states have special considerations in place for how to handle very high or very low combined incomes. Whereas you might hear of an outlandish amount of child support paid by a celebrity in California, in other states, there is an explicit cap on the amount of income considered in the child support calculation. Charlie Sheen was featured in *Forbes* magazine because he was ordered to pay upwards of $100,000 a month in child support for his twins. Recently Britney Spears made news because her ex-husband was seeking an increase to the $20,000 a month she previously paid. These are unusually high amounts that come about because there is considerable discretion in the system at higher levels of income.

Percentage models of child support determination base their calculations solely on the income of the noncustodial parent and use either a flat or a varying percentage based on the number of children. The income shares model combines the income of both parents and determines a dollar amount that represents what a family with that combined income would spend on their child. That amount is then divided proportionally between the parents.

The Melson model seems more nuanced and is much more complicated because it takes into consideration that each parent must be able to meet their own basic needs first before paying child support. After these needs are met for each parent, the model operates like the income shares model. In each of these, additional expenses outside of the usual living expenses are taken into consideration. For example, if a child is disabled, there may be additional costs to consider. The costs of expenses like braces, sports, piano lessons, tutoring, and summer camps can be added to the basic child support amount. When children turn eighteen (or in some cases twenty-one), child support ceases. In most states, that means that a parent cannot be compelled to pay for a child to go to college, but parents may incorporate provisions for paying for college in their divorce agreement.

At first glance, child support obligations that use percentage calculations seem fair because the percentage is based simply on the paying parent's income and the number of children. Parents who earn less money pay a lower dollar amount but the same percentage as parents who earn more. Consider a parent who makes $20,000 a year and has to pay 20 percent of their income in child support. This parent is left with $16,000 to cover all of their other living expenses. In the same scenario, a parent who makes $100,000 a year would pay much more in an absolute sense but would have $80,000 to cover their own living expenses. At lower income levels, the same 20 percent could arguably make it difficult for parents to support themselves in a minimal way. The income shares model works a little differently because each parent pays their relative proportion of the amount of support calculated. However, on the income charts used by different states, families with higher combined incomes pay a smaller percentage of their monthly income in child support, resulting in child support calculations that are regressive for both women and men at lower income levels.

Just like fathers who pay child support, noncustodial mothers face penalties if they do not or cannot make timely payment of their child support. Every state has some sort of penalty that can be brought to bear on parents who do not make their child support payments (National Conference of State Legislatures 2014). Jeanne got behind in her payments right after they were adjusted upward and then applied retroactively: "They made all of that retroactively due. I couldn't pay it right away all at once and it's on my credit. So I lost my driver's license, was jerked out of my car, and had a warrant for my arrest."

In California, parents who are more than thirty days behind in child support risk losing their driver's and other licenses, including occupational and professional licenses. In Connecticut, the penalties are triggered at ninety days, but they also take effect if the parent fails to maintain court-ordered health insurance. While there are both male-dominated and female-dominated occupations that require occupational licensing (for example, physicians, attorneys, plumbers, nurses, accountants, barbers, and teachers), two of the most sizable occupations that require licensure are nursing and school teaching, occupations that are heavily dominated by women. Individuals employed in semiprofessions, the building trades, and service-sector jobs that require licensing on average earn less money than those in licensed higher-status professions like engineering, medicine, law, and accounting. These jobs are stratified by gender and race. Nonpayment of child support by professionals likely has less to do with their ability to pay than it does for those in lower-paid licensed occupations. Furthermore, those with higher incomes can afford legal counsel to guide and defend them when necessary. Occupational licensing, known for its positive effects on diminishing gender and racial wage gaps within occupations (Blair and Chung 2017), becomes a mechanism of social control affecting some groups more than others.

Recall that many noncustodial mothers had difficulty affording or keeping legal counsel. This lack of legal counsel has important implications when it comes to child support and any potential penalties. I heard from participants and observed routinely in online support groups the ways in which noncustodial mothers ran afoul of the child support system. A few mothers I spoke with paid their support directly to their child's father only to find that these payments would not be counted as having fulfilled their obligations, sometimes even with proof in the form of a canceled check. Angela made this mistake but eventually prevailed in court because she kept good records of her cash transactions: "Of course he filed a motion saying I was in arrears and that's just not true. I know over the course of 8 years, I've given him cash at some points because he'd say, "I can't get to the bank and the kids need stuff." I wasn't totally dumb so I got cash out right near his house in the exact amount I needed to give to him. I was lucky I saved all that because they tried to say I didn't pay it."

Other mothers found themselves in immediate arrears upon the issuance of child support. They faced the loss of a driver's license or other licenses. The nurses I spoke to mentioned this as a frequent worry. Or, as Sandra experienced, being in arrears caused constant anxiety of being penalized even further:

> I've just declared bankruptcy a couple months ago but I still have debt that I need to pay back. You can't just discharge child support in any form. So I'm behind. I'm in arrears to him for about $3000 because I just couldn't keep up. And so I just wait every day for a summons that they're gonna put me in jail or something for not paying. I wouldn't be surprised, which is dumb because then I couldn't work and still couldn't pay. And then I'd probably lose my job. If I can't pay now, how am I going to pay if I'm not working? It's the dumbest thing I've ever heard.

Of course, the newer or more tenuous the job, the more apt parents are to find themselves in arrears and facing penalties that could further affect their employment and thus their ability to pay child support.

Increasingly companies are running preemployment credit checks that might show a past-due child support obligation or the existence of a wage garnishment. Unlike fathers, however, noncustodial mothers face a gendered stigma when they apply for jobs with child support arrears or garnishments. Shannon explained,

"When I got turned down from jobs, I could never know if it was because of the back child support I owed from when I didn't have a job. If they checked my credit, they would've seen it. And when they see that, they assume I must have been a crack addict to lose my kids and have to pay child support." Mothers like Shannon felt judged for having a garnishment or a record showing they paid child support. They felt a potential employer's knowledge of a child support obligation was particularly problematic because of the assumptions the employer would make about them.

Among all of the noncustodial mothers I interviewed and observed, former stay-at-home mothers had the most difficult time with the child support system. First, as mentioned earlier, because child support can be retroactively placed in effect, some mothers found themselves immediately in arrears and with no job. Daisy was unable to find work when she first got divorced, so she immediately got behind on her child support payments: "It was so fast. Like right away and no grace period. I thought it was $80 then all of a sudden I got a bill and I saw it was $200. I'm thinking maybe it's interest and that's why it went up. But I'm starting school next month too to be a medical assistant. I can't wait. I'm just not sure how I'm gonna pay all that." Their time out of the workforce worked against both the speed with which they could get a job and also the kind of job that they could secure. Before being a stay-at-home mother, Amy worked in a good office job: "When they busted my ass for child support, I was only able to get a part time job about four hours a day. I went from being an office manager and working in health care to assembly line, sweatshop work. I couldn't get a good job up here without a degree. I brought home $116 a week and the judge gave him half of that." Labor market transitions for stay-at-home mothers are understandably difficult under even the best of conditions. Depending on the field, finding a comparable job upon reentry can be very difficult.

When child support is at issue, a noncustodial mother might find herself paying child support amounts well in excess of what she can afford on her current job. Judges have the discretion to impute income to parents whom they perceive as underemployed. I was surprised at the number of times that noncustodial mothers reported having their income imputed for the purposes of child support calculations. A quick review of child support guidelines across states shows that judges have leeway to impute income to a parent; however, that is usually reserved for times when the court does not believe a parent is earning up to their capacity (National Conference of State Legislatures 2002).

In Christine's case, her child support was assessed on what the judge thought she ought to earn based on her level of education: "I am unemployed because I was working on applying to be a licensed teacher in this state. I had my master's degree and taught preschool when I was first married and moved here. The court said that I wasn't attempting to work and that our kids could have gone into day-care. They based the child support on what a tenured teacher with a master's degree would make. That's $700 a month, which is most of what I take home right now." Christine had a master's degree in education but was not licensed to teach in the state where she lived while married because she was a stay-at-home mother who had taken time out of the labor force. After her divorce, the only job that she could find in her field of expertise was as an unlicensed preschool teacher in a private care setting, which paid significantly less than would a licensed teaching job in a unionized public school environment. She had hoped to work toward getting licensed in her state rather than working at a job that paid barely above minimum wage. Her child support payment made it impossible for her to obtain the credential she needed to make the income that had been imputed to her.

By far the mothers who struggled most to pay child support were former stay-at-home mothers who had been in an abusive relationship where financial abuse was involved. Domestic violence is discussed extensively in chapter 7. Many non-custodial mothers hesitated to bring up domestic violence in the custody deter-mination process, but even when they did, it had no impact on child support, which is handled separately from custody. The disconnect means that domestic violence, and in particular financial abuse, is not on the radar when child sup-port determinations are made.

Gender and Employment Status

Difficulty with child support is but one manifestation of the gendered (and classed and racialized) organization of work and employment. Mothers' employment sta-tus and the household division of labor were also frequent topics in interviews and online discussions. Work and employment are social institutions that are deeply gendered and come into play when custody decisions are made, whether through courts or not. When I spoke with noncustodial mothers and asked them to make sense of their situation, their employment or lack of it was a recurring theme. While it is impossible to know for certain precisely how much of a role these mothers' employment situations played in their custody decisions, work and employment arose as an important factor for them at some point in the process. In addition to the mothers' perspectives, my examination of official standards and documents concerning custody determination augments their perspectives.

In situations that were voluntary and largely collaborative between parents and where the courts were not involved, noncustodial mothers report talking through work demands and schedules with their ex-partners in ways that were flexible and malleable over time. In Virginia's situation, for example, her job and her child's father's job were not the driving factors in their calculus for determining parenting time, custody, or child support:

> All of our arrangements are between us. We never went to court or anything of that nature. It varies because he's getting older. In the past, I always had him for Christmas break and summer and all the holidays. Now that his dad lives further away, we meet in the middle and each drive an hour and a half. As he gets older and has friends, the summer that used to be the entire summer is now broken up into a couple of weeks at a time because he wants to do things with his friends. It's really flexible. Last year when he played soccer and they had a game every Saturday, I went there for some games but I didn't see him as often from March through May.

For Angela, however, the decision to be noncustodial made sense for all involved because of their respective job demands, but not in ways that invoked gendered reasoning:

> I was our primary financial provider while we were married. But he had a job but it wasn't a job that required him to be there all the time. It wasn't a job that paid a whole lot. It was just a job. So when we got divorced, he had his parents' marital home, where we lived. As far as I was concerned it was not my house, but it was the house our children grew up in. I couldn't imagine rippin' 'em out of their house and their school. As far as I was concerned we were just taking care of our kids the best way we could despite the fact that we were no longer married. So he stayed home and took care of everything and made sure they got to school, except that I registered them. I took them to the doctor. I saw them every weekend, birthdays, holidays, everything I could and I worked 85 hours a week. So it was the most logical scenario.

While Angela's relationship with her ex-partner could be strained at times, they were on the same page about what custodial arrangements made sense for them given their work demands and how they divided the household labor.

Noncustodial mothers who entered the child custody determination system found that their employment status took on importance in ways that were gendered and often disadvantageous to them. Noncustodial mothers who had jobs where their status or income far exceeded that of their ex-partner mentioned that as an important factor in the decision to award custody to an ex-partner. For example, in the midst of a custody evaluation, Monica received a promotion, which was something that she thought would work in her favor in the custody determination. Monica's job allowed her to work at home frequently. She enjoyed the idea of having family dinners and so was able to arrange her work schedule to be available after school and through dinnertime. When her son went to bed, she carried on with her work, usually by reading and sending emails or putting together presentations. However, when she spoke about the promotion to the evaluator, she felt that it was a strike against her.

> The evaluator seemed concerned that I wouldn't have time to care for my son because I recently got a promotion. That worried me. Not because I thought he was right, but I saw where he was going with it. He said that with all that responsibility, I would have to put in more hours. [My ex-husband's] job seemed more flexible to him, but he can be called in at night and on the weekend. My job is really flexible. I can drop off in the morning, pick up in the afternoon, and make dinner every night. I can do my emails at home at 1 a.m. if I want. I would handle things exactly the same way that I've been handling them for the past eight years. The exact way that I'm handling them now.

In contrast, Maggie felt that her employment mattered only insofar as she was the one able to pay more child support. Maggie's ex-husband had a work history that was spotty at best, but he was not a very involved father either. He did not do any of the routine childcare or household duties. When I asked Maggie whether childcare responsibilities were taken into account, she explained, "Their dad got primary residence because I worked and he didn't. In other words, in my opinion, whoever can pay support is noncustodial. The court said, 'Ok you work and he doesn't, so he gets the kids during the week and you get them every weekend.'" Maggie felt this standard she perceived left her at a disadvantage but contained a logic that generally applied to men because in heterosexual couples they often earned more than their partners.

Regardless of where noncustodial mothers stood in their individual case, there are underlying assumptions at work in custody determination when mothers like Maggie and Monica have high-paying or high-status jobs, particularly in relation to their ex-partners. The first assumption is that such jobs require long work hours and provide decreased flexibility. While this was true in some cases, it was not in others. It is a myth that occupations dominated by women, typically lower status, are more flexible than male-dominated jobs (Glauber 2011). For example, elementary school teachers cannot just step out of the classroom if their own child is sick. Nurses cannot easily cut short their shift to see a child's after-school sporting event. Even individuals who work temporary jobs that are touted for their flexibility often find that, in reality, they cannot shape their hours or turn down assignments (Rogers 2000). The second assumption at work in cases like these is that when a mother's work is primary, the male partner will take on the additional household labor. In other words, their status relative to their ex-partners' was used to extrapolate to a configuration of household labor. In both Maggie's and Monica's cases, they still managed the lion's share of household labor when they were married, including cooking, cleaning, shuttling children around, caring for sick children, and most other routine needs. Postdivorce and despite their noncustodial status, these mothers still did the bulk of the caregiving work for their children. This was very typical of noncustodial mothers who participated in the online support groups as well.

Research on the household division of labor unfortunately has focused on married, cohabiting, heterosexual couples and does not address household labor postdivorce.[1] What we do know from decades of research on work, family, and household labor is that this body of work does not support the assumption that men will take over the bulk of household duties if their female partner has a high-status job. Certainly, over time, as women's labor force participation has increased, women have collectively reduced their time spent on housework and childcare, which has somewhat closed the gender gap in household labor time. Fathers have increased their relational time with children when compared with previous generations, although the increase is centered on days that they do not work (Maume 2011). In short, men's contributions to housework have been more resistant to change than women's contributions to household earnings.

There are important differences among women when it comes to employment and housework. In heterosexual, nondivorced families, women with high status or longer work hours do less housework than women with low status or fewer work hours and stay-at-home mothers (Gupta 2007). These mothers are able to buy out of some household duties by hiring household help or utilizing outside services. Even with this ability, women at all levels of work status and income do more household labor than their male partners. Women's lack of time available for household labor and childcare does not necessarily translate to men picking up the slack (Maume 2011). Instead, women are known to forgo leisure as well as quality sleep for their second shift (Hochschild 1989; Mattingly and Bianchi 2003; Maume, Sebastian, and Bardo 2009; Venn et al. 2008). This time crunch for women was particularly acute when a newborn was present. Jill Yavorski, Claire Kamp Dush, and Sara Schoppe-Sullivan (2015) found that immediately following the transition to new parenthood, women's total labor increased dramatically over men's, yielding an eight-hour-longer week for women. Routine, daily, necessary care and planning for that care (the mental burden) remain largely the work of women in heterosexual marriages.

Women's increased earnings relative to those of a male partner have had some effect when it comes to increasing male partners' share of the household and care burden. There is much debate about this relative-resources hypothesis, under which conditions it applies, or whether it applies at all. Researchers identify some increase in men's contributions up to the point where men's and women's incomes are nearly equal (Maume 2011), but men whose masculine identity is threatened at work, by, for example, low-status or feminized work, do less household labor, particularly when their earnings are similar to their spouse's (Arrighi and Maume 2000).

The situations of many noncustodial mothers reveal that when women's work is seen not as secondary but rather as equal to or higher in status than their partner's work, decision makers are assuming they are following a specialization model of the household division of labor (Lachance-Grzela and Bouchard 2010) in which one partner focuses on paid work, while the other focuses on unpaid household labor. This specialization model evokes the hegemonic image of a 1950s white, middle-class suburban family with a breadwinning father and a homemaking mother,[2] but it does not reflect contemporary arrangements in heterosexual families, where typically both spouses are employed. The result of these embedded assumptions is that a male partner with lower relative employment status becomes constructed as the primary caregiver simply by virtue of the mother's greater income or occupational status. Thus, women's jobs with higher status or pay can work against them by rendering their household labor invisible and inflating the efforts of a male partner.[3] In other words, high-status jobs that confer a mark of stability on fathers become a liability when held by mothers seeking custody. Pam felt that her high-status job in a male-dominated field played a significant role in the custody decision made by the judge: "One of the things that mattered was my job. I have been judged by people over the years because I have a better job and make more money than my ex-husband. And the fact that I have a job is suspect in and of itself. That I actually loved my job and was good at my job was just completely considered to be abnormal. Why didn't I just quit and stay home when I had a chance?"

Note that Pam mentioned the she earns a higher income than her ex-spouse. Monica also felt that her job relative to her ex-partner's was a significant factor in the opinion rendered by the custody evaluator in her case, from whom she felt hostility: "I also think that this evaluator was somehow trying to make up for my husband having the lesser job or less education. Like it was a criticism or a punishment or something for emasculating him. And the big, bad wife, she couldn't possibly take care of her children. Let's give them to him. That'll show her." Comments such as these were not unusual in the support groups online either. In terms of sheer numbers, the social pattern is still largely that women earn less and have lower-status jobs than their male partners, and motherhood still has a significant impact on women's earnings (Budig and England 2001; Waldfogel 1997). Yet there has been an increase in families in which wives outearn husbands by more than $30,000, from 6 percent in 2000 to 9 percent in 2015 (US Bureau of the Census 2015). My research suggests that mothers in this category may be at a disadvantage in this regard when it comes to child custody determination. Whether these perceptual issues outweigh the benefits of being able to afford legal advice remains an empirical question.

If high-status mothers' work is seen as interfering with their ability to care for children, one would expect that unemployed or stay-at-home mothers would have an advantage over employed ex-partners in child custody determinations. I expected to find it hard to locate noncustodial mothers who had been stay-at-home mothers. These mothers, however, did not feel that their status was an advantage. To the contrary, these mothers expressed a sense that they had been portrayed as lazy or dependent in the custody determination process.[4] To what extent judges actually felt this about the noncustodial mothers is difficult to determine; however, in our broader culture, negative attitudes toward stay-at-home mothers coexist alongside our cultural imperatives for at least some mothers to be full-time mothers. Fernanda's situation is instructive because it highlights the ways in which an arrangement considered beneficial when talking about a father can be construed as precisely the opposite when a mother is in the same situation. Fernanda explained how she thinks their employment and housing statuses played into the decision in her case. She had expected that the children would remain with her.

> The children had been with me since he left them with me, but then like six months after the temporary hearing, the judge made a different decision. I had been a stay-at-home mom and did some part-time work on the side. The reasons I think were number one, he was and is full-time employed with the federal government and I was not. I had finished this training before I moved out. He was working full time and had the steady income and the stable household. He was living in a house that his parents owned[,] and I was renting. My mom had just moved here. His lawyer argued that I was relying too much on my mom and the judge believed that. But her final ruling was that he should not be using paid daycare. She was going to order me to pay for it but she didn't see that he would need it because his mom was available. Then I kind of got the sense that she ruled this way kind of to make me go get a job, which is a really lousy thing in my opinion.

Fernanda felt that the judge's decision was in part designed to make her seek full-time employment and become independent. She was seen as too dependent for having household assistance from her mother, but her ex-husband's living in his parents' house and having his mother care for the children was seen as beneficial and as a means to keep the children out of paid childcare. Thus, irregular employment or lack of employment, which we have seen constructed as beneficial for men in child custody determinations, can be a liability for women.

Fernanda's situation highlights an underlying assumption about higher-paid fathers, that there is a full-time caregiver in his household. This assumption worked to mothers' disadvantage. It was common for noncustodial mothers to relay that another woman in her ex-partner's household (a stepmother, a grandmother, or even a girlfriend) was seen in a favorable light in custody determination. So common was this viewpoint that I heard it referred to as custody-by-stepmom or custody-by-grandma by more than a few mothers. This seemed especially common in situations where the noncustodial mother had been married to a very high-status man, but it also occurred in working-class families. Among the noncustodial mothers I interviewed, fewer than five had ex-partners who did not have a new wife, a girlfriend, or a mother involved in the day-to-day care of their children. My participation in online support communities yielded similar findings, thus suggesting the need for more systematic investigation of whether there exists implicit preference for male-breadwinner, female-homemaker families in custody determination processes.

At first, it seems perplexing that care from a stepmother or a grandmother could be preferred to care by a stay-at-home mother; however, we are at a cultural moment that combines imperatives of intensive motherhood and neoliberalism such that mothers *must* be employed, but for utilitarian and selfless purposes rather than for personal gain or self-actualization. Cultural constructions of bad mothers frame them as doing either too much or too little or both, and in that context former stay-at-home mothers and mothers with high-status jobs both fail on this account (Ladd-Taylor and Umansky 1998). High-status employed mothers fail because they are seen as excessively working, while stay-at-home mothers fail because they are seen as excessively mothering (Rose 1998; Starnes 2007).

In contrast to highly paid fathers, the highly paid mothers in this study did not have the benefit of the assumption that they would have a caregiving partner or parent available. Heterosexual mothers who remarried saw the presence of their new spouse as a detriment in terms of providing care for the children, even though a new spouse might confer some additional financial status. In some cases, ex-partners, attorneys, or custody evaluators problematized the presence of a new husband. In online support groups, noncustodial mothers warned each other that having a live-in boyfriend, or sometimes any boyfriend, was a strike against them in the process. Another man in the house was seen as a risk to the children, often in terms of diverting the mother's attention from her children. In extreme cases, a new husband might be characterized as potentially either violent or a child molester.[5]

Actual gender and work patterns reveal that having a full-time caregiving partner or other relative in the home is a poor assumption even for men.

The breadwinner-caregiver model is increasingly rare and represents a histori-cal anomaly (J. Anderson 2016). Although post-2008 recession statistics have shown a slight increase in the percentage of mothers who are stay-at-home, this increase is partially driven by low-wage workers' inability to find employment during the recession (Cohn, Livingston, and Wang 2014). While the popular myth is that stay-at-home mothering is something that highly educated women opt into, stay-at-home mothers are actually less educated and poorer than em-ployed mothers (Fondas 2013; Kuperberg and Stone 2008).

For poor mothers or former stay-at-home mothers of any class, the need for them to be employed resonates with the work-first approach of welfare reform that came out of the 1996 Personal Responsibility and Work Opportunity Rec-onciliation Act (Albelda 2001; Mink 1998). The work-first approach declines to acknowledge structural constraints on poor women that require effective supports such as affordable childcare and training for jobs that provide a living wage that can support a family. For middle-class women, the work-first approach applied to stay-at-home mothers fails to recognize work in the home as labor, as well as the realities of what it takes to reenter the workforce even if one had a career be-fore motherhood (Starnes 2007). In the case of custody, poor women seeking social safety net supports are seen simultaneously as bad mothers and bad work-ers and citizens.

This combination of intensive motherhood ideology and a moral imperative for women to work, when joined with mistaken assumptions about men's con-tributions to household labor, disadvantages both stay-at-home mothers and high-status employed mothers. The message is that a mother must work, but her employment should not upset the gender order by being of higher status than a father's employment. A remaining empirical question that is difficult to answer with existing data is how mothers across the employment spectrum fare in rela-tion to their ex-partners. Mothers employed in traditionally female-dominated jobs of a status that is equal to or lower than that of their male partner's job *may be* in a sweet spot where they face less scrutiny for their employment status in the process of determining custody. It is possible that gender ideologies help construct some female-dominated jobs like elementary school teachers as favorable in the custody determination process because they are seen as typical, respectable middle-class jobs that afford mothers the flexibility of short workdays and sum-mers off without being too ambitious. Although nurses have similarly typical middle-class, female-dominated jobs, in my interviews and observations, they fre-quently reported that the irregular schedules or potential night work often as-sociated with nursing was a real detriment in their cases even if they were not on such a schedule at the time of the custody dispute. Sandra felt that a central factor in the judge awarding custody to her ex-husband was her work schedule. She was a nurse who, having just started a new job, had to work some long night shifts and pay her dues before having a more regularized schedule: "The judge was deliberating whether it would be okay or not. He wanted me to prove that I had significant circumstances all set up. The house. The job. A support system. Childcare. I'm on call so it's kind of tricky because sometimes I'm at home and sometimes I'm not, but I can't predict it. It's not regular hours. So I had made arrangements for somebody to move in with me to be available on those nights where I'd be on call so I could just come and go as needed and she would have somebody there." In contrast, Elaine was perplexed that her ex-husband's erratic work schedule did not seem to matter in their case: "I was a stay-at-home mom and he worked third shift so he was gone all night and asleep during the day. His schedule would change a lot and that was something I brought up in court. Well, how stable is he if his schedule is always changing?" Taken together, these mothers' understandings of how their employment status shaped their custody decisions point to the importance of understanding work institutions that are gendered in different ways depending on one's social location. Whether high status or low status, mothers' employment, or lack thereof, is fraught with contradictory gender ideologies that provide reasoning that can work against any mother who is challenged for custody.

Overrecognition of Men's Caregiving

Assumptions about gender and the household division of labor play out in custody determinations through the overrecognition of men's caregiving. Gendered caregiving norms in general and in the custody process in particular set the bar for fathers rather low. Noncustodial mothers who had done the bulk of household labor, whether they stayed at home or not, frequently expressed their disbelief at the outcome of their custody determination. They believed that the best-interests standard for custody determination should favor whoever was providing the day-to-day care of the children but often felt instead that the court overly recognized and rewarded fathers' caregiving and devalued both women's employment and their caregiving.

It was common for primary caregiving mothers, whether employed or not, to feel that their household labor was devalued or rendered invisible in the custody determination process. Monica, who worked outside the home, felt that her day-to-day caregiving went unrecognized and was irrelevant to the custody determination:

My life isn't anything like I imagined. I always thought when I grew up I'd be in one of those laundry commercials with the sheets blowing outside in the sunshine. I'm not that mom. I could be more patient. Well, let's face it, I'm not a patient person. I can't be the mom I'm supposed to be. But I was working like fifty hours a week and always feeling sick. My ex didn't do anything really but watch t.v. with the baby and that supposedly made him a great dad. We'd be somewhere and my hair would be falling out and there's bags under my eyes because I was up all night and up early cleaning in the morning and putting everything together for the family outing. So I was grouchy. I'm always grouchy. But he sleeps like a baby and carries our son around at the party and everyone's like "Oh what a great dad!" Conspicuous parenting. That's what he does. I'm a horrible bitch. I'm a horrible bitch because I want to be left alone for like an hour or I don't feel like building sandcastles. Someone has to throw out the moldy cheese and flush the dead goldfish and know that we're almost out of diaper cream. So what does a court see? They see The Horrible Bitch and The Great Dad. There's your next new Disney film.

The other side of women's invisible household labor is the overrecognition of men's parenting.[6] Many noncustodial mothers felt that custody determination favored fathers who expressed a desire to be more involved with their children. They characterized the custody process as one that sets the bar for fatherhood rather low, identifying both a readiness of courts to believe that fathers were equal partners in childcare and a reluctance of courts to appear biased in favor of mothers. In one online support group, the term Father of the Year was used sarcastically to refer to minimally involved fathers who played up their involvement in order to gain advantage in the custody dispute. Rhoda believes the overrecognition of men's parenting is a contemporary phenomenon born of the desire to see more men involved in children's lives: "Dads used to have a harder time. These days, I think it's easier for them. If the dad shows interest, the court makes him Father of The Year and says you're showing interest so you must be the perfect dad. I think they can screw up and make mistakes and then say I'm sorry and look gold. Whereas I think these days moms have to be drop dead perfect and that's not even enough." Sandra believes that the trend is due in part to successful campaigns by those in the fathers' rights movement.

I looked through all the fathers' rights sites because I knew he was gonna look there. It's such, it's like, how do I describe it? It's such a movement for fathers' rights that it's almost militant. It seems like it got started because it assumed that mothers had all the rights and fathers didn't have rights. And now it seems like it's swung all the way to the other side where almost everybody I talk to seems like the fathers are the ones that are believed and get more rights than the moms. And I thought, well, how did this happen? It seemed like moms used to always get the benefit of the doubt and fathers had to fight back. And now fathers get the benefit of the doubt just because they're doing whatever they're doing. You know what I mean? Traditionally, I guess moms have been the one to take care of the kids and dad's out doing the hunting and gathering, you know, caveman stuff. And now it's like, it's dad will do a little thing and he expects a medal for doing it. It's like it's your kid too, that's what you're supposed to do. You get a paycheck and go to the grocery story, so you gotta do something else besides hunting, you know! I think the old boy thing just hangs on. That fathers just get rewarded for doing the smallest things because they're fathers and they're doing it. Whereas mothers are expected to do it because that's what needs to be done and they just do it. And I think fathers are getting a lot more than they used to, a lot more attention and a lot more favoritism and rights, but I don't think it's necessarily because they deserve it. I think it's just because it's fathers doing something.

Bonnie thinks that the overrecognition of men's parenting goes hand in hand with gender stereotypes about unfit mothers such that continuity in day-to-day care for a child is irrelevant.

I think any bad gender stereotype or double standard that they can throw out there works in their favor. "She's a slut! She's emasculating him! She's selfish!" Literally anything that I did was evidence that I'm selfish. All that dads have to do is pop their head up and say they want to be a good dad. Or yell in advance that, "Moms always get custody!" We're at a time now where we want gender equality so badly that we jump the gun. Yes, dads can be moms, but they aren't usually. And if he can make me look bad, then somehow that translates to he's doing all of the mom stuff. It's not a popularity contest, but it is. Why is it so hard to figure out who has been doing what all along and just stay with that?

These mothers identified a readiness of courts to believe that fathers were equal partners in childcare and a reluctance of courts to appear biased in favor of mothers. What emerges is that the discourse of gender bias in the context of child custody refers to bias against fathers. Fathers' rights groups have indeed been successful in transforming the idea that fathers cannot get custody into a common-sense understanding of how things are.

Even the language of primary caregiving has come to be understood as promoting gender bias against men, and it is absent from state laws and official guidance on custody determination. The shift to gender-neutral terms like *parenting time* further obfuscates gendered patterns of household labor and childcare. One effect of the rejection of gendered language is that parenting becomes conflated with caregiving. The gender-neutral framing of caregiving as parenting does a disservice to women, who remain the primary group doing most of the caregiving today. Conflating parenting with caregiving elides important differences in the actual content of what parents do, which is often unfortunately still quite gendered. Recall that the one significant change in fathers' behavior over recent decades concerns increased interactive time with children. In the language of caregiving, fathers have become more relational with their children than earlier generations. Thus, the understanding of parenting for men increasingly has come to include nurturing, as well as economic support and discipline of children. These are positive developments for men as well as children.

There is a tension in scholarship on caregiving that revolves around whether to recognize and celebrate women's greater share in these crucial activities or to press for caregiving responsibilities, which constitute a form of labor, to be distributed more equally across genders in society. Such an ethic of care explicitly values nurturing work involved in raising small children. However, care work involves a substantial amount of work that is not nurturing or relational. *Reproductive labor* is a term that is inclusive of nurturing but also includes the quotidian, devalued, and often invisible tasks like cleaning, cooking, and bathing, along with the mental burden of knowing what medicines, household supplies, and foodstuffs are in the cupboards or need to be purchased. For example, in caring for a very young baby, cuddling, feeding, or bathing the baby is relational, while making sure there are clean clothes, baby food, or fresh diapers in the house is not. When we reduce caregiving to its relational aspects, we continue to devalue or render invisible the work that, when paid, is most often done by poor women and women of color (Duffy 2007). In the context of custody, the focus on parenting *as nurturance* highlights precisely the areas where we have seen men increase their efforts. These are important social changes; however, this focus renders invisible the myriad other tasks involved in caregiving that are not relational.

The gender-neutral framing articulates a socially desirable state of gender equality that we have not yet achieved. While women have increased their representation in the workforce and in many formerly male-dominated fields, men have not embraced all aspects of the home to the same extent.[7] Custody decisions that overrecognize men's parenting are perhaps well-intentioned attempts to reverse engineer gender equality in the home. The consequences for many of the mothers I interviewed included having their primary caregiving roles discounted. How might we recognize women's (still) disproportionate share of caregiving responsibilities and reproductive labor without cementing those gender divisions of labor in place? Perhaps the time to ungender reproductive labor is not when a custody decision has to be made but rather continually from the formation of each new household. At the very least, all parties involved in making custody determinations should have a greater, nuanced understanding of gender and reproductive labor.

In place of any gender markers, sometimes the language "a willingness to parent" is embedded in custody guidelines. This language elevates stated intentions over evidence-based assessment of caregiving arrangements. One potential way out of the gendered consequences of gender-neutral language is to follow the approximation rule, which involves determining how household labor was allocated before the dissolution of the relationship and then reflecting those arrangements in the custody agreement (Emery, Otto, and O'Donohue 2005). Amy discussed something similar:

> There needs to be more investigation into who's raising these kids. When dad has 'em, is grandma getting them when dad's supposed to be with them? Are the daycares raising the kids when mom doesn't work and can be home with them? My daughter goes into daycare at 7 a.m. and isn't picked up until 6:30 in the evening. When she was here with me, she was driven to school, got up to a full breakfast in the morning. She was picked up at 2:45 and brought home. We did homework at the table and had family dinner. Then me and her did whatever she wanted to do after the homework was done. We spent time together. Versus going back into a home with a dad that throws a tv dinner on the table at 7:30 whenever they get home. Do your homework by yourself. They need to investigate more into what dad is doing. No, wait a minute. That's woman-chauvinistic of me. There are good physical custodians and there are bad physical custodians. There are good dads and moms just like there are bad ones.

Fernanda felt that stability in terms of employment was overemphasized relative to caregiving. She too favors a practice that sounds like the approximation rule.

> I think what matters is who's going to be the available parent to the child. I understand the financial stability factor, but I think who's available to care for the kids is important. I mean, not just when they're young either. The more I hear about friends of mine who have teenagers, it seems like they need you more then. I'm not saying that it needs to go to the stay-at-home mom and I understand financial stability. I'm not sure I would agree with somebody being granted custody who's never going to work even though they could, just stay at home and take care of the kids and

expect the ex to pay their way. I don't really agree with that. I think part of the divorce process is deciding how you're gonna stand on your own two feet and what you're gonna do with your life because obviously being a mom is not gonna pay the bills.

What these mothers' experiences reveal is that judges and other parties to the custody determination process may operate with deeply gendered understandings about what constitutes appropriate employment and caregiving for parents of all genders. Popular discourses of gender bias against men reinforce the appeal of gender-neutral standards that are anything but gender neutral. Individuals' gendered understandings are an important piece of the story. But individuals do not arrive at these understandings on their own. Gender is also embedded in the language of official standards and guidelines used for custody determination.

Examining Guidelines, Statutes, Commissions, and Recommendations

Issues of gender, work, and employment make their way into the official and unofficial criteria employed by judges, evaluators, and other parties to making a custody determination despite the formally gender-neutral approach. This section focuses on the content of publicly available guidelines and documents that lay out the multifaceted criteria for custody determinations. This analysis is not an exhaustive accounting of materials. States vary in their standards and the language they use regarding factors that matter in custody determination; however, there is significant borrowing of language and standards from state to state. Professional associations like the American Bar Association and the National Center for State Courts exert a kind of normative institutional isomorphism (DiMaggio and Powell 1983) through groups such as the American Law Association and the Uniform Law Commission and publications such as *A Judge's Guide to Making Child-Centered Decisions in Custody Cases* and *Determining the Best Interests of the Child*. The push for uniform handling of domestic cases across state lines has resulted in much continuity among states (Appelton 2014).

Carefully analyzing the state codes concerning how to define the best interests of the child reveals very few mentions of gender at all. When gender is mentioned, it is most often similar to the approach in Pennsylvania, which states that the criteria are to be the following: "Gender neutral.—In making a determination under subsection (a), no party shall receive preference based upon gender in any award granted under this chapter" (PA Code § 5328 [b]). South Carolina goes even further, specifically addressing the elimination of any advantage that the tender years doctrine may have conferred on mothers. Its statute reads, "The 'Tender Years Doctrine' in which there is a preference for awarding a mother custody of a child of tender years is abolished" (SC Code § 63-15-10 [2012]).

In general, these resources and documents are framed as gender neutral. It is that very gender neutrality, however, that obfuscates the manner in which gender continues to enter into custody decisions. Not all states have laws that prohibit wealth from being a determinative factor in child custody decisions (Frantz 2000), so women's relative economic position can disadvantage them in custody disputes. In the case of former stay-at-home mothers, they appear to have run afoul of a concept sometimes referred to as the capacity to provide. Heavy reliance on a capacity to provide would advantage fathers. Take, for example, the following language: "A person who has voluntarily accepted a reduction in income below the parent's earning capacity may be considered to lack the disposition to provide for the child's basic needs. A parent who has an excellent employment history but who has recently become self-employed may still be considered to have a greater capacity than a parent who has a less successful employment history and whose earnings in her most recent position depend on future sales" (Friend of the Court Bureau 2016, 10). Note the valuation of an excellent employment history, which appears to compensate for a parent whose income has recently decreased at the time of the custody issue. A parent in a similar situation but with a less successful employment history is considered to have less capacity to provide. The elevation of the standard of an excellent employment history reinforces the ideal-worker norm, which is "framed around the traditional life patterns of men" and "excludes most mothers of childbearing age" (Williams 2000, 2). Even though women's labor force participation patterns increasingly are coming to resemble men's, childbearing still negatively affects mothers' incomes and careers. In the context of heterosexual families, there remain gendered patterns of wives' jobs being secondary to husbands' jobs, meaning, for example, that job relocations that benefit him may end up in a career disruption for her.

An important subgroup of noncustodial mothers consists of those who had been in a relationship that involved domestic violence, which is the focus of chapter 7. In relation to employment, there was a pattern among these mothers of having their ex-spouse restricting their employment hours or opportunities in some fashion. At her ex-husband's insistence, Amy quit her job and did in-home daycare instead. Angela's ex-spouse was frequently jealous and accused her of infidelities when she was going to work, so she eventually quit her job and stayed home full time. In the context of understanding the intersection of gender, work, and custody, domestic violence complicates employment in ways that are rendered invisible in gender-neutral discourses. What appears to be voluntary underemployment may actually be the result of interpersonal control tactics used by an abuser.

Women's secondary labor force location reinforces men's relative economic advantage. According to census data, one-quarter of heterosexual couples have earnings that are within $5,000 of each other. Wives outearn husbands by more than $30,000 in only 9 percent of heterosexual couples, but husbands outearn wives by more than $30,000 in 35 percent of couples. These data do not parse out mothers and fathers from married couples without children. Considering the motherhood wage penalty, these numbers likely underestimate the extent of wage disparity between spouses in heterosexual families. Given that the median household income was $57,617 in 2015, women outearning men by more than $30,000 per year is a small and distinctly upper-middle-class phenomenon (US Bureau of the Census 2015). In most heterosexual families, the gender disparity in income is not as great, but it still favors men. Women's median share of household income is around 30 percent (Golan and Kerdnunvong 2016).

In the foregoing language regarding capacity to provide, the issue of self-employment arises as a reason that a parent might have a decreased capacity to provide. However, if the recent dip in income is preceded by a pattern that reflects the ideal-worker norm, self-employment is seen as less problematic. This framing constitutes another advantage for men. We know that patterns of women's and men's self-employment differ. White men, in contrast to white women and men of color, are more likely to have higher-status self-employment (Lee and Rendalli 2001). Self-employed men are more likely to be incorporated and hire employees than other groups (Kochhar, Parker, and Rohal 2015).

The other voluntary reduction in income that goes unspoken in these guidelines concerns stay-at-home mothers. Echoing the experiences of noncustodial mothers, Cynthia Lee Starnes (2007) identifies the tendency of the legal system to see unemployed mothers as lazy and self-indulgent, resulting in an imperative for employment of divorcing mothers of children older than a certain age, which varies by state. In this framework, being a former stay-at-home mother is a disadvantage, particularly if one is living in poverty or does not remarry. This kind of work-first approach to motherhood fits neatly in the neoliberal model of motherhood (which I discussed in greater detail in the introduction and chapter 3) seen on full display in the 1996 process of welfare reform via the Personal Responsibility and Work Opportunity Reconciliation Act (Mink 1998). Although intensive motherhood is a cultural imperative, poor women and women of color are more constrained by work requirements that make it difficult to meet those cultural ideals. In both contexts, women's household and caregiving labor is devalued or rendered invisible just as we see with many mothers who have lost custody to a male ex-partner.

Closely related to capacity to provide is the concept of stability. As seen earlier, *stability* was a word that frequently came into play in interviews and online discussions. In the online support groups, many mothers like Fernanda characterized their situation as hinging in part on the judge seeing them as less stable than their ex-partners because they were reentering the workforce or made less money. Mothers' relative economic disadvantage is encoded in the following example that discusses housing in terms of the need for a child to live "in a stable, satisfactory environment" (Friend of the Court Bureau 2016, 13). The full entry on housing stability reads, "Factor (d) examines the stability of the child's home. For instance, a stable environment is not demonstrated when a parent moves several times, remarries and divorces in the short time since the parents divorced, and now plans on marrying *her* boyfriend" (13; emphasis mine). Frequent moves for "evictions, foreclosures, or broken relationships" (13) are identified as introducing unnecessary instability into the child's life.

Although gender neutral, the concept of stability supports male advantage to the extent that stability is connected with either economic self-sufficiency or maintenance of the family home. Stability sounds very much like a middle-class construct, but in working-class families, it can still be conferred on fathers because of their economic position relative to their ex-partner's, particularly if the family home is involved. Noncustodial mothers with higher-status jobs were not exempt from the notion of stability, and several felt that it factored into the decision in their case in unexpected ways. Monica explained, "I kind of felt that anything I did was going to be called unstable. I had the better job, but he was stable because he wasn't going anywhere. I don't see how you can be more stable than me. Look in the dictionary next to the word, stable. I'm there. But I moved out so I'm unstable." This seeming fetishization of the family home is actually rooted in the history of family law. Susan Frelich Appelton (2014) provides a detailed analysis of how the concept of domicile (or home) embedded in family law represents a remnant of women's inequality in heterosexual marriages that affects outcomes of today's family law cases in ways that disadvantage women. Standards of custody determination privilege domicile stability in the primary physical residence of a child. Given the gender wage gap and the likelihood in heterosexual couples that the man will have a higher income than the woman, stability as a direct or indirect criterion for custody determination is a male standard, particularly because the motivation underlying child support payments or alimony is to ensure the economic well-being of the household where a child resides.

In the codes of states that specify criteria for the best interests of the child, the importance of stability is frequently more directly connected to housing and a parent's willingness to use their resources for a particular kind of housing arrangement. The following example is given in Michigan's *Custody and Parenting Time Investigation Manual*: "A parent who had sufficient income to provide secure and adequate housing was found to be lacking in this factor when *she* decided to save money by sharing an apartment with an adult couple who had negative aspects to their relationship and where the child slept on a sofa bed and cot" (Friend of the Court Bureau 2016, 10; emphasis mine). In a sea of gender-neutral language, the explicit gendering of the parent with the unstable arrangements in the previous two examples is unusual and puzzling, perhaps reinforcing the worn stereotype of women's flighty nature. It is not capriciousness but women's relative economic position that places them at an economic disadvantage that can translate to a housing disadvantage, particularly if the woman is a former stay-at-home mother reentering the workforce. Another stereotype embedded in these criteria is that women spend selfishly on themselves, but economic studies from around the world confirm that "when women have control [of] household spending, the money goes toward more family-targeted goods" (Thompson 2011).

Data on who is more likely to leave the family home are mixed at best (Mulder and Wagner 2010), but they do show that women's relative economic status has an effect. It is not uncommon for one divorcing spouse to buy out the other rather than sell the family home. The spouse must be able to take on the mortgage on their income or trade any potential alimony for the equity in the house. Even so, judges' reluctance to award alimony (Starnes 2007) further reinforces the gendered nature of the stability standard. Home ownership is tied to race and class as well. Although 64 percent of people own their homes, whites' rates of home ownership are over 70 percent, and the rates for Black and Hispanic homeownership are under 50 percent (US Bureau of the Census 2018).

This construction of a particular type of housing as a marker of fitness for parenting is not unique to custody determinations postdivorce. It resonates with the experiences of poor women and people of color who interact with the child welfare system. Lack of housing support is identified as a significant barrier for families seeking reunification with children placed into foster care. There is a nationwide affordable housing crisis resulting in more than 38 percent of households being characterized as rent burdened—that is, they spend more than 30 percent of their pretax earnings on housing (Pew Charitable Trust 2018). Casting housing difficulties as a set of poor choices or reflective of unwise spending decisions reifies a set of stereotypes of individuals on public assistance.

What we see in the context of the custody guidelines very much echoes those stereotypes and imports them into the system unladen with race, class, and gender markers so that these criteria appear objectively in the best interests of the children. In this context, falling short of the unspoken ideal of a white, middle-class, two-parent family in a single-family suburban home translates to instability. Considering men's wages and that men are more likely to remarry and remarry sooner than women (Shafer and James 2013), they are advantaged in meeting the criterion of stability insofar as it is understood in this system.

Middle- and upper-middle-class women who had well-paid jobs and housing arrangements arguably were stable, but as seen earlier, other aspects of their situation seemed to trump their stability. Finally, the emphasis on stability (in the form of a domicile occupied by a white, middle-class, two-parent family) is the link that helps us understand the custody-by-stepmother phenomenon mentioned by so many participants. It also helps us understand how, in the foregoing passage, a parent intent on saving money on housing is cast in a negative light.

The term *bias* represents another means through which a gender-neutral framework reproduces women's disadvantage in the custody determination process. A 2014 report by Maryland General Assembly's Commission on Child Custody Decision-Making identifies biases such as those concerning religion, race, and disability as a significant issue in child custody determination. The question of gender bias in the report specifically focuses on whether fathers are disadvantaged in the family court system. The subcommittee on bias includes individuals representing groups that have a stake in addressing issues relating to gender, such as the Baltimore Responsible Fatherhood Project, the House of Ruth (domestic violence survivor advocates), and the Women's Law Center. The report contains witness lists from public hearings that demonstrate a routine presence of fathers' rights advocates and individual fathers. Some of the mothers who testified spoke in support of the men in their lives who they felt experienced bias in family court because they were fathers. While there were a few mothers speaking *as mothers*, most of the group spoke either as advocates of children or as survivors of domestic violence. Taken together, witnesses speaking to fathers' concerns outnumbered all others by a ratio of two to one.

Among the recommendations from the bias subgroup is to quantitatively investigate bias against fathers in custody determinations, but that study was not completed because these kinds of data are not routinely collected and are difficult to construct from existing records. The group also recommended bias training for judges: "Since many litigants in custody matters appear to believe that trial judges make custody decisions in a way that reflects gender bias, judicial education should address explicit and implicit bias" (Maryland General Assembly, Commission on Child-Custody Decision-Making, appendix G, 29). Note that the recommendation for training is based on the *belief* by litigants that judges engage in gender-biased decisions. Since the empirical study of gender bias was not completed, the recommendation is not evidence based but rather appears to reflect the concerns of those who testified at the public hearings. Taking the over three-hundred-page document as a whole, the recommendation for gender bias training for judges should be understood as training to prevent bias against fathers. But as we have seen, those weighing in on custody decisions may already be self-monitoring for bias against fathers.

The section of the report on disability bias provides a stark contrast to the section on gender bias because it identifies specific problematic language and criteria that contribute to the disadvantage of people with disabilities in family court. The recommendations concerning disability bias rest on federal disability legislation, such as the Americans with Disabilities Act, and disability bias in court is seen as continuous with biases seen in other social institutions like employment and education. In other words, disability bias is not framed as bias against the socially dominant group, the nondisabled. The recommended actions to prevent disability bias are not based on mere perceptions that the socially *dominant* group is actually the one at a disadvantage. Therefore, we do not find recommendations to avoid discrimination against the nondisabled. Contrast this with the handling of gender disadvantage, which results in a call for training judges to prevent bias against fathers, a bias that is empirically unsubstantiated as well as discontinuous with men's treatment across other social institutions.

Concerns of bias are not unfounded. Judges do have extraordinary discretion in interpreting and applying the guidelines, and many statutes contain a phrase similar to one in the statute of Virginia, which includes the broad category of "such other factors as the court deems necessary and proper to the determination" (VA code § 20-124.3 [2012]). At least ten states have similar phrasing that opens up custody criteria to the broadest possible interpretation. Scholarship on discrimination in employment reveals that bias enters most easily into decisions when criteria are expansive and discretionary (Heilman 2001; Uhlman and Cohen 2005). Implicit or unconscious bias enters when standards are unclear, and explicit bias can easily be couched as something else. Given what is a well-documented phenomenon, it would be foolish to assume that the absence of clear standards does not generate biases against some groups. Analysis of the experiences of noncustodial mothers and the documentation on custody criteria suggests that there may be biases, but they are not against fathers.

Having a good job works against mothers, but so does having a bad job or no job. Mothers work too much and mothers work too little. Because we are still conflicted as a society when it comes to mothers working and work is such a polymorphous thing, discourses can be harnessed against women no matter what their employment situation. In either case, custody determination tends to erase women's unpaid labor in the home. On the other hand, male ex-partners' good jobs were seen as an asset rather than a liability. When a man was employed in a job that paid less than his ex-wife's job, his relative position could be seen as a benefit, providing him the flexibility to care for the children. Class and race ideologies help to construct middle-class white fathers seeking custody as the new, involved father while simultaneously failing to challenge the trope of deadbeat dads, a racialized and class-marked concept.[8]

Gender-neutral discourses and myths about equality contribute to creating this contradictory set of affairs. The assumption that gender equality already exists in social institutions undergirds the gender-neutral discourse, creating experiences that have everything to do with gender. Even though there is formal gender equality under the law, labor markets and contributions to household labor are indeed very gendered. We confuse "equality of status with identity of contribution" (Starnes 2007, 231). Thus, in our desire as a society to reach a gender-equitable state, we have prematurely encoded illusory equality into law in ways that perpetuate gender inequalities.

Maternal employment resonates quite well with the imperatives of the neoliberal state. The ever-shrinking safety net of the neoliberal state pushes women out of welfare roles and into a labor market that is stacked against women, people of color, and those with less education. In the realm of child custody, the tender years doctrine cedes to neoliberal demands for maternal employment. Maternal employment, however, must be instrumental rather than self-actualizing. Mothers "should be in the paid labor market providing a model for their children, and should be able to accrue the financial resources necessary to support their family independent of government assistance" (Gross et al. 2014, 166). This imperative has bled into custody determination such that mothers must be employed enough to not require public assistance, but they should not be working in ways that disrupt gender hierarchies. In other words, they should not be in charge or earning more than men.

Mothers will be ordered to pay child support without regard for gender, but they are subject to different labor markets or may have been out of the labor force for childbearing. Because noncustodial mothers remain routinely involved with their children in ways that fathers often do not, removal to the paternal household does not result in deadbeat mothers who drift away and are difficult to track down to collect child support. In addition, although child support is conceptualized as paying for the necessities in the custodial home, mothers are more likely to spend additional money directly on children's necessities than men. Noncustodial mothers impoverished by child support orders share this burden with poor white fathers and poor fathers of color who find themselves losing their driver's licenses or worse when they cannot make their full child support payments. Children with residence in a male-headed household, however, have lower poverty rates and are less likely to require public assistance than if they resided with their mother (Chalabi 2015). Noncustodial mothers remain caught in the contradictions between neoliberal motherhood and intensive mothering where mothers must be breadwinners and stay-at-home mothers at the same time.

MANUFACTURING BAD MOTHERS

The field of psychology intersects with child custody determination everywhere from the incorporation of psychological discourses in the standards applied to determine custody to the actual involvement of psychologists and therapists as mediators or as custody evaluators who render an expert opinion on a given case. Contemporary Western psychological frameworks rest on and support neoliberal ideas about individualism, individual responsibility, and privatization. Individual, psychological-based interventions in the form of psychotherapy represent neoliberal answers to social problems. Rather than challenging social structures that create traumatic or troubling social milieus, therapeutic approaches are founded on promoting individual accommodation or adjustment to existing circumstances (Foucault 1988; Rustin 2015). Cultural and psychological ideas about what fathers do for children include cultivating independence, which positions them well vis-à-vis mothers in the neoliberal context. At the same time, the impossible demands of intensive motherhood when assessed through a therapeutic lens serve to "manufacture bad mothers" (Swift 1995) during a psychological custody evaluation. Our neoliberal, postfeminist cultural moment sets up a rocky terrain mothers must navigate when it comes to custody. Because of the connections among gender, psychology, motherhood, and neoliberalism, the strong therapeutic presence in child custody determination is worthy of analysis.

Of the mothers I interviewed individually, about half mentioned mental health as a factor that arose in their custody case. Having a history of mental health issues was also a frequently discussed topic in the online support groups. While it is not possible to know whether mental health was *the* issue that mattered in each case, it is instructive to analyze patterns in the ways in which mental health or mental health practitioners were approached in their cases.

Past Mental Illness as a Factor

Among the women who mentioned mental health as a factor in their custody case, there were just a few who had ever been hospitalized for what are thought of as more serious mental illnesses, such as bipolar disorder. Katie, for example, had undiagnosed bipolar disorder while she was married. As she shared, her husband filed for divorce and custody of their two children while she was being hospitalized after a suicide attempt: "I had an untreated medical condition, but because of the stigma since it's mental health, my husband was able to use this to his advantage. I had a mental illness that was untreated. It just needed to be treated. We're back in court again and I had my psychiatrist in to testify and maybe I could get some overnights." At the time of our interview, Katie was still married but under a temporary custody order that allowed no phone contact and required supervised visits with her children, who were both under five years old. After her discharge from the hospital, Katie did not see her children for a few months. When she did finally see them, she was allowed one hour of supervised time a week. At the time of our interview, Katie's psychiatrist felt that she was capable of caring for her children enough to have them for overnight visits. She hoped that his letter of support would convince the judge before the final custody order was issued.

Katie's case illustrates a trend among the mothers for whom serious mental illness was a factor in their custody determination. Once they had been labeled as having a mental illness and custody restrictions were implemented, they had a difficult time making any changes. Sometimes, their time with their children remained restricted to a few hours a week despite documentation from their psychiatrist or psychologist regarding their continued successful treatment. This was true in Lydia's case. Although she had a part-time job and documentation from her psychiatrist that she had been stable and on the same medication for nearly five years, it was not enough to modify her time with her children.

In other cases, it was a combination of the label and a lack of economic resources that kept supervised parenting time in place. Elaine originally split custody fifty-fifty with her ex-husband. While she was divorcing her second husband, her first ex-husband took her to court for a change in custody, citing a history of mental illness that she had disclosed to him while they were together:

> When he and I got together, I confided in him about previous emotional issues growing up. And those were things that I shared with him, so when

it came to court, of course he does the mudslinging and bringing those things to the table. I thought it was in my interest to be up front and not be ashamed. But being honest, I actually handed him his entire case on a silver platter. He brought up a psychiatric visit I had in a hospital when I was 18 years old, which was three years before I even met him. And that was five years before I had my son.

Elaine had no record of *recent* mental health issues, but her attorney said that the case did not look good for her. With her economic resources spread thin, Elaine could not afford to continue to pay her attorney, who ended up dropping her in the middle of her custody case. She felt she had no alternative but to accept what was offered to her, which was to have supervised visits. Although her ex-husband allows her to see her child unsupervised from time to time, she lacks the resources to go back to court to have the orders changed. In lieu of a change to the court order, Elaine's ability to see her children without supervision remains dependent on the goodwill of her ex-husband.

More typically, however, the noncustodial mothers in this study had not been hospitalized but had experienced more run-of-the-mill depression and anxiety. Amy put it most succinctly: "Every time we go into court, the first thing that they say is that mom has a mental illness and some physical ailments. And that's all that matters." Ruth spoke about her own experience and her observations of the support group that she participated in: "I think a common thing is mental illness, depression, those struggles. I've heard stories from several women who have a situation very similar to mine where they went through depression and the results were that the ex was able to use it to their advantage."

A common topic of discussion in the support groups was that simply having a record of any kind of mental health issue could spell trouble for mothers in terms of custody. Rhonda's situational depression was considered a mark against her even though she held down a full-time job and was the primary caregiver of her children: "The evaluator talked to my therapist and she said, 'She's depressed.' Well, who's not? My mother just died. She said it was situational depression. Yes, I'm on antidepressants. I have been since my daughter was four because I was in a horrible marriage. I'm on them because I feel like it helps me wake up every morning and get all the stuff done that I need to do. I've never had an alcohol problem. I've never taken drugs. I don't sleep. When I'm feeling overwhelmed, I go see a therapist. But then you're dinged for that too."

Pam was taking antidepressants at the time of the custody dispute. She felt strongly that if she went to court, she would lose because of her record of mental health issues:

> After her birth I had postpartum depression. There was this inner voice that I could never shake no matter how much I thought I was doing the right thing. There was always this voice in the back of my head saying, "You're gonna fuck this up." I would just be so afraid of doing something wrong and not being as perfect as I thought she deserved. I would get angry at myself and take it out on my ex-husband. He's not a bad guy. I wasn't crazy. I wasn't suicidal. But I knew it mattered, so I gave him what he wanted.

Postpartum depression was also problematic for mothers in the custody determination process even if they currently were not depressed or being treated for depression. Sandra felt strongly that her record of having postpartum depression would be held against her, so she avoided treatment for the current situational depression she was having throughout her divorce and the custody determination process.

> He told everyone that I'm crazy. I have had depression. I think it came out mostly as a result of my divorce, but I coped, managed, it was fine. I had postpartum depression after both kids pretty badly. And I had no support whatsoever and it was terrifying for me. I wasn't postpartum psychotic or anything, nothing like that. I couldn't make decisions. I couldn't concentrate. It was classic depression symptoms that I had never experienced before I had my kids. When we were going through the custody thing, it was really hard to cope. But I never sought help there because I knew that medical records could be subpoenaed. I went to a therapist once because I needed someone to talk things through with. But I never sought treatment because I knew he would subpoena those records. If my mental health was brought into it, I'd be sunk for sure.

A subgroup of noncustodial mothers said that they had developed their anxiety or depression as a result of an unhappy or abusive marriage. These mothers felt that even though their mental health issues were clearly situational, it made no difference in terms of the damage that could be done by being labeled mentally ill. In Amy's case, the court was aware of the domestic violence in her marriage: "I felt like sayin' to the judge, you know why I'm depressed? Because I was married to [my ex-husband]. I tried to please him every which way and he'd tell me I was nothing but a piece of trash. He slapped me when I was pregnant. His girlfriend put her hands on my daughter. Duh. Who wouldn't be depressed? Why does that give me a bad mark and make it like I'm a bad mom?" In online support groups, noncustodial mothers shared their experiences of having depression or some other mental illness being used against them in the custody dispute. Many of the discussions focused on these kinds of negative experiences of being disadvantaged by having even routine mental health issues. It was not unusual for mothers like Sandra, in the midst of a custody dispute, to report that they were considering delaying treatment for depression and anxiety, even if it was garden-variety situational depression, for fear that it would be used against them regardless of how well they might be functioning.

In contrast, there was a lot of sharing of information about mental health experiences in the online support groups in an attempt to destigmatize them. Val, who is a nurse, echoed these efforts at destigmatization when I interviewed her.

> I see parents who have bipolar and as long as they are on their meds they're fully capable people. I mean I work with someone who has bipolar and she holds down a professional career, you know. What I see too often, both in the online group and in my professional life, is somebody who had one bad episode of psychosis or mania or something, even depression, they go for treatment and then, "My god, you can't ever have your kids! You're mentally ill!" That's like wait a minute, if I had cancer instead and went through chemo and radiation, you wouldn't say you can never have your kids again. I remember Hannah who supposedly had a suicide attempt and was in the hospital for a week and when she came out he was there saying he needed to have custody of the kids. Some parents are so severely mentally ill that they can't do overnights, but even a schizophrenic deserves to have a few hours a week of supervised playtime with their kid. And kids deserve to know the good, bad, and the ugly about their parents.

Lydia observed differences in her treatment relating to her physical disability in comparison to her bipolar disorder:[1] "If you go to court and they label you mentally ill, then you're a killer or a psycho. You may have depression and you may take antidepressants and that's all. Or you may have anxiety and take anti-anxiety meds. They need to understand. They understand my physical disability. They understand if someone can't walk or see or hear. But when people deal with the mind, they think you're gone and you'll never come back."

In contemporary US society, there still exists significant stigma when it comes to mental health, so it should not come as a complete surprise that the same stigma would be present in the context of custody determination. Indeed, state guidelines frequently mention mental health as a factor that affects the best interests of the child. In Pennsylvania, for example, the factors include "the mental and physical condition of a party or member of a party's household," and "the mental and physical health of all individuals involved" can be taken into consideration in Delaware. Colorado's statute is a little more careful: "the mental and physical health of all individuals involved, except that a disability alone shall not be a basis to deny or restrict parenting time." Twenty-one states explicitly reference mental and physical health in their best-interests factors, but at least a dozen states have an additional category like New Hampshire's, which states that "any other additional factors that the court deems relevant" (Maryland General Assembly, Commission on Child-Custody Decision-Making 2014, appendix I, 10).

There is very little specific guidance regarding which mental illnesses should be determinative in custody cases and under which circumstances. With the vague standard of the best interests of the child, a simple history of situational depression can be given significant weight. Judges do not have mental health expertise, and their judgments about the salience of a particular diagnosis or history of diagnosis will be shaped by the argumentation of lawyers and the presentation of expert testimony in the context of an adversarial legal system. How does one determine whether primary custody with a mother who once had postpartum depression is more or less in the best interests of the child than primary custody with a father who was minimally involved in the day-to-day parenting of that child? Given the fact that women are more likely to reveal and seek treatment for mental health troubles than men (Addis and Mahalik 2003), the incorporation of a vague standard around mental illness leaves room for systemic bias that will disproportionately affect mothers.

Psychological Custody Evaluations

Not surprisingly, there has developed a trend of increasing involvement of psychology professionals as neutral expert arbiters in child custody determination (Emery, Otto, and O'Donohue 2005). As far back as the 1960s, mental health practitioners were incorporated into California's family courts to provide conciliation services (Press 2013). The American Psychological Association (APA) has even issued a document titled "Guidelines for Child Custody Evaluations in Family Law Proceedings" (2010) for psychologists who participate in child custody evaluations. While there has been an increased desire to support legal decisions with empirical data, the use of empirical data remains problematic (Huntington 2018). There are important gaps in empirical support for custody arrangement outcomes in general and in relation to psychological factors specifically (Tippins and Wittmann 2005), but employing mechanistic, purportedly objective measures "focuses attention on outcomes rather than on competing values, cloaks normative judgments, and risks replicating historical, state-sponsored discrimination" (Huntington 2018, 303).

Nevertheless, it was not uncommon for the noncustodial mothers I spoke with to participate in a psychologically based custody evaluation, and custody evaluations were a frequent topic in the online support groups. In these groups, mothers shared information about the process as well as ideas about how to best present oneself in the context of a custody evaluation. Some mothers embraced the idea of having a psychologist involved in the custody determination process for various reasons, including their sense that it would provide a neutral party or because of their own positive experiences with individual therapy. Nevertheless, custody evaluations were a major source of discontent in interviews and online. In their criticisms of the process, noncustodial mothers identified issues such as cost, thoroughness, and bias. Costs of the evaluation ranged from $300 to upwards of $10,000. Sometimes the costs were borne equally by both parents, but other arrangements were not uncommon. Custody evaluations took anywhere from a few days to over nine months. The APA guidelines acknowledge significant variability in the length of time needed for an evaluation but urge that they be completed in a timely fashion.

Angela felt that the length of the uncertainty and the process were detrimental to her child, so she dropped out and turned over primary custody to her ex-husband in the middle of the evaluation: "It was torture. It was ridiculous. If I was stressed out of my mind, I can only imagine how my son felt. Well, no. I know how he felt and I didn't know how to comfort him. So I just dropped it. I couldn't keep going." In Monica's case, the evaluation was scheduled to take three months but ended up taking almost a year: "My ex-husband kept delaying his meetings because he knew I had to move. He was trying to drag it out so I would have to move without my son or give up my job. He was just fucking with me. Ten months! And the evaluator just let it happen and didn't see any problem with it."

Maggie's initial custody recommendation from the friend of the court, a kind of court-supplied mediator in Michigan, took six months: "After we went through all of the evaluation, the recommendation itself took three or four months because it was over the summer. Everything gets dragged out because of holidays and summer vacations." Although the initial recommendation was that Maggie would have sole custody, her ex-husband's attorney argued successfully for a full psychological evaluation. Like many others I spoke with in interviews and online, Maggie felt that the process was highly flawed: "The whole time she interviewed me, it was only 45 minutes, I was like this is just wrong. The questions she's asking me. And as I'm talking to her, it was like she wasn't paying attention. She wasn't listening. And I'm just like, 'Wow!' When I left it felt weird and wrong. She asked me things like do I spend time with the kids. Do I drink? I answered truthfully. She didn't pay attention. She didn't write anything down." Maggie's husband joined in our conversation at this point to tell me that the same evaluator interviewed him and was clearly not listening because she was doodling and would not make eye contact.

There is a tension in the process between thoroughness and completing an evaluation in a timely manner. Noncustodial mothers who experienced lengthy or very short custody evaluation processes found them to be the most problematic. Truncated custody evaluations leave room for bias—when we lack adequate information on a person we are evaluating, our biases tend to fill in the blanks. Far-reaching custody evaluations leave room for bias to enter another way through mission creep, which is why the APA guidelines for custody evaluations caution evaluators to carefully define and stick to the scope of their evaluation. In a case where the dispute involves two *good enough* parents (Winnicott 1960), extensive psychological evaluation seems out of place.[2]

In her sessions with the evaluator, it was clear to Monica that her ex-husband was trying to frame her history of depression as a chronic issue: "I had depression when I had a miscarriage some years ago. I even gave written permission for the evaluator to get my medical records and talk to my therapist. He decided that this was a negative for me but I found out after the fact that he never actually contacted them." Since the evaluator did not contact her physician or therapist to obtain the actual documentation, Monica was left not knowing whether and to what extent her history of depression played a role in the final decision in her case. She felt the evaluation lacked thoroughness even as it was too lengthy.

APA guidelines advise evaluators to avoid conflicts of interest; however, it was not uncommon for noncustodial mothers to mention perceived or demonstrable conflicts of interest on the part of the evaluator. In Monica's case, the custody evaluator took on her ex-husband and his family as clients at the end of the evaluation. She said, "I'm not sure how that's ok. I mean, they're now seeing him as a family. What if we need to go back to court? He's all chummy with the evaluator. It also seems really manipulative. Stick the kid into family therapy so he can keep presenting his case to the evaluator, but that's also putting pressure on our son. And what about the fact that the family he just gave custody to is now back in his office because they're a dysfunctional mess? How is this ok?"

Elaine felt that the evaluation in her case was tainted by the fact that her ex-husband chose and paid the evaluator, and that the evaluator had been careless in conducting the evaluation and preparing the report: "The psych eval was done back in 2004 and that was somebody he hired so it wasn't someone appointed. So I think the opinion was already leaning and biased in one direction because of who she was receiving the check from. The report had a lot of inaccuracies in it whether it was misquoting from people she interviewed, or I was actually referred to by the wrong name in several places. And I was trying to fight it. Are you kidding? How can you say this is credible if she doesn't even know who she's talking about?"

In Bonnie's case, she felt that the evaluator's questions were inappropriate and ventured into areas that had nothing to do with who should have custody: "He asked me if I was promiscuous. And I was like, 'What?!' What kind of a question is that? My jaw dropped. I asked what he meant. He asked if I cheated on my ex, so I'm sure that's what my ex told him. Which is priceless because he's the one that was doing the babysitter. But I just froze and so I'm sure he thought I was lying when I eventually said that I didn't cheat. I should have told him it was none of his business but then that would have been worse, I'm sure."

Noncustodial mothers felt that their presentation of self was very important in the custody evaluation in the same ways that it mattered in front of a judge or when revealing their stigmatized status to new acquaintances. Frequently, concerns about presentation of self centered on doing gender. Social class, race, and other dimensions of social inequality are always implicated in doing gender. Interviews by evaluators gave many mothers a sense that they were being judged on how they measured up to the evaluator's image of motherhood. In her interview, Hannah described herself to me as "less girly" than other mothers: "I felt the need to be some way that I'm not. Sweeter? Happier? I don't know. I'm blunt. I have resting bitch face. I curse. I guess I'm not what he imagines as a great, nurturing mom. I dropped the f-bomb in front of him and I'm sure that was a negative. Mother curses, check!" She felt that she did not fit the mold and that her failure to do gender in a certain way had negatively shaped the evaluator's opinion of her.

It was not uncommon for mothers to feel that there was much more pressure on them than on their male ex-partner to present themselves well to the evaluator. Dee Dee said, "I was under a microscope and I'm sure that my ex was not. At our final session where he announced his recommendation, the evaluator seemed to fall all over himself praising my ex. It makes me wonder whether it's enough for dads to just say they want kids and then talk sports." Patrice also felt that she was harshly interrogated. The evaluator in her case asked her directly to address issues that her ex-husband had raised:

> He tried to make it sound like I was this completely off the wall unfit mother. Which he couldn't. There was one example he gave where he had been traveling all week and got home and I handed him the girls and said I needed a nap. Clearly she can't handle being a mom. And I'm like he left me alone with them, always, every week for like ten years. I needed a nap. Yep, I needed a nap. I have three little kids under the age of four and I'm alone with them for five days in a row. The house is clean. They were clean. They were fed, the laundry was done, groceries were in the house. But I needed a nap, so I'm an unfit mother.

What many noncustodial mothers describe is something called effortless perfection, a term that originated with college-age women's feeling the need to be perfect while also appearing to extend no effort in attaining perfection. The need to display effortless perfection shaped mothers' presentation of self and the ways they tried to do gender in the custody evaluation. Many felt that they had to demonstrate that they practiced intensive motherhood with seemingly no difficulty. The further one fell from performing normative notions of gender, which are also classed and raced, for example, the less likely they would be seen as good enough mothers.

Some mothers' evaluations included observations of them and their children. These were particularly stressful times. In Hannah's case, her evaluator did not review her interactions favorably: "My son hadn't slept and we had to squeeze this visit with the evaluator in between school and baseball. So we're in there and he's antsy and won't listen to me. I'm thinking I already screwed up by cursing so I better be on my best behavior. What I wanted to do was yell, 'knock it off!' but I kept patiently trying to get him to focus. So apparently that wasn't right either. In the report it said that I wasn't authoritative enough or something." Hannah was doing what any good parent would do by trying to get her son to focus on the situation at hand. To the extent that effortless perfection requires that mothers accomplish these difficult tasks of parenthood without losing a beat, much less losing one's temper, it is a manifestation of intensive motherhood extending to the presentation of self. In the context of a psychological custody evaluation, the stakes of doing intensive motherhood poorly (that is, without effortless perfection) are high.

It was not unusual for mothers undergoing custody evaluations with psychologists to say that they felt it was intrusive and extended well beyond what was needed to determine whether they were competent parents. Anyone undergoing a custody evaluation is likely to feel that it is intrusive, but what comes through in interviews and from the online discussions is the imbalance of power in the custody evaluation context. Custody evaluations are often seen as a deciding factor that judges will not go against. If the interaction with the evaluator goes poorly, it can prompt a mother to drop out before the evaluation is complete. Bonnie was one of those mothers. She said, "I saw it was going down the tubes and I had already spent a ton of money. Every hour of his time was like $150. I could see the strikes piling up against me so I had to stop." In Monica's case, she felt her evaluation had been biased but that she had no recourse because of what her attorney told her at the outset.

> My attorney said that she thought we should do a custody evaluation but she told me that I would have to accept the outcome. I didn't

think anything of it at the time. It seemed a little weird. She said if I wanted to contest the findings in court, she would drop me as a client because she has to work with these people on a regular basis. Ok, so in the middle of the thing, it's clear to me that the psychologist does not like me. I have no idea why, but I know that I feel contempt coming from him. Did we date? I just had this sense of dread and like there was nothing I could do about it. Sure enough, when the report came in and I'm sitting there in shock, I felt helpless. There wasn't anything I could do.

In addition to in-person interviews, most noncustodial mothers who participated in a custody evaluation reported having taken some sort of psychological test. Few could remember the exact name of the tests they were given, but for those who did, the Minnesota Multiphasic Personality Inventory (MMPI) was the most common. Few who had the test reported being told anything specific about their results.

Neither Rhonda nor her ex-husband had results on the MMPI that indicated anything extreme; however, each of them scored outside the range on the lie scale. Highly educated, Rhonda is aware of many of the faults of the MMPI: "My scale was off. I have tons of education and they say that affects it. So that was odd. They brought it up. His lie scale, sneaky, conscious lying was waaaay out and nothing was said. You'd think that they'd be able to figure out someone who has a pathological personality, but no. You know that 45 minutes sitting with a psychologist and taking the MMPI is not going to diagnose anything."

In Abby's custody evaluation, she and her ex-husband were interviewed and given psychological tests: "When I got the report, I was just floored. Apparently, when she interviewed my ex-husband, she interviewed him twice as much as she interviewed me. He said all of this horrendous stuff about me that isn't even true. It was stuff that he expected to be accused of. He actually said that I had been violent and he said that I was promiscuous. She didn't investigate anything. It was a complete shock." She had a similar experience with the results, which said that she had a personality disorder, prompting her to do additional research.

You know, it's very hard to take these tests, especially when they are not recommended for every situation, especially a custody dispute. I actually talked to several friends who are psychologists and psychiatrists and they say it's not for use in custody evaluations and it's actually a gender biased test because a man and a woman can answer the exact same way, but because it operates on base rates the base rate for personality disorder is ten points lower for women than it is for men. So if you get a man and a woman who answer the exact same way, the man will appear confident but the woman will appear as having narcissistic personality disorder.

It is in fact common practice in custody evaluation to administer psychological tests like the MMPI, which is one of the most popular (Ackerman and Ackerman 1997; Erickson, Lilienfeld, and Vitacco 2007). Critics of the MMPI have demonstrated that both sexism and heterosexism shape its findings (Chernin, Holden, and Chandler 1997; Lindsay and Widiger 1995; Rosewater 1985). Personality and cognitive tests have been criticized in other contexts, such as employment. The use of psychological tests in employment can run afoul of employment nondiscrimination laws on several grounds, including race, gender, and disability. *Karraker v. Rent-a-Center Inc.* in 2004 and the recent settlement of Target with the Equal Employment Opportunity Commission are two recent examples that demonstrate the problematic nature of psychological testing used outside the context for which it was developed. The Equal Employment Opportunity Commission has gone so far as to issue guidance on the proper use of such tests, which can be found on the agency's website. Among the principles for using such tests is that they must have been validated for the purposes for which they are currently being used. While viewed skeptically in an employment context, psychological testing remains more uncritically accepted in child custody determination despite extensive critique (Emery, Otto, and O'Donohue 2005; Erickson, Lilienfeld, and Vitacco 2007).

Tests like the Rorschach inkblot test and the thematic apperception test, although characterized as valid in documents like the *Judge's Guide*, do not meet the standards of scientific validity necessary for inclusion in court proceedings. The MMPI and the Millon Clinical Multiaxial Inventory were developed as general psychological assessments rather than being specifically designed for the custody evaluation context, where contextual factors associated with a custody dispute can shape the results in ways that make the findings unreliable (Erickson, Lilienfeld, and Vitacco 2007). Even the Bricklin Perceptual Scales test, which is used to identify the parent of choice in the context of custody determination, has been subject to serious criticism: "These measures assess ill-defined constructs, and they do so poorly, leaving no scientific justification for their use in child custody evaluations" (Emery, Otto, and O'Donohue 2005, 7).

In short, the most routinely used psychological tests are highly problematic because they are not validated for the custody context. Even if such general psychological tests were found to be valid and reliable in the context of custody evaluations, two problems remain. The first is that once psychological measurements are made, there remains no clear path to actions from a given set of findings. For example, once we know the child's attachment, in which direction should custody proceed? Should the child spend more time with the parent to whom they are more securely attached or to the one to whom they are resistant (Mercer 2009)? That decision requires a value judgment that psychologists are no more or less able to make than judges. Or parents. The second problem is the lack of empirical research testing whether custody decisions made through psychological evaluations produce optimal outcomes for children and families (Mercer 2009; Tippins and Wittmann 2005). Do psychological evaluations produce better outcomes than decisions rendered by judges or through mediators? Given the cost and time involved with psychological custody evaluations, these are important empirical questions.

Robert Emery, Randy Otto, and William O'Donohue (2005) provide a much broader critique of the custody evaluation process beyond psychological testing. They find problematic the profession's tendency to pathologize children's responses to parental separation and divorce, noting a conceptual elision between a child's exhibiting distress and having a disorder, moving the emphasis of evaluation away from factors such as parental conflict, which has strong empirical support for shaping children's postdivorce well-being. The issue of parental mental health diagnoses should be situated in the proper context. That is, in the context of custody determination, it matters whether a mental health issue is being effectively treated, is severe (for example, schizophrenia or substance abuse), or creates a situation of harm or neglect for a child that would have otherwise involved child protective services. In other words, the incorporation of parental mental health in custody evaluations should not be used as a tiebreaker when a parent with a mental illness is otherwise a good enough parent (Emery, Otto, and O'Donohue 2005; Winnicott 1960).

Some perceive the entire enterprise of custody evaluation as narrowly focused on the psychological rather than economic or other factors:

> Alternative experts the courts instead might employ include accountants who have evaluated each parent's ability to provide for their children economically, educators who can comment on the parents' relative commitment to promoting success in school, religious leaders or philosophers who have assessed the quality of each parent's moral values and training, or perhaps dieticians who have evaluated each parent's preference for healthy versus convenience food. These suggestions may seem outrageous, but so is the idea that custody should be awarded to a parent who has an edge over another parent in promoting children's psychological well-being, particularly when the construct is ill defined or undefined. (Emery, Otto, and O'Donohue 2005, 20)

Forensic psychology more generally has been subject to intense questioning (Arrigo 2003; Caplan 2004; Heilbrun 1992; Nicholson and Norwood 2000; Ogloff 2000). What is the proper role of mental health and psychologists in legal matters even outside of custody determination? Given what is at stake and the issues that arose for these noncustodial mothers, it is an important question to continue to ask. Indeed, there is a significant body of literature that questions the effectiveness and the ethics of the psychologist's role in the legal system in everything from competency determination and criminal responsibility to threat assessment and child custody.

Why place routine mental health diagnoses under scrutiny when it comes to child custody? It is not common practice to remove children from a competent married caregiver who has been diagnosed with depression, so why would it become a consideration that would upend existing parenting divisions of labor upon divorce? The broad criteria of the best interests of the child mean that a perceived deficiency of any kind (such as depression) can become fodder for disqualifying a good enough mother in the context of a custody dispute. For parents with more serious mental illness, why not focus on whether they are successfully being treated and have an ongoing relationship with the appropriate mental health practitioners? I also observed that once marked by the stigma of mental illness in a custody dispute, mothers had a very difficult time returning to unsupervised parenting time or regaining parenting time that they lost in the process. It should be stressed that most of the mothers who had mental health diagnoses, even some with bipolar disorder, had been at least adequately parenting their children before the divorce. They were primarily responsible for the day-to-day care of their children, and their mental health did not become an obstacle to their caregiving until it was included in the custody dispute. Given the fact that women are more likely to seek mental health care and to have mental health diagnoses than men, uncritical and ill-defined inclusion of mental health as a factor in child custody creates a gender disadvantage for mothers.

The indeterminate nature of the best-interests standard, coupled with a narrowly defined psychological evaluation process and problematic assessment instruments, leaves room for biases to enter the process, whether they be biases of the individual evaluators or biases of a more systemic nature. While it is impossible to know whether bias is operating in any given situation, the structure of the social context of custody determination also leaves little room for recourse when it happens. To the extent that psychology and child development literature reflects the values of upper-middle-class, white, heterosexual families, psychological evaluations will also reflect an unspoken bias in these directions. Issues of class, gender, race, sexual orientation, and disability shape not only how mothers are perceived by evaluators but also the power dynamics in a process that is already highly asymmetrical. For various reasons, lawyers may not want or be able to contest a custody evaluation that came out against their client. Mothers' on average lesser economic resources continue to be a source of inequality in the custody dispute because of the potentially high costs involved in employing a psychological custody evaluator or contesting unfavorable findings.

Feminist Critiques of Psychiatry and Psychology

The observations of noncustodial mothers regarding how mental health issues or psychological custody evaluations shaped their case may be seen as idiosyncratic or the result of a single biased evaluator, but what ties them together is the ways in which biases embedded in the fields of psychology, psychiatry, family therapy, and child development shape evaluations of mothers in custody disputes. These fields and associated practices have been extensively deconstructed and critiqued in terms of biased theoretical underpinnings and the reproduction of institutionalized social inequalities such as those of gender, race, class, and sexual orientation (Burman 2017; Contratto and Rossier 2005; Leslie 1995; McLellan 1999; Worell 2000). The long tradition of feminist critique of these areas has taken place both inside the respective fields and in more general feminist theory. While there has been significant progress in some subfields of psychology through feminist critique, much work needs to be done. While women, girls, and gender have become valid areas of psychological research (Stewart and Dottolo 2006), forensic psychology and child development are areas that are still in need of feminist remaking and intervention (Worell 2000). Some feminist principles have been incorporated into therapeutic practices, albeit often without the label of feminism.

The Association for Women in Psychology started in 1969 as a response to problems of sexism in the academic field of psychology as well as in the APA (Caplan and Cosgrove 2004; Tiefer 1991, 2009). Today, the field of psychology has feminized, with women forming more than two-thirds of the therapeutic workforce, yet people of color remain vastly underrepresented in the field despite some recent progress (Lin et al. 2015). Before and since the inauguration of the Association for Women in Psychology, feminist psychologists both repudiated and built on Freudian psychology that constructed women and girls as inferior psychological beings. Karen Horney (1967) contested the hegemony of Freudian psychoanalysis, both deconstructing and countering the notion of penis envy with a more contextual and less biologically based understanding of women's social power vis-à-vis men. Flipping Freud on his ear, she proposed that men suffered from womb envy, which drove them to seek status and material success in place of being able to reproduce human life. In 1972, Phyllis Chesler, one of the cofounders of the Association for Women in Psychology, published an exhaustive work in which she lays out a critical psychology of women that recognizes gender and power imbalances in psychological theory and practice, coining the term *psychiatric imperialism*. Nancy Chodorow's (1978) landmark monograph reframed Freudian perspectives on women, particularly with regard to motherhood, by using object relations theory to understand *why* women want to mother. The critique of androcentrism in the field of psychology continued in other classic, although perhaps gender-essentialist, feminist work like that of Carol Gilligan (1982) highlighting the androcentric nature of Kohlberg's moral development scale, on which women never quite measured up to men. Generally, much of this early critique of psychology and psychological constructs focused on the stereotypical and dichotomous gender order, in which women and men were polarized across traits that were socially valued according to the primary holders of those traits. Women therefore fell short of men on traits like ambition and logic but demonstrated more dependency and neuroticism.

In the years since these and other critical foundational works, feminist criticism of psychology and psychiatry has grown even more expansive, multifaceted, and complex (see, for example, Caplan and Cosgrove 2004; Chesler 2005; Leslie 1995; McLellan 1999). This body of critique rests on the foundational notion in critical social theory that mental health and mental illness are socially constructed (Foucault 1988; Goffman 1961; Linder 2004; Lorber 1997). Indeed, terms like *syndrome* and *disorder* signal the social construction of mental illness, and factors as such race, gender, social class, sexuality, and others that are the site of social inequalities structure mental illness as they do other social phenomena.

Although the profession of psychology has feminized over the past forty years, it remains androcentric, centering men, men's concerns, men's ways of being, and men's lives.[3] Specifically, contemporary psychology reflects the values of white, middle-class, heterosexual families (Contratto and Rossier 2005), and their class, gender, race, and sexuality shape the treatment a patient receives. Whether one is sent on one's way, diagnosed, given medication, seen by a therapist, committed to an institution, or jailed depends on to which social categories one belongs (Ali 2004; Bullock 2004; Chesler 2005). For instance, instead of being able to participate in individual, non–institutionally based psychotherapy, women of color are more likely to face hospitalization than other groups (Chesler 2005). Psychological custody evaluations take place on this terrain, and that has profound implications for potential outcomes. The feelings that noncustodial mothers had about the process, including the need to do gender to counter these biases, should be understood in that light.

Psychology also individualizes and depoliticizes human troubles rather than situating them in their social context. The field seeks to help individuals accommodate to the social order rather than recognize and challenge social inequalities and oppression (Cosgrove and Riddle 2004; Landrine, Klonoff, and Brown-Collins 1992; McLellan 1999). Psychological distress is pathologized rather than being perceived as an understandable response to the dehumanizing and traumatizing effects of social inequality and oppression by gender, race, social class, and sexual orientation (Bullock 2004). When it comes to domestic violence, for example, psychology has been faulted for failing to recognize abuse, instead blaming the victim or labeling women's responses to abuse as mental illness (Chesler 2005).

Psychology and many forms of therapy are blind to power dynamics, particularly gendered power dynamics in heterosexual families that derive from the different social valuations of men and women and fathers and mothers (Leslie 1995). Power dynamics in families are always present, not just in cases of domestic violence. Gendered labor markets, for one, shape women's opportunities and likelihood to articulate dissatisfaction in a heterosexual marital relationship. This kind of contextual thinking is lacking in most clinical frameworks. Instead, approaches like family systems theory presuppose an egalitarian power relationship (Ault-Riche 1986; Goldner 1985; Knudson-Martin 1994). Problems in the family are attributed to the functioning of a reified family system such that families characterized by violence against women, wife beating, or even child sexual abuse are reframed as *high-conflict families* or even *incest families*, and the violence within them is reframed as family violence (Leslie 1995; McLellan 1999). Terms like *high-conflict families* are echoed through legal language and in judges' manuals. Responsibility for family dysfunction thus rests equally in both partners, with each contributing to the problematic dynamic. This lack of context has implications for anyone participating in a psychologically based custody evaluation, whether it be in the context of domestic violence or something as simple as situational depression. The *Diagnostic and Statistical Manual of Mental Disorders (DSM)* lays out five axes for mental illness diagnosis but relies mainly on Axes I and II, the mood disorders and personality disorders that we tend to think of in lay terms as mental illnesses. Psychology's underutilization of *DSM* Axis IV (Bullock 2004), which identifies social and environmental stressors affecting the individual's mental health, contributes to the problematic acontextuality we observed in noncustodial mothers' accounts of how their mild mental health issues were interpreted.

Psychology can operate as a type of social control conserving the status quo. Historically the social control exercised through psychology has been even more direct. From the nineteenth century to the mid-twentieth century, psychologists and psychiatrists have collaborated with husbands to institutionalize wives or daughters who were rebellious or promiscuous or had failed to adjust to "the feminine role" (Chesler 2005). Chesler (2005, 95) notes the gendered power structure in psychotherapy that infantilizes women: "The mental asylum closely approximates the female rather than the male experience within the family." Even though the gender composition of the therapeutic workforce has changed dramatically since the mid-twentieth century, power in the therapeutic relationship manifests itself in gendered ways regardless of the gender identity of any individual therapist. The experiences of my participants suggest that psychological custody evaluation can serve as a (perhaps less harsh) form of gendered social control.

Feminist psychologists, like other feminist social theorists, have questioned the value neutrality of psychological science and practices. Gender and other biases are embedded in the scientific discourses articulated through the use of the *DSM*, although some have argued that psychological diagnosis more properly belongs in the realm of art than science (Caplan and Cosgrove 2004). Diagnostic categories fail both on reliability,[4] the ability of different observers to provide the same diagnosis, and validity, the ability of the diagnosis to represent an actual phenomenon that exists outside the therapeutic context (Cosgrove and Riddle 2004). Psychological practice nevertheless carries with it the status and power of scientific discourse, obfuscating what can actually be highly variable and capricious practices.

Some noncustodial mothers sought out psychological custody evaluations with the hope that they would be neutral arbiters. Judges also put a lot of faith in the expertise of psychologists. It is not, however, the individual expertise that is at issue but rather the notion of neutral, scientific expertise itself. Despite claims to scientific neutrality, biases are deeply embedded in the structures and practices of psychology. They can enter the diagnostic process, or they can be found in the articulation of the diagnosis itself, particularly those diagnoses seemingly reserved for women only.

In Freud's time, for example, women were said to suffer from hysteria. Until 1980, hysteria remained a clinical diagnosis in the *DSM*, later being replaced by histrionic personality disorder and borderline personality disorder, diagnoses applied mainly to women (Gibson 2004; Jimenez 1997). These diagnoses rest on constellations of behaviors that either echo culturally accepted displays of femininity or mark the patient in opposition to them. The diagnostic criteria for histrionic personality disorder include "consistently uses physical appearance to draw attention to self," (American Psychiatric Association 2013, 667) a practice that one could argue all women are more or less trained for, especially in a contemporary culture that's permeated by social media. Similarly, inappropriate anger is one of the criteria in the diagnosis of borderline personality disorder. Women's anger, and in particular Black women's anger, is pathologized and negatively sanctioned in everyday interactions as well as in psychotherapy (Ashley 2014).

Some disorders seem to present nearly exclusively in women. Take, for example, Munchausen by proxy, a disorder found mainly among women and seemingly limited to mothers who sought attention by creating and treating illness in their children. Munchausen by proxy was a precursor to the contemporary parental alienation syndrome developed by Richard Gardner (Caplan 2004). Parental alienation syndrome was originally attributed only to women (and only in the context of a child custody dispute) but has since been reframed in gender-neutral terms. In the fifth edition of the *DSM* (*DSM V*), there is a short note about "culture-related diagnostic issues" and "gender-related diagnostic issues" with many of the diagnostic labels in the *DSM V*. These caveats note the sex ratios of the diagnosis or point toward the possibility of under- or overdiagnosing based on gender: "Certain personality disorders (e.g., antisocial personality disorder) are diagnosed more frequently in males. Others (e.g., borderline, histrionic, and dependent personality disorders) are diagnosed more frequently in females. Although these differences in prevalence probably reflect real gender differences in the presence of such patterns, clinicians must be cautious not to overdiagnose or underdiagnose certain personality disorders in females or in males because of social stereotypes about typical gender roles and behaviors" (American Psychiatric Association 2013, 648).

Note the assumption of real gender differences in mental illness, which renders both gender and mental illness in essentialist terms. Exhaustive meta-analyses of psychological studies reveal that the vast majority of measured gender differences in psychological phenomena are small or close to zero. In fact, psychological measurement is influenced by the social context of gender, as well as gender acting as a stimulus (Hyde 2007, 2014). In other words, any observed gender difference is largely a product of how a society constructs gender, including opportunities and constraints on each gender's life chances. Cross-cultural differences in women's and girls' math ability demonstrate that math ability, like other cognitive and psychological traits, is not hardwired by gender.

Despite the nod to cultural issues by the *DSM V*, anger as a symptom of mental illness raises more problems for women than men when psychological frameworks are deployed in custody determination. While in the midst of a custody dispute, it is likely that all parties feel and express anger, but women's anger is construed differently. Women's anger is pathologized and decontextualized in the psychological custody evaluation such that it becomes a symptom of something deeper that ultimately says something about their ability to mother. The noncustodial mothers I encountered both online and in person were keenly aware of the limitations on their ability to express anger.

The *DSM* also uses the term *cultural issues* to stand in for race, ethnicity, and national origin. For example, schizotypal personality disorder includes the criterion of "behavior or appearance that is odd, eccentric, or peculiar," (American Psychiatric Association 2013, 656) with the caveat that "pervasive culturally determined characteristics, particularly those regarding religious beliefs and rituals, can appear to be schizotypal to the uninformed outsider (e.g., voodoo, speaking in tongues, life beyond death, shamanism, mind reading, sixth sense, evil eye, magical beliefs related to health and illness)" (American Psychiatric Association 2013, 657). The general discussion of cultural differences in the *DSM* instructs clinicians to seek additional information to understand individuals better: "It is useful for the clinician, especially when evaluating someone from a different background, to obtain additional information from informants who are familiar with the person's cultural background" (American Psychiatric Association 2013, 648). However, critical psychologists caution that this well-intentioned approach can result in reifying racial and ethnic stereotypes rather than situating the experiences of people of color in a system of race and class inequality that affects mental health (Leslie 1995). Although there is ample evidence of heteronormativity and bias against lesbian, gay, bisexual, and queer individuals and families, the *DSM V* does not have a similar section for caveats relating to sexual orientation in personality disorders and how one's social location might shape behavior in ways that look disordered to an uncritical eye. Despite some recent efforts to acknowledge how social inequalities shape diagnosis, psychological custody evaluation proceeds within a framework that is historically shaped by distortions around gender, race, class, and sexual orientation. Psychological practice, like other social institutions, is susceptible to cultural lag.

Biases are also embedded in the psychological axioms or principles that underpin much of child development theory and psychology. The first of these that is relevant to the question of noncustodial mothers is mother blame (Burman 2017; Caplan 2002; Ladd-Taylor and Umansky 1998; Rich 1976). There is a vast literature on mother blame in psychology and elsewhere that is too dense to review here, so the focus will be on the major strands of that literature. Mother blame is an axiom applied unevenly to mothers across social categories like class and race, and it is evidenced in part by a much more developed language with which to lay blame at the feet of mothers than fathers (Leslie 1995). An early twentieth-century manifestation of mother blame is encapsulated in Leo Kanner's (1943) term *refrigerator mother*, which pinpointed a cold and uncaring mother as a cause of autism. Everything from schizophrenia and personality disorders to ADHD and invisible disabilities are attributed to bad mothering (Armstrong 2004; Blum 2007; Singh 2004). And single mothers are, by definition, inferior to married mothers when it comes to the psychological well-being of their children (M. Smith 1997; Worell 2000). Lest we believe that the mother-blaming phenomenon belongs in the past, "the new science of blaming moms" (Metzl 2014) identifies something called "maternal imprint syndrome," which holds that mothers' behaviors while pregnant can have long-term consequences for their offspring, including everything from obesity to high blood pressure. It is no wonder, then, that there is a clinical distrust of mothers that is not limited to male clinicians (Chesler 2005, 16). Distrust of mothers is embedded in the foundation of psychology.

The child development literature has also contributed to mother blame when it relies on attachment theory that constructs mothers as mere vessels to fulfill children's needs (Athan and Reel 2015; Burman 2017). As Erica Burman (2017,

143) writes, "Mothers have been portrayed as so central to, and absorbed within, their children's development that any assertion of power or independence on their part appears to be at the expense of damaging children." The field has been so focused on the mother-child dyad that it is the one relationship that psychological custody evaluators have the most knowledge about. Given the dearth of research or discourse on fathers, siblings, or other relationships in the child's life, it is not surprising that an evaluator's focus is on mothers. My research suggests that when there is any attempt at involvement from a father (recall from chapter 5 that just asking for custody can be seen as involvement), any failing on behalf of the mother tips the scales toward the father. In a custody evaluation, the mother-blame axiom shapes how psychologists understand children's functioning in school and elsewhere. If children are doing poorly, the blame rests with the mother.

Critiques of contemporary child development literature raise concern that by constructing children as passive, lacking in self-knowledge, highly suggestible, and constantly in need of protection, we silence children's voices (Burman 2017). Each of these characterizations of children mirrors the contemporary social construction of childhood that predominates documents used to guide custody decisions. For example, in the *Judge's Guide*, the section on child development pertaining to early elementary-age children warns that children in this age group may be "particularly prone to suggestibility or 'brainwashing'" (American Bar Association 2008, 61). Yet children frequently do not have a voice in custody proceedings, particularly in preadolescence. The State of Georgia is unusual in that it allows children to actually choose their residential household when they reach the age of fourteen. In other states, whether to hear from children is left to the sole discretion of the judge, but many judges are hesitant to take testimony from younger children. Sometimes a guardian ad litem is appointed to represent the interests of a child. In interviews and in online discussions, I found that many noncustodial mothers had balked when faced with whether to seek input from their children. At a general level, these mothers felt that good mothers did not allow their children to be involved in the custody dispute. Mothers were also concerned that they would be seen as manipulating their children or alienating them from their fathers. Since their motherhood qualifications were already under the microscope, it is hard to know whether their stance was more about how they presented themselves as mothers or the actual harm they felt could come to their children.

The second axiom is what Miriam Greenspan (1983) called "father knows best." The therapeutic relationship is one that mirrors the patriarchal family, with the therapist as man/expert/father and the patient as woman/patient/child (Chesler 1972). Thus the typical therapeutic relationship is one of symbolic and interpersonal inequality (Contratto and Rossier 2005). In contrast, feminist psychotherapy seeks to remove hierarchy from the therapeutic relationship (Chesler 2005).

In the context of a psychological custody evaluation, this gendered power relationship shapes mothers' experiences, as well as their ability to counter inaccurate information or negative findings. Many of the mothers I spoke with felt infantilized by the experience of the custody evaluation. The expert status of the psychologist is reinforced by the courts, which narrows the scope of relevant best-interests factors to the psychological (Emery, Otto, and O'Donohue 2005).

This father-knows-best axiom is embedded in psychological approaches in other ways. Although fathers may be constructed as peripheral to the day-to-day happenings in the family, their presence in the family is what marks the family as healthy (M. Smith 1997). The gender complementarity of developmental psychology casts the father as the parent who provides discipline and encourages a child to explore (Burman 2017). Although the axiom of mother blame centers mothers in psychology, the corollary principle of father-knows-best devalues motherhood and furthers the invisibility of mothers' household labor. In this way, mothers who have been primary caregivers of their children can have that labor discounted in favor of a father who has never put his children to bed and does not know the names of their teachers. Developmental psychology helps to set the bar for father involvement very low.

Closely related to the father-knows-best axiom is the idea that mothers are gatekeepers to their children, marginalizing fathers and other well-intentioned helpers. Family therapy proceeds on the construct of the overinvolved mother who is the origin of family dysfunction, which, of course can be corrected by her *allowing* the father to become more involved in the child's life (Leslie 1995). This construct is also racialized when Black single-mother families are labeled matriarchal. Embracing the trope of an overinvolved, gatekeeping mother requires discounting power and privilege in creating and maintaining deeply gendered imbalances in household labor. Women have a second shift not because they jealously guard access to their children (and the laundry, the dirty dishes, and the vacuuming) but because men's social status enables them to opt out of this additional and often unsavory work. The concept of maternal gatekeeping masks well-known gender and power dynamics in heterosexual families. The implications of this axiom for psychological custody evaluations are clear: if we believe that mothers want to marginalize fathers and are responsible for their detachment, then mothers must be persuaded (or forced when necessary) to make room for fathers, irrespective of the quality of existing relationships. When those relationships are poor, the mother is the likely culprit. We can see this axiom manifest in friendly parent provisions and in mothers' own censoring of their concerns about domestic violence in the next chapter.

"Children need both parents" is a refrain found in virtually all forms of documents pertaining to custody, including custody evaluation guidelines, state legal statutes concerning custody, and judges' manuals. Whether children need both parents for their well-being is an open question with answers that depend on what we mean by well-being (economic outcomes, educational attainment, health measures) and the quality of the relationship between the two parents (M. Smith 1997). Research on children's postdivorce adjustment shows that the key to understanding children's responses is the level of conflict between the divorcing parents rather than any given custody arrangement (Emery, Otto, and O'Donohue 2005).

Many negative outcomes of single-parent families can actually be attributed more to poverty than to the absence of a second parent. A second parent is potentially a second earner who may help lift a family out of poverty, particularly if the second earner is male. Because of gendered labor markets, women are less likely to hold jobs that provide a family wage. Therefore, outcomes that appear to be attributed to the absence of a second parent are actually the economic by-product of such absence (Downey 1994; Rowlingson and McKay 2005). But again, psychological custody evaluations rest on a body of knowledge that does not readily dispute the idea that mothers marginalize fathers and that children always need both parents. Fathers' rights groups have mobilized many of these ideas, using them to sway public opinion and to lobby for a presumption of joint custody of children (Crowley 2008). Thus, these axioms have become persuasive in the public discourse.

In addition, these assumptions are embedded in various documented guidelines for custody determination and evaluation. For example, Michigan's *Custody and Parenting Time Investigation Manual* suggests that evaluators should determine which parent a child goes to for "sympathy, consolation, or to share in a victory" but cautions that the child may go to that parent "because of interference by the other parent" (Friend of the Court Bureau 2016, 6). In this light, it becomes more than conceivable that a father's lack of engagement in a child's day-to-day life will be dismissed as irrelevant in the custody evaluation no matter what the reason. In this same document, words like *capacity*, *disposition*, *willingness*, and *ability* are emphasized over status quo caregiving arrangements. Pared with society's general overrecognition of men's caregiving and household contributions (as seen in chapter 5), psychology's assumption that women *prevent* men from being more involved ignores decades of research on gender and power dynamics in heterosexual households.

Even though not all noncustodial mothers have gone through custody evaluations, the psychological and child development framework is implicitly present in all custody disputes. Take, for example, the explicit inclusion of a child development framework in the *Judge's Guide* (American Bar Association 2008), which makes reference to Jean Piaget, Erik Erickson, and John Bowlby and the attachment orientation of their theories. An entire chapter of the guide is devoted to an in-depth exploration of the developmental needs of children at various ages. The report published by the Maryland General Assembly's Commission on Child-

Custody Decision-Making (2014) gives a similar nod to the place of child development in the custody determination process. Burman (2017) provides an extensive critique of child development literature (including Piaget, Erickson, and Bowlby) that considers how the field is shaped by assumptions about gender, class, and race. We cannot separate the outcomes of custody disputes from the biases embedded in the frameworks used to make those decisions.

Custody determinations rely heavily on the field of psychology, whether it is in using mental health as one of several best-interests factors or through a full psychological custody evaluation. In either case, contemporary custody determination rests on a field replete with problematic gender, race, class, and other assumptions. Despite the increased representation of women in the fields of psychology and psychiatry, outcomes of custody evaluations will continue to be shaped by stereotypes and inequalities because these are built into the foundations of the field. The highly individualistic nature of psychology means that the whole endeavor of custody evaluation is acontextual, whereas a feminist lens views "women's symptoms as their best attempts at dealing with pathological situations rather than as reflecting pathology within the woman" (Worell 2000, 190).

Many of the cases that get to the stage of entering a full psychological custody evaluation do not involve two apt and well-meaning parents who more or less shared equally in domestic labor and childcare. Those families were represented among the interview participants and online support groups as having largely voluntary arrangements with better communication and co-parenting relationships than families that went to this stage of intervention. Mothers who lost custody after a psychological evaluation process had often been doing the bulk of childcare and household labor despite their employment status. When one considers the axioms of mother blame, father knows best, and mothers as gatekeepers, we can understand how fully competent mothers who were primary caregivers for their children, even when they were full-time stay-at-home mothers, could come to lose custody to an uninvolved or even abusive father (taken up in detail in chapter 7). The bar for involved fatherhood is indeed low. Adding to these tendencies are the effects that fathers' rights groups' discourses, which have come to take on the status of common sense, may have on judges' or evaluators' interpretations of family dynamics. In addition to rendering women's unpaid work inside the home invisible, state laws that eschew the term *primary caregiver* or instruct explicitly that gender cannot matter when it comes to child custody may make it difficult for judges and evaluators to justify maternal custody. As in other social institutions, premature but perhaps well-intended standards of gender neutrality can work to women's disadvantage.

Because of the ways in which mother blame permeates culture and psychology, my work suggests that it may be easier to search for a reason to disqualify a mother than to give her custody. Other work bears this out. Emery, Otto, and O'Donohue (2005) contend that custody evaluations and the notion of best interest are used as a tiebreaker in custody disputes. In my research, however, the criteria of best interests are deployed to operate more as a disqualifier than a tiebreaker. When fathers ask for custody, mothers *only* need be disqualified. There can be no such thing as a good enough mother in the custody context because all of the cultural contradictions of motherhood find their nexus in a custody dispute. Mothers are too strict and they are too permissive. They do too much and they do too little. Either way, they are to blame. Social surveillance of parents, particularly mothers who are poor and of color, has increased (Burman 2017). Custody disputes become a semiprivatized extension of the state's interest in increasing social control of mothers because outside the custody dispute context, the disqualifiers identified by noncustodial mothers do not garner attention by the state. This is particularly true if the mother in question is married, white, heterosexual, and middle class. Postdivorce, mild transgressions of motherhood like cursing, being unladylike, or merely having a history of depression can result in losing primary custody. Mothers must perform white, middle-class, heterosexual femininity with effortless perfection (no complaining about the children or their father), and the further they fall from that mythical norm (Lorde 1984), the more precarious their position in a custody dispute.

Given the historical role of psychology in the social construction of motherhood and the social control of mothers, one wonders whether psychological principles or psychological custody evaluations have any proper place in the custody determination process. There likely would be tremendous resistance to eliminating any and all involvement of psychology and psychologists in custody determination, in part because custody evaluation and psychology are constructed as scientific enterprises that engage neutral experts. There is, however, no objective custody arrangement that works best. We lack empirical evidence that shared custody, mother custody, father custody, or any other arrangement produces the best outcomes, however these are defined. Nor would it be easy to gather such data or to study them in a randomized experimental trial. All arrangements are at the nexus of values and beliefs, but participants in the system, including judges, attorneys, psychologists, and even parents, talk about custody determination as though there were actual, objective criteria. Scientific discourses hold tremendous power. In discussing scientific testing, Burman (2017) cautions about overinterpreting such discourses' significance. Similarly, the idea of an impartial psychologically based custody evaluation is one where "the moral evaluation which underlies the description is rendered invisible and incontrovertible" (26) by scientific discourse. The framework of child development means that mothers are expected to accept the outcome as legitimate both because it is scientific and because good mothers would do so.

Recalling the experiences of the noncustodial mothers I interviewed and observed, I would cautiously approach any recommendations to extend the opportunity to partake in a psychological custody evaluation to those who might otherwise not be able to afford them. In addition to gender, race, class, and heteronormativity are intertwined with the standards by which mothers are judged in psychological terms in systemic and intersectional ways that disadvantage women. Given the issues outlined here, the extent and means of involvement of psychological principles and practitioners in child custody determination are deserving of much assessment of their own.

STILL IN AN ABUSIVE RELATIONSHIP

The plight of domestic violence survivors in custody disputes is common enough that there exists an annual conference. Since 2006, the Battered Mothers Custody Conference (n.d.) holds and annual conference that "aims to inform, support, and advocate for these survivors, allowing them to network with each other and with the professionals and advocates who come to present at the conference." Neither are the dynamics of abuse in child custody cases unknown to the judiciary. In 2001, the first edition of *A Judge's Guide: Making Child-Centered Decisions in Custody Cases* was published by the American Bar Association thanks to a grant from the State Justice Institute. In the second edition (American Bar Association 2008), the eight-page section on domestic violence outlines the effects of domestic violence on children who witness the abuse, noting, "A significant percentage of contested custody cases are in families where domestic violence occurs" (131). The document urges judges, even in jurisdictions where it is not required, to count domestic violence as a serious factor in the determination of child custody, arguing that an abuser acts de facto against the best interests of the child by virtue of their abuse. The section also includes recommendations for training all parties engaged in custody disputes in a domestic violence context, including mediators, custody evaluators, psychologists, and judges.

Similar resources exist elsewhere, such as the *Custody and Parenting Time Investigation Manual* prepared by the Friend of the Court Bureau (2016) in Michigan, which has a four-page section about domestic violence screening. The National Council of Juvenile and Family Court Judges (Bowles et al. 2008) has published *A Judicial Guide to Child Safety in Custody Cases*, and the Battered

Women's Justice Project provides a range of resources, including interview guides, forms, and worksheets for decision-making in custody cases where abuse may be involved.

Nearly every state has some consideration of domestic violence built into its state custody laws (Legal Momentum 2005; Levin and Mills 2003). For example, some states waive their presumption of joint custody in the context of domestic violence, creating a "rebuttable presumption that it is detrimental to the child and not in the best interest of the child to be placed in sole custody, joint legal custody, or joint physical custody with the perpetrator of family violence" (Haw. Rev. Stat. Ann. § 571-46(9) 2004, quoted in Legal Momentum 2005, 16). Other states specify that a move away, with or without the child, will not be held against that parent if they are fleeing abuse. After more than two decades of the Violence against Women Act and advocacy for survivors of domestic abuse, attention to domestic violence is encoded in child custody procedures. How, then, can mothers still lose custody to their abusers?

There exists some academic literature on the phenomenon of custody in cases of domestic violence. Much of this work focuses on the individual actions of attorneys and psychologists who operate to the detriment of mothers. Phyllis Chesler (1984, 2011) offers thick description of the psychological mechanics and outcomes in custody cases where domestic violence was involved. She documents manipulation of children resulting in what she calls psychological matricide, a phenomenon that partially resembles the concept of parental alienation. "Smother-fathers" use these and other tactics to seek to displace the mother by gaining custody. The psychological costs to embattled mothers were enormous, ranging from physical illness and increased alcohol consumption to depression and even suicide attempts. Of particular importance in Chesler's (2011) work is the fact that "many custodially embattled mothers are not 'likeable'" (213), which predisposes them to losing custody. In these cases, judges' and custody evaluators' decisions have more to do with the mother's disposition than with the facts of her abuse. Amy Neustein and Michael Lesher (2005) frame their study in terms of the backlash against mothers, particularly when it comes to protective mothers, those mothers trying to prevent access to their children by an ex-partner who sexually or otherwise abused them. An important finding of their work, echoing that of Chesler, is that mothers are often judged more for their disposition than for the legal claims they are making. My findings resonate with this earlier work.

The internet is also peppered with blogs detailing heartbreaking personal stories from mothers who lost custody to or share custody with an abusive ex-partner. Doreen Ludwig's book (2015) details her deeply personal account of fighting her abuser for custody. In that process, she ended up impoverished and in jail. The focus of her critique is fatherhood policy initiatives that have the unintended consequence of empowering abusers in a custody dispute such that a child's father having access to them has been given primacy over a mother's safety.

At least on the surface, there does not seem to have been a lack of attention to the problem of domestic violence in custody cases. While doing background research for this book, I found a veritable library full of legal analysis on domestic violence and child custody mainly taking place in law journals. We seem to know that the system is failing domestic violence survivors in custody disputes with their abusers. Some laws have been changed, and various groups have created guides or sets of best practices. Nevertheless, the disadvantage faced by an abused mother persists.

The answer does not only lie in individual mistakes or biases or in crafting better laws. Although attention to those issues is imperative, we need an analysis of the full picture that ties together the various institutional pieces when a domestic violence survivor finds herself in a custody dispute. While it seems that we merely are talking about men versus women and the social pendulum that swings to and from each group in turn, we need to move beyond simply noting that mothers do not fare as well as fathers. We need instead a thorough analysis of how gender is implicated in the structures, practices, culture, representations, and interactions that surround child custody decisions. Joan Acker (1990) understands gender as something other than a simple binary designation between women and men. In other words, when we say a phenomenon is gendered, we mean, "Advantage and disadvantage, exploitation and control, action and emotion, meaning and identity, are patterned through and in terms of a distinction between male and female, masculine and feminine. Gender is not an addition to ongoing processes, conceived as gender neutral. Rather, it is an integral part of those processes, which cannot be properly understood without an analysis of gender" (Connell 1987; also see West and Zimmerman 1987; Acker 1990, 146). Understanding the intersection of child custody, the law, and domestic violence requires looking through the lens of gender as an analytical framework. We might note gender disparities in outcomes, but that is only the beginning of the analysis. Just as important are the gendered meanings we make, the gendered assumptions that underlie our practices, and the places where our understandings or social processes are framed as gender neutral. Gender, although socially constructed, operates in the world as a social force. Gender is real insofar as our social institutions, beliefs, and practices are organized around it.

This chapter builds on the work of others who have drawn attention to failures in determining child custody in a domestic violence context. Using an institutional approach provides the framework for connecting individual experiences to the social structures that enable a gendered enactment of power that results in abusers gaining custody of their children. One might speak of a custody assemblage (Deleuze and Guattari 1988) that consists of the courts and judges, attorneys, custody evaluators, psychologists, mediators, schools, medical offices, and individuals, all imbued with gender, participating in creating custody outcomes that can seem to defy best practices as well as common sense in the context of domestic violence. In that sense, then, this chapter builds on all of the chapters that precede it. Keep in mind that gendered stigma, intensive motherhood, work, employment, household labor, and psychological interventions in custody determinations may all intersect in the experiences of mothers who lost custody of their children to their abusers.

Using a subset of interviews with participants who were domestic violence survivors, I explore dimensions that were common across interviews and in online support groups. These more detailed accounts, like mini case studies, allow for more contextualization, which enables us to see the different threads of gender and institutions intertwine. While this chapter is based on cases involving domestic violence, I certainly found threads that are continuous with experiences of noncustodial mothers who have not experienced domestic violence. Cases involving abuse are at the extreme in terms of gendered power and control in relationships, but they remain instructive for their insight into a more normalized continuum of gender and power dynamics in heterosexual families.

Out of the thirty-five interview participants, ten had been in an abusive relationship with the father of their child. In addition, another five participants described relationships where controlling behavior was a significant feature. These numbers are not surprising given that a large percentage of contested custody cases involve families where violence has been a problem (Dore 2004). As in more general cases of domestic violence, some noncustodial mothers experienced existing abuse that escalated after separation had begun. For others, the abuse seemed to be triggered upon separation. This was so particularly if the mother was the one who left, was getting remarried, or had had an extramarital affair. It is important to reiterate here that there is a continuum of gender and power, with the extreme end representing domestic violence. You will recognize some of the dynamics in these stories because they are present to a lesser extent in many "normal" heterosexual relationships.

Verbal, emotional, financial, and physical abuse were also common topics of discussion in the online support groups. In those discussions were women who had long, documented histories of violence at the hands of their ex-partners. It was not unusual for these mothers to have obtained restraining orders or other forms of documentation of the abuse at some point in their relationships. Some of these situations resulted in arrest of the abuser. And yet these mothers lost custody to their abusers too.

Mediation and Domestic Violence

Amy's husband was verbally and physically abusive to her throughout the course of their marriage. Throughout their marriage, he had sex with other women and would berate Amy when she objected. Being a religiously devout woman, Amy tried hard to keep their marriage together and arranged for marriage counseling with a Christian counselor. On the way home from what would be the last of these sessions, Amy's ex-husband told her that she was "a stupid bitch" and that the counseling was "ridiculous." As the abuse continued, Amy's son from a former marriage kept begging her to leave, as he was sometimes a target of the abuse.

Financially unable to leave and living at a great distance from her own extended family, Amy kept working on her marriage. During those years, Amy went to individual counseling and talked about her husband's behavior with other women in her church, who urged her to stay. She thought that having a child would make things better, but when she was pregnant with her daughter, her ex-husband slapped her in the parking lot of her obstetrician's office for not getting out of the car quickly enough. Eventually, Amy sought help from a social services agency, but before she could make any plans of her own, Amy found herself locked out of her marital home without her daughter. With no money and unable to see her daughter, Amy went to stay with a friend.

Amy's ex-husband filed for divorce, and as part of that process, they saw a mediator to discuss custody of their daughter. At one point, the mediator left Amy alone in the room with her ex-husband, and he threatened her:

> He come across the desk at me and he said, "if you don't sign this fuckin' paper you'll never see your daughter again. I'll see to it." And he said, "you'll be payin' child support and alimony to me, bitch." So I'm cryin' and she come back in and she asked "honey, do you want to sign this?" I said "no, but if it's to get my daughter, yes." She never explained joint custody or physical custody or any of that. Then afterwards, he didn't bring my daughter to me like he promised, and when I went home and calmed down, I saw what I had agreed to.

What Amy had signed after being threatened was an agreement to joint legal custody with primary physical custody going to her ex-husband. Amy had just gone from being a stay-at-home mother to seeing her daughter every other weekend and for a few weeks in the summer.

Three years later, a physician reported Amy's ex-husband on suspicion of child abuse. It turned out that her ex-husband's new live-in girlfriend had slapped their daughter repeatedly. There were pictures of hand marks on the child and social services found credible evidence of abuse. Amy was given temporary custody of her daughter for about a year. After his girlfriend moved out, her ex-husband sued for custody again. Amy did not want to go through another frightening mediation, so she took her chances going to court. Custody was returned to her ex-husband. She said, "So much should have been in my favor. The fact that I was married. We had been married for almost 4 years. We are a stable environment. My daughter was in school and on honor roll. My daughter was in dance class. She was in softball. She was in chorus. She was in everything! She was blooming! She was doing great in counseling."

Since the 1980s, mediation has increasingly become part of the landscape of custody disputes (Emery 1995; Garner 1989), with many states adopting mandatory mediation as a first-line practice. While there seem to be benefits and positive outcomes of mediated versus litigated custody disputes (Emery et al. 2001), numerous areas of concern have been identified that raise the question of whether mediation can be used in cases of domestic violence at all (N. Johnson, Saccuzzo, and Koen 2005; Rivera, Zeoli, and Sullivan 2012; Saccuzzo, Johnson, and Koen 2003). Concerns of psychologists, activists, and scholars have not gone entirely unheeded. When mediation does take place in the context of domestic violence, some best practices have been identified, such as utilizing shuttle mediation and not leaving the victim alone with the abuser (Schepard 2004). The publication, *A Judicial Guide to Child Safety in Custody Cases* acknowledges the fundamental issue of power imbalance: "To be successful, mediation requires an equal balance of power across the table. Situations that involve coercion, whether physical violence has occurred, are generally not suited for mediation. Although there are circumstances under which mediation can be configured to maximize safety, it is best avoided in cases where coercion and safety are factors for either a parent or a child. *This is so even if no civil protection order has been entered in the case*" (Bowles et al. 2008 24, emphasis mine).

Despite a body of literature that includes guidance for the judicial system, Amy was subject to coercion at the hands of her abuser during their custody mediation. Fearing for her safety and the safety of her daughter, she unwittingly signed and gave primary physical custody to the man who also physically and emotionally abused her and her older son.

Patrice no longer has legal custody of her children and only sees them every other weekend and for four weeks in the summer. When her divorce was final, however, the orders required her to reside in the family home with her abuser on a rotating schedule. They rotated into the home on a week-on, week-off basis. This arrangement was put in place despite the fact that Patrice had a five-year-long active order of protection against her ex-husband. She explained, "We moved in and out of the house. Yeah, and I had a domestic violence protective order against him at the time and they still made me share a house with him. One day, I came back from my weekend and he had left a hunting knife in my bed." Before they went to trial, Patrice's attorney convinced her to drop the protection from abuse order and meet with her ex-husband because she feared the order would be used against her.

> She's like, "Well, you've gotta talk to him 'cause I'm hearing he's going to take your kids." And I'm not going to have any money left to pay for an attorney, so she's like "I'm not going to be able to represent you any more since you can't pay me." So we went in without [the protection from abuse order]. And in the judge's decision, it says both parents are good parents and father gets sole custody. That's all it says. In this state, if you can prove the inability of the parents to get along, but they aren't unfit, then typically custody would go to the parent who's staying in the marital home. Well this was a huge house that I could never afford.

Because domestic violence was not broached in the custody process, Patrice's case was labeled merely as high conflict, and other factors took on greater significance.

Patrice felt that she continued to be in danger even well after custody was turned over to her ex-husband.

> This is way after our divorce and I was just walking down the street with this guy I know. Not holding hands, we're just buddies. He saw my ex-husband down the block. Then he circled again and backed up and squealed his tires as he drove by. Then he circled again and was leaning out the window yelling at me in front of our son who was in the car. [He was] calling me a whore and saying that I had broken up the family. I was shaking and crying and when my friend stepped in to try to intervene, [my ex-husband] said, "I have an unregistered handgun and if you take another step, I'll shoot you." He actually reached for the gun in front of our son.

Although there is ample research that domestic violence does not end and often escalates when a relationship terminates, and this research is acknowledged in judicial guides and handbooks, noncustodial mothers' experiences reflect that continued danger to them is downplayed or completely ignored once custody has been decided. In Patrice's case, when her lawyer convinced her to abandon the little protection that she had from her ex-husband, it placed Patrice at a disadvantage in the custody conflict and exposed her to continued threats of violence.

Underidentification of Abuse

Shannon had been a stay-at-home mother for sixteen years when she separated from her husband. She emphasized that her husband had never been directly vi-

STILL IN AN ABUSE RELATIONSHIP

olent with her, but he was known to punch holes in the walls or break chairs or windows during his outbursts. He was emotionally abusive and very controlling toward Shannon during their marriage, something her neighbors talked to her about after she had separated: "They used these nicknames for him, shithead, psycho, when I wasn't around because they all hated the way he treated me, talking down to me in front of people, making fun of me, calling me names, yelling to get his way. He didn't hit me so I didn't know this was abuse. But they were all afraid to say anything. I think they were afraid of him too." When she asked for a divorce, he threatened in a text to kill her. Shannon was able to get an order of protection but was unable to get the police to seize the firearms he took with him when he left the house.

Shannon's husband stopped paying the household bills and removed nearly all of the money in their bank accounts on the day he left the house. There was not yet a temporary order of spousal or child support, and within a month the house was out of heating oil. Shannon had to choose between heat and food for her two children in November in New York. Friends lent her cash so that she could get gas for her car to go to the food bank. One night while she was asleep, he came to the house and took the car, claiming it was his. She remembered, "I had nothing. I hadn't been working and he took everything. He kept paying the mortgage because he owned the house. I wasn't on it. He said he owned everything and that I owned nothing. He said he paid for it all and it's his. I didn't know if I had any rights to it. I couldn't afford food. I had to stand in line at the food bank on Tuesdays. Where was I going to get an attorney if I couldn't even pay for my own food?" Shannon continued to scramble to keep the house afloat with loans from friends and family. She was still looking for a job when he filed for sole custody. During that time, he would call and berate her for being lazy because she did not have a job. He told her repeatedly that she would lose the children, that she was unfit because she could not pay her bills. At the initial hearing in front of the referee, his attorney used Shannon's financial instability, the instability that her ex-husband had created, against her. His evidence included Shannon's running out of heating oil and having the electricity and cable turned off for nonpayment. Shannon's ex-husband had also called child protective services (CPS) and reported her for neglect. When CPS workers came to the house, they expressed a great deal of concern regarding the lack of food in the house. Shannon was scared: "I couldn't do it anymore. I knew there's no way I'd win. I couldn't keep the big house going even if I did get a job. I have a college degree, but I haven't had a job since the kids were born. I just sat on my kitchen floor and rocked myself back and forth, crying and screaming. He won. I moved out and he had the house and the kids and the cars and everything." Shannon's ex-husband's campaign of financial abuse was successful in creating a self-fulfilling prophecy regarding her ability to care for her children. He created the conditions under which she could not adequately care for her children. She was afraid of him and demoralized from his repeated calls to berate her. Not knowing the process or having access to legal advice, Shannon became convinced that she had no recourse but to relinquish custody.

Despite an order of protection, the verbal, emotional, and financial abuse did not stop when she separated from her husband. The laws on the books and the guidance manuals for judges and mediators could not help Shannon because the abuse itself led her to remove herself from the legal process. It was over a year later by the time Shannon regrouped from the upheaval of losing everything. She had a job and a small apartment in the same town as her children. When she finally was able to consult with an attorney, she learned that a new status quo had been established: her children were living in the marital home with her ex-husband. The attorney felt that her being away (if only a few miles away) for that year was an insurmountable obstacle to getting a change in custody.

Even though Rhonda felt she was highly educated about domestic violence, she did not readily identify her unhappy marriage as abusive. At most she thought he was a bully. When she went in search of legal assistance, she connected with a domestic violence shelter.

> When I went to the shelter, I felt stupid for going there. I've never been hit. I've never filed charges. And yet, when they gave me the checklist, I could check off an awful lot of them. During the marriage, I wouldn't have told you [it was abuse]. I would have said, "He doesn't hit me." But all of that got worse when we separated. He wanted to control everything. And when I moved out, he felt he could come over any time and take food for the kids. When I changed the locks and put a stop to that, things began to really get bad.

If Rhonda herself found it difficult to identify her situation as abusive at first, it is not surprising that various parties to her custody dispute were not able to see her situation as one of domestic abuse.

As was the case with other mothers I spoke to, Rhonda's abusive ex-husband used third-party proxies, including repeated filing of motions with the court, as a way to continue the abuse. Rhonda identified the custody evaluation as particularly problematic. During her psychological evaluation, Rhonda was asked whether she had ever tried to commit suicide. She said, "He has a medical background, so he knew what to say and that he took care of me, just made me throw up the pills I took. I've never tried to commit suicide! Ever. I had no clue that he was manipulating them this way. I read it in the final report. Now all of a sudden, I'm in denial because I won't admit that I tried to kill myself!" Recall how people negatively evaluated the affect of noncustodial mothers in custody disputes where domestic violence is not a factor. That dynamic is intensified when domestic violence is present and actually contributes to the underidentification of domestic violence. Chesler (1984, 2011) and others refer to these mothers as protective parents and document the ways that they do not fare well in custody disagreements. They are judged on their presentation of self (Goffman 1959) rather than any danger to the child.

Protective mothers and survivors of domestic violence do not fare well in the family court system because they do not present well. These mothers are viewed unfavorably when they are too emotional (fragile or hysterical), outspoken, critical (of the court or the abuser), or angry (Chesler 2011; Ludwig 2015; Neustein and Lesher 2005). Patrice observed, "A lot of times, I think victims can't afford to fight back. They're not unfit, but they are traumatized. So they look hysterical in court and you know, there's such a big disadvantage when they can't pay and have someone guide them. So they're hysterical or they try to appear tough and that doesn't go over well." All of these emotions are appropriate responses to an abusive situation. However, a mother's lack of emotion can also be perceived negatively (Chesler 2011). Patrice described her experience:

> I had an evaluation the first time he sued me and to make matters even more complicated, I was pregnant. I was furious at having to take these tests and knowing that he would say that I was hysterical. That's what all batterers say. I didn't know at the time that they also say, "She was the violent one, and she was promiscuous, and she was this and that." I just knew he would say that I was hysterical. So I took the MMPI [Minnesota Multiphasic Personality Inventory] and my MCMI3 [Millon Clinical Multiaxial Inventory, third edition] and tried really hard to be tough and non-emotional. One came out normal and the other said that I had narcissistic personality disorder.

As with gender in the workplace, the sweet spot of acceptability of women's affect is very narrow. We saw earlier that mothers who had depression or anxiety find themselves harshly judged for having mental health issues or taking antidepressants. In the context of domestic violence, there is a lack of recognition of how a mother's affect can be shaped by the abuse, resulting in a kind of self-fulfilling prophecy. Depressed and anxious mothers, even when they have documented evidence of domestic violence, may be deemed unfit to care for their children. Gender violence, then, creates a mother who appears unfit to care for her child, and she is consequently stripped of custody. If a mother tried to harm herself at any point during her violent relationship, she could find herself having only supervised visitation. I spoke with several domestic violence survivors who were paying for supervised visitations as well as child support, which left them few resources to care for their mental health. This situation created a vicious cycle in which they did not have the proper affect, a mental health care provider to vouch for them, or the financial means to go to court to have supervised visitation lifted.

How we see abusers and survivors plays to well-worn gender stereotypes. But more than just stereotypes are involved. The earlier critique of gender bias embedded in the heavily psychological framework applied to custody determination is even more pertinent in the context of domestic violence, where the stakes are so high. Custody evaluators frequently have a therapeutic background. Noncustodial mothers like Rhonda expressed deep concern about the ability of an evaluator to do a fair job, particularly in a case like hers that involved abuse:

> If that evaluator calls him for what he is, he's going to go after her just like he's going after me. That's his personality. She doesn't want to lose her license so she's not gonna say anything. So she does the scarecrow and points in two different directions. Now nothing is done. He said he was the primary caregiver, and she said there's no proof either way even though I provided them years of documentation from the schools with only my signature on it. Nobody seems to call that bullshit. It's not really even that they're not believing me. They're saying the truth is somewhere in the middle, but his lies are skewing everything. So I must be half crazy.

Similar to Patrice's, Rhonda's situation was labeled a high-conflict divorce. Rhonda's ex-husband was not seen as abusive; therefore, a parenting facilitator was put into place, requiring Rhonda to attend regular meetings with her ex-husband present. These meetings with the parenting facilitator gave her ex-husband another opportunity to continue the abuse: "I'm scared of him. Literally, my heart pounds. I've got a meeting with the facilitator and he's in the room and we meet every month and I hate it. I come out of that meeting and I'm just drained and exhausted. It's horrible. He's a bully and they don't do a thing."

Many of my participants reported self-censoring about issues of even physical abuse in court. In contrast, Christine raised the issue of emotional abuse: "I told the truth. I told what a monster that he really was. And told the judge about the 'cunt' and 'bitch' and 'fucking this' and 'fucking that.' She said that although it was uncomfortable to hear, it didn't rise to the level of domestic violence. Yeah, of course it's uncomfortable to hear. I wonder if she would like to hear her son calling her daughter-in-law that?"

Christine's and Rhonda's experiences resonate with studies finding that various components of the system (such as mediators, evaluators, and guardians ad litem) are underdetecting or underrecognizing domestic violence, which can result in continued abuse, escalating abuse, or revictimization by the very process itself (Grams 2004; Haselschwerdt, Hardesty, and Hans 2011; N. Johnson, Saccuzzo, and Koen 2005; Saunders, Faller, and Tolman 2012). The recognition of domestic violence becomes all the more difficult when the abuse is not physical (Dutton, Goodman, and Bennett 1999; Hart 1990; Jaffe, Crooks, and Poisson 2003; M. E. Johnson 2008; Rivera, Zeoli, and Sullivan 2012). Online support group discussions echoed these experiences that the only abuse recognized was physical abuse. A narrowed understanding of domestic violence by important parties to the custody determination puts mothers at a disadvantage and in harm's way. Note that in early 2019, the US Department of Justice (n.d.) narrowed its definition of domestic violence to encompass only "felony or misdemeanor crimes of violence." In other words, emotional, verbal, and financial forms of abuse and controlling behavior are no longer considered domestic violence. It remains to be seen how this change will reverberate in custody cases.

Another fashion in which domestic violence is downplayed is with regard to the connection between abuse of mothers and abuse of children. There is a substantial body of research that identifies the substantial overlap between domestic violence and child abuse, as well as the harm to children that comes from witnessing domestic violence and experiencing its aftermath (K. Anderson 2010; Appel and Holden 1998; Edelson 1999; Herrenkohl et al. 2008). For about half of the participants who experienced domestic violence, there was physical abuse of their children at the hands of their ex-partner or someone else living in the custodial household. Janet's children experienced emotional and physical abuse by both their father and their stepmother.

> She started texting me and telling me that she wanted to come and live here. And I asked her why and she's like "There's just a lot of things going on over here that's upsetting me." We made an appointment with the attorney and she told him that her stepmom had grabbed her by the hair and smacked her upside the head. Not once, but twice. And she had spanked her while she was doing her punishment of running stairs, they have to run stairs depending on the punishment. I wish my daughter hadn't made a face at her. Her stepmother grabbed her by the arm, flipped her over and started spanking her. My daughter was trying to stop her and put her arm back there and her stepmother just kept hitting her.

As seen earlier, noncustodial mothers thought that a new boyfriend or husband in their household had been a disadvantage to them in the custody dispute process. Indeed, some fathers' rights groups raise the specter of physical and sexual abuse of children, arguing that father custody is safer for children, particularly if there is a new man in the mother's household. While there are plenty of negative cultural representations of stepmothers, these do not include their being a danger to children. In fact, in the context of custody, a stepmother can be an asset. Having another woman in the house, whether it was a stepmother, a grandmother, or simply a girlfriend, signified a safe, warm home atmosphere, not a potential danger. The result is that this is one more manner in which domestic violence was underidentified for these noncustodial mothers.

Use of Proxies

Daisy had recently filed for divorce when her ex-husband was arrested for domestic violence that was witnessed by their eldest daughter. At the court hearing, his attorney argued for a suspended sentence, saying that his client was afraid that Daisy would take his children while he was serving his sentence, however short. When her ex-husband was released on a suspended sentence, he called CPS and reported her for using marijuana.

> They told us that either the kids can go to foster care until we figure it out or I can just agree to them living with their dad because he was out of jail and the kids wanted to see their dad. So he and I came up with an agreement that was so stupid of me. I signed that we would have shared custody and of course, when I gave him the kids, he just never gave them back. Since he had them and I willingly let them go, they said they could either go to foster care or they could do in-home wards of the court in the father's home. And of course, I don't want them to go to foster care, so I let them stay with their dad. I mean, I'm sure that if I made the call, he'd test dirty for weed too. But if I did that, the kids would go to foster care and I just don't want that.

Daisy had a court-appointed attorney who did not bring up the domestic abuse during the custody proceedings, and the court-appointed guardian ad litem did not interview Daisy. She said, "The [guardian ad litem] came into the court and told the judge that he interviewed my kids and they were better off with their dad, but he never spoke to me. I don't know if their dad was in the room when he talked to them or not. That's why I don't understand. How can you say they're better off with their dad if he never spoke to me?" Daisy ended up with in-home supervised visitation that had to be changed to a neutral location because her ex-husband continued to harass her and her family during drop-offs and pickups. Daisy has not been able to exercise her six-week summer parenting time in over two years and has no court order in place mandating phone contact. Her ex-husband does not answer the phone when she calls, but he leaves abusive voicemails on her phone: "He's screaming. Irate. He tells me that 'you don't know these kids and you're not ever gonna see them,' and it's like of course I don't know them. I haven't seen them in two years. You won't let me. My daughter, I just found out last night that she went to prom and I missed it. If he finds out that we're in contact, he takes her phone away from her."

During the times when Daisy did have the children in her home, her ex-husband routinely called CPS and told them she was taking drugs and there was no food in the house for the children. None of the repeated visits by CPS revealed any neglect or drug use on Daisy's part. Eventually, the CPS caseworker recommended that she call 911 if the harassment continued. Given her past experience with reporting physical domestic violence, Daisy did not feel she would get anywhere by calling the police. Neither did she feel that she had any recourse through the courts without hiring her own attorney when he violated their court orders.

Daisy's situation reveals a few additional dynamics about custody in domestic violence situations. It is common for abusers to enlist others to contribute to the abuse. Proxy abuse can happen at the unwitting hands of outside agencies like CPS, psychologists, or guardians ad litem, as well as family members. Repeated calls reporting Daisy to CPS and manipulating the guardian ad litem without any due process or input from Daisy were manifestations of this kind of tactic by her abuser. As a result of her ex-partner's campaign, Daisy was given supervised visitation for a nonviolent charge, while her ex-husband continued to harass and intimidate her. The court failed to recognize not only the history of domestic violence in this case but also that harassment via the legal proceedings were a continuation of that prior abuse. In fact, given how deeply intertwined custody is with gender, one could argue that in cases like this, the custody dispute itself constitutes a form of gender violence.

The manner in which Daisy's ex-husband continued to harass her would likely be treated differently outside the family context. One could not as easily file repeated baseless police reports against a coworker or neighbor without the person having recourse to harassment statutes. That custody disputes take place in the discursively private realm of family and home subjects them to a different kind of logic from disputes taking place in the discursively public realm, such as in business. The deconstruction of the false binary of public-private is a familiar and important analytical contribution by feminist theorists. The private realm is devalued in relation to the public, which is what allows for a result where the court appears to be more concerned by a parent who uses marijuana than by one for whom there is ample documentation of being arrested for abuse against the other parent.

Daisy's case demonstrates how abusers utilize third parties to help them carry out their abuse. In psychological parlance, *triangulation*, *abuse by proxy*, and *third-party abuse* are common terms used to describe this phenomenon. One of the most common methods of third-party abuse was to make reports of child abuse or neglect that at the very least mothers would have to spend time, energy, and even money addressing. Jeanne offered another example where her ex-husband called CPS and other organizations, including building inspectors and the Internal Revenue Service: "He would call CPS on me even though the children had never been to my house. He'd say that I don't live in a place that's habitable. CPS would show up and bring building safety people because he'd call them too. So it looks extra bad and puts my job in jeopardy. It takes time and money. It was just crazy and he's always there calling a special agency on me even if it had nothing to do with him." In Jeanne's case, she managed to defend herself against the spurious claims of neglect; however, in other cases, noncustodial mothers found themselves with reduced visitation, supervised visitation, or no visitation. Carla's summer time with her daughters was approaching when her ex-husband called to say that he would not be sending them. He told her that he was sure that her new husband was sexually abusing their daughters. While CPS was investigating her current husband, there was a no-contact order in place for him. Carla was only allowed supervised visits even without her husband present. Because of the no-contact order, the three-hour drive, and the cost of supervised visitation, Carla could only manage to see her children for a few hours once a month at most. This arrangement continued for three years, and when Carla later became pregnant with her third child, her ex-husband filed a protective order against her. Unable to travel, Carla could not defend herself against the newest charges. The result was that Carla had no contact whatsoever with her daughters for over three months. Eventually, both Carla and her husband were cleared of any wrongdoing.

A couple of years later, Carla regained custody after her ex-husband was arrested for domestic violence against his new wife. He underwent investigation for child neglect and sexual abuse, and all charges were ultimately deemed credible. However, the time apart had taken its toll on Carla and her daughters: "It's constant repetitive thoughts. I never get a break from it. I thought nothing is ever going to change. I'm just done. I'm tired. The girls don't seem to want to have anything to do with me. My oldest really doesn't want to have anything to do with me. I'm not mommy to either one of them."

In their efforts to inflict harm on the mother of their children, abusers also attempted to enlist therapists and custody evaluators with varying degrees of success. In interviews and in online discussions, noncustodial mothers relayed how their ex-partners had manipulated these professionals. Maggie spoke with one such custody evaluator for less than an hour: "There were no phone calls, no emails, nothing but a 45-minute interview in which she decided that I was basically a prostitute, that I was an alcoholic, and a drug addict and that there was nothing wrong with him. He was a struggling single father who was a great dad and I'm basically the selfish bitch. Oh, and I'm obsessive-compulsive and custody should go to dad. She was an actual psychologist, but obviously not a very good one." In these situations, the abusers were adept at appearing calm, professional, or beleaguered (Rivera, Zeoli, and Sullivan 2012).

Abusers also enlisted former friends and other family members, including stepmothers and paternal grandmothers, to berate or put pressure on noncustodial mothers. It was not unusual for noncustodial mothers who survived domestic violence to talk of third parties who repeated, nearly verbatim, insults or accusations the noncustodial mother frequently heard from her ex-partner. These noncustodial mothers felt especially betrayed by family members, and they became increasingly isolated with even fewer social supports than they had going into the custody disagreement. As Maggie said, "I didn't really have anybody in my corner to testify for me. As I now know, he intentionally separated me from everybody. They have to keep that control so he kept me separated from my friends, my family. Nobody was willing to come forward. In fact, my oldest friends took his side even knowing [the abuse] that was done to me because he was such a great manipulator." Abusive ex-partners also frequently attempted to recruit children to further their efforts at continued abuse. Rhonda shared,

> My ex kept telling them I never did anything for them. My son started saying this too, "Well you don't care. You never drive me to football." He said this as we were driving to football! Then my ex would tell them they couldn't go on the school trip, "The schools says you can go but your mom says no and she's doing it just because she's mad at me and so she's punishing you." Every year, I'd have really pissed off kids! That wasn't the only thing. It was, "Well you could do this if your mom would let you. I could afford to buy this if your mom would pay more child support."

Discussions in the online support groups revealed multiple ways that children were recruited to punish and harass their mothers. Some children were enlisted to take items from the mother's home, including tax returns, bank statements, and copies of emails. Other children berated their mothers using words that echoed the abuser. When Jeanne saw a copy of her son's college application essay, she was surprised at what her son appeared to believe about her: "I knew they weren't talking good about me but I didn't know the story they were telling. I was shocked to see that the story that my kids tell is that their drug-addicted mother abused them. It went on to say how abusive I was. And he really threw me under the bus saying that I tried to kill myself."

The success of this tactic was highly variable. Sometimes it resulted in noncustodial mothers losing contact with their children, but other times, noncustodial mothers took actions to placate their abusers in order to protect the children.

One of the reasons that Maggie cited for pulling out of the custody dispute and turning over primary custody to her ex-husband rather than going to court was that she felt the children were being harmed by the negative talk they were hearing about their mother: "He's pulling some nasty shit on the kids, you know. Trying to [say], you know, 'Love Dad! Hate Mom!' We all know that alienation thing works. Honestly, they were in such bad shape from being stuck in the middle for all this time, I says, 'My god, I can't keep doing this to them.'" Maggie's children had observed physical and emotional abuse of their mother while she was married to their father. She told me how the children were sometimes caught in the crossfire emotionally, but also physically, like the time when her ex-husband threw car keys at her and hit her infant son in the head. She felt that she could best protect her children by turning over custody to her abusive ex-husband.

Many of the noncustodial mothers I spoke with actually embraced the concept of parental alienation syndrome (PAS) because they had an ex-partner attempting to have their children participate in this kind of third-party behavior. A few mothers had not seen their children in years because of such tactics. PAS was also a frequent topic of discussion in the online support groups. There was not much controversy for them around using the term because it so aptly described what some felt about their experiences as noncustodial mothers.

The Friendly Parent and Parental Alienation Syndrome

The mothers I interviewed and observed in support groups online did not feel empowered to bring up domestic violence in the context of a custody dispute, regardless of the severity of the abuse or any documentation they may have. In interviews and in the online support groups, noncustodial mothers regularly cited high-profile cases as cautionary tales. In addition, it was not unusual to hear from them that an attorney recommended against bringing up anything negative about the father, even when that extended to domestic violence and, in several cases, when there were allegations of sexual or other abuse of the children. These mothers told me that their attorneys feared that raising any allegations against the father would be seen as an attempt to undermine his relationship with the child. At the very least, their concern was with friendly parent provisions that are based on the idea that if custody is contested, primary custody should go to the parent who is more likely to encourage the relationship with the other parent (Dore 2004).

Friendly parent language usually looks something like that seen in Michigan's Child Custody Act § 722.23. The following is listed as one of the factors used to determine what custody arrangement is in the best interests of the child: "The willingness and ability of each of the parties to facilitate and encourage a close and continuing parent-child relationship between the child and the other parent or the child and the parents." A more extreme situation that is not unusual in the context of domestic violence is when abuse allegations by the mother are portrayed as a means to turn a child against his or her father. Several of the mothers I interviewed stated that they knew their ex-husband had a fathers' rights attorney who would very quickly seize on any domestic violence allegations as a means to discredit them. Fathers' rights groups routinely use terms like *malicious mother syndrome, the Medea complex*, and, most commonly, *parental alienation syndrome*.

PAS is a nonvalidated psychological phenomenon that has been discredited in the scientific community. It is said to stem from one parent's successful campaign to poison the relationship children have with their other parent. Children then turn against that parent and may refuse to see them. The fear or anger that ostensibly alienated children demonstrate in the presence of the targeted parent is said to be due to tactics of the mother rather than abusive behavior of the targeted parent. A psychiatrist, Richard Gardner, branded the syndrome unique to the child custody context based on his experiences providing expert testimony on behalf of fathers who were accused of sexually molesting their children (Gardner 1985).

Gardner is as controversial a figure as his work on PAS. He is known for his defense of pedophilia and his creation of a Sexual Abuse Literacy Scale as a means to cope with what he characterized as an epidemic of illegitimate child sexual abuse allegations (Bruch 2002; Emery 2005). Gardner initially framed PAS as a syndrome that applied solely to mothers, but rebranded it as gender neutral in later incarnations (Bruch 2002; H. Smith 2016). He contended that at least half to nearly all contested custody cases involved PAS, and that any claims of sexual abuse by children in a custody dispute are likely to be false and a manifestation of PAS as a form of revenge. In order to determine the truth of the allegations, Gardner (1985, 6) recommended placing the child and accused parent in a room together because "when the accused and the accuser are in the same room together, with the opportunity for an 'eyeball-to-eyeball confrontation,' there is a much greater likelihood that the two individuals will be honest with one another. After all, they were both allegedly there. They know better than anyone else the details of the alleged encounter and each one is likely to pick up the other's fabrications in the most sensitive way. Of course, the younger the child, the less the likelihood he or she will be able to engage effectively in such confrontations, but they can still be useful." Once a conclusion is reached that a child has fabricated abuse, Gardner's remedy for PAS is a change in custody, placing the child in the accused's home and denying any contact with the protective parent for "a month or so" (7). Fathers' rights groups have embraced the concept, which is based on the "taken-for-granted stereotype of the 'scorned woman'" and some catchphrases from psychoanalytic theory and psychology more generally (Adams 2006, 327). In other words, PAS is appealing because it reflects deep-seated beliefs about women and it invokes the cultural weight of scientific discourse. For example, when children make accusations of sexual or other abuse, mothers "relish the accusation and deny conflicting evidence. Mothers of children who are genuinely abused commonly deny the abuse or react with horror and grief" (Gardner 1985, 6). Mothers are portrayed as petty and jealous, and unlikely to change even with therapy, preferably family therapy that includes the child and their abuser: "Of course, psychotherapy can be useful at that time as well, but it must involve both parents and the child in the same room together. The treatment of the mother, however, is not likely to succeed unless she can work through her ongoing animosity toward the father. Often a central element in her rage is the fact that he is reestablished in a new relationship and she is not. Her jealousy is a contributing factor to her program of wreaking vengeance on her former husband by attempting to deprive him of his children, his most treasured possessions" (7). Gardner constructs the children as possessions that the vengeful mother wants to take from the father because she is jealous of his new relationship. Statements like this do not mesh with the fact that most heterosexual divorces are initiated by women (Braver, Whitley, and Ng 1994) and that many noncustodial mothers found that abuse began or escalated upon their own dating, remarrying, or having a baby with a new partner. Michele Adams (2006) identifies a growing body of legal and psychological scholarship on PAS that is formulated as gender neutral but that nevertheless rests implicitly on gender stereotypes that undergird its formulation. Adams contends that these subsequent formulations of PAS put forth by researchers, although gender neutral, actually continue to promulgate gender bias.

Despite efforts of the proponents of PAS, there is a lack of scientific and legal support for its legitimacy (Dallam 1999; Meier 2009; Pepiton et al. 2012). In 2012, the American Psychiatric Association declined to accept PAS for inclusion in the fifth edition of the *Diagnostic and Statistical Manual of Mental Disorders* (H. Smith 2016). PAS has not met the scientific standards of peer review and does not hold up under close examination of scientific reliability and validity (Bruch 2002). Neither does it meet legal standards for inclusion as evidence. For example, *A Judicial Guide to Child Safety in Custody Cases* instructs judges not to accept expert testimony regarding PAS "under relevant evidentiary standards" (Bowles et al. 2008, 12) derived from *Daubert v. Merrell Dow Pharmaceuticals* because it does not meet the scientific standards for use in the courts. Under the Daubert standard, references to PAS "should therefore be ruled inadmissible and/or stricken from the evaluation report" (Bowles et al. 2008, 24). Nevertheless, PAS remains a powerful concept that has social power and an air of legitimacy. At the very least, it shapes whether noncustodial mothers self-censor or are preemptively silenced by their attorneys.

Despite the Daubert standard and the American Psychiatric Association's skepticism about PAS, there are indications that some custody disputes are being influenced in favor of fathers who bring accusations of parental alienation against a mother who is protective of a child she had with an abusive partner. For example, one notable case in the news was that of Anna Cooper, who, despite having expert medical testimony on her child's abuse, lost custody to her ex-husband and was limited to supervised visits after her children were labeled as suffering from PAS because they did not want to remain with the man abusing them (Stelloh 2014). More extensive discussions with additional examples can be found in Neustein and Lesher (2005) and Chesler (2011).

Since being labeled with PAS can result in protective mothers losing custody to their abusers (Emery 2005; J. Kelly and Johnson 2001), it would be useful to reframe how we understand accusations of PAS in contested custody cases as part of a broader pattern of abuse that often solicits third-party proxies. In this case, the proxies are family court, attorneys, mediators, and custody evaluators who, in their professional roles, help the abuser continue the abuse. When abusers use children third parties as proxies, the term PAS resonates strongly with noncustodial mothers because they are in a system where the term is pervasive regardless of its lack of scientific acceptability. It has the currency of common sense. Ironically, it is abusers who have been granted custody who seem to display behaviors that are more reflective of Gardner's construct of PAS. The abusers' actions, though, are continuous with their prior abusive behavior rather than constituting a discrete psychological phenomenon that only occurs in the context of a custody dispute.

We do not need to name a syndrome in order to understand that people recruit third parties to their side in a dispute. That this practice occurs with children in the context of divorce and child custody within an adversarial legal system should not be a surprise. However, there is no reason to suspect that these attempts at shaping children's understandings of the divorce are enacted by one gender more than any other. To be sure, many behaviors that are labeled as evidence of PAS (a child refusing to see a parent) can and do happen in the context of a divorce with typical amounts of conflict (J. Kelly and Johnson 2001), and they do not signal any insidious actions on behalf of the mother or anyone else. Joan Kelly and Janet Johnson (2001) make a distinction between children who are inexplicably refusing to see a parent and those who do so for more mundane reasons having to do with a child's developmental stage (separation anxiety), the child's reaction to the stress of the changes brought by a divorce or remarriage, or dislike of one parent's rules or parenting style. They contend that there are very few alienated children and that most children who are labeled this way actually fall into their category of the estranged child. The estranged child is not brainwashed but rather is reacting in an arguably healthy way by setting boundaries with an abusive, neglectful, or otherwise seriously deficient parent.

The notions of both the friendly parent and PAS rest on gendered ideas about families and parenting that are appealing for their seeming face validity or common sense, as well as the way they make use of psychological discourses. In a custody dispute context where domestic violence or abuse has been present, these concepts can become weaponized not only as seemingly legitimate concerns encoded into guidelines and practices but also because mothers internalize the threat and change their behavior or whether they even raise the issue of past abuse.

Bargaining Power

The domestic violence survivors I spoke with and observed in the support groups reported that they tended to ask for less (time, money, flexibility) in the custody process than they otherwise might. Their having to placate their ex-husbands was a continuation of the dynamics in their former relationship. Noncustodial mothers commonly used the phrase "walking on eggshells" as a descriptor for how they felt during the custody determination process but also in their postrelationship status with their abuser. As Rhonda shared, "It got to the point where he would tell me to jump and mostly, if it was for the kids' sake, I'd do it. I would do all the stuff they needed and do all the driving and pay for everything." These mothers are very aware that they are asking for less and that they are doing so out of fear. Participants like Nina cited fear of physical retaliation, of emotional and psychological abuse, of abuse to their children, and of continued litigation: "I agreed to pay all the travel costs and agreed to my own screwing for lack of a better way to put it. I didn't have anybody there to say, 'Well you might want to think about this or this tax write-off or something.' I just was very intimidated at the time and scared of losing. How many people do you run into who have an ex who is hell bent to destroy them at all costs? So I agreed to child support and all the travel expenses and health insurance. He got all the tax deductions."

Echo Rivera, April Zeoli, and Cris Sullivan (2012) raise concerns about women's diminished bargaining power when they are physically present in custody mediations with their abusers. Indeed, there were ample examples of this in the interviews and in the online support group discussions. Noncustodial mothers like Rhonda who had experienced domestic violence rejected the usefulness of mediation in their situation: "What mediators do is try to come to an agreement between two parties who want two different things, but what you want is reasonable and what they want is completely unreasonable, like wanting to destroy me. So you end up giving a lot." Rivera, Zeoli, and Sullivan (2012) and others have correctly noted that abusers' ability to be calm and even charming in a mediation context can sway mediators toward them in the negotiation. This was certainly the case with the noncustodial mothers I spoke with; however, even when an ex-partner was combative in the mediation session, it did not help the mother's case in the end. A mediator may have expressed empathy or validated the mother's perception of her ex-husband as unpleasant, but the combativeness was not enough to sway the mediator even when documentation of abuse, including arrest records, was provided.

In addition to this dynamic, noncustodial mothers spoke at length about the dynamics outside the actual mediation itself that influenced their decisions to decrease their ask whether they engaged in mediation, went to court, or settled outside court. Most mothers did not use the term *rebuttable presumption*, but they talked about trends in custody that they observed or read about. Abby recounted how they came to their second custody arrangement: "All the judges started doing fifty-fifty custody even in domestic violence cases as long as nobody beat the child and neither parent had a drug problem. The presumption was fifty-fifty because it was a very liberal county. So my ex-husband asked for fifty-fifty and I felt I had to give it to him."

Shortly after Abby married at age twenty, her marital relationship turned violent. Her son's pediatrician recommended that she remove herself and her son from the violent situation. When she left her husband, he began to harass her. The pediatrician advised her to look into taking out a restraining order against her abuser, which she did. After the divorce and a custody evaluation, Abby was granted primary custody of her son, and her ex-husband made frequent requests of her to change the custody arrangement. Abby explained, "But within five years' time, he had gotten a good job and I thought, well ok, if he takes me to court, I've already spent tons of money on the first lawsuit. It's very expensive and if he takes me to court, I'm gonna end up with fifty-fifty anyway because he's never beaten the child and he doesn't have a drug problem."

When Abby's new husband took a job promotion that required him to relocate for two years, Abby and her ex-husband maintained the fifty-fifty split, with her frequently traveling back and forth. When Abby became pregnant, they arranged to shift much of her time to the summer to accommodate the birth and restrictions on her air travel in the later stages of the pregnancy. Her ex-husband refused to allow their son to visit that summer and then filed for a change of custody. She countersued and underwent another evaluation: "So I didn't say anything bad about him. All I said was that I was surprised by the lawsuit. I was scared to death that if she knew about the domestic violence, she would think I had parental alienation syndrome going on." Despite her ex-husband's arrest record for domestic violence and public intoxication and his failure to abide by their agreement, Abby ended up with phone contact and only two weeks with her son over the next six months while the custody evaluation proceeded.

In Abby's case, several dynamics are at play. The dynamic that sets the stage for Abby's loss of custody is the strong, explicit preference of the courts in many states to default to fifty-fifty custody arrangements (DiFonzo 2014). In states like New Hampshire, Iowa, and Louisiana, joint custody is presumed to be in the best interests of the child and is therefore the default, the rebuttable presumption. Jurisdictions are increasingly being asked to consider variations on the practice of joint custody, including provisions for increases in the minimal parenting time and routinely finding for joint custody even when one parent objects (Ellis 2014). In the statutes, domestic violence is rarely a disqualifying factor for joint custody and the burden is frequently on the parent asking to deviate from fifty-fifty custody. In Amy's case, she felt the burden on her to demonstrate the need to deviate was insurmountable. She estimated that she had spent over $30,000 in attorney fees by that point.

Economic power played a role in the dynamics that noncustodial mothers experienced outside the domestic violence context. However, for those mothers who lost custody to their abusers, the negative impact of unequal economic power was intensified. In Jeanne's case, she had very little contact with her sons. Out of fear of retaliation, she felt that she could not ask for any changes or even protest when her ex-husband refused to comply with their court orders: "All those years I said nothing because I was told if I rocked the boat, their family is all lawyers and judges and I would find myself in so much trouble. I don't know but they always had a knack for suing me. I was sued for everything. If I showed up looking stupid, I was sued. I was sued for saying this, I was sued for saying that. It doesn't mean they won, but I still had to go to court. I always showed up with my lawyer there even though I was making next to nothing."

These dynamics affected how noncustodial mothers approached continuing conflicts, including violations of their court orders. This was a frequent topic of discussion in the support groups. In situations where noncustodial mothers showed up to pick up their children and their ex-partners refused to turn over the children in accordance with their court order, participants received advice from attorneys to simply document that they had been there and were denied access to their children.

When Nina forced the matter and stayed on her ex-husband's front porch demanding to see her children, her ex-husband called the police on her for trespassing. She told the police that she was trying to pick up her children in accordance with the court order, but they declined to get involved, stating that it was a family court matter. Other noncustodial mothers have sought help from local police departments when they were denied their time with their children and were told that police did not enforce family court orders.[1] Their recourse was to go back to court to have the agreement enforced; however, lack of funds and fears of additional retaliation meant that these actions were infrequent. Noncustodial mothers' bargaining power is often diminished in comparison to an ex-partner with greater resources, but the context of domestic violence magnifies these and other imbalances, so these mothers ask for less and try not to rock the boat.

I Would Have Stayed

More than a few mothers said that if they could do it all again, they would stay with their abusers rather than go through losing custody and continued abuse. They felt that at least they would have their children, would know how they were doing, and would be able to protect them better than they were able to as noncustodial mothers. As Patrice explained, "If you're not physically in danger and you really believe that he's going to try and take your kids, stay. Stay and protect your kids and go when they're older because he's going to take them. Believe what's in your gut. He will do it and he will probably win. I wish I could say something different than that."

These noncustodial mothers had not anticipated that their ex-partners would continue or escalate their abusive behavior when they left the marriage. Friends, family, and even professionals they encountered like physicians, attorneys, and teachers advised them to leave sooner rather than later. Some mothers felt pressured to do the right thing and leave. Patrice elaborated,

> I had so many people in my ear telling me, "You have to leave," and "He's going to end up hurting you." All of this stuff and really pushing me against my better judgment. I knew what he was capable of doing and it wasn't going to be specifically hurting me, although things were escalating. He broke down a door. He was raging drunk on New Year's Eve and broke through a door and a whole doorframe to get to me. It was an absolute nightmare. It was escalating, I could see that, but I also knew how to keep things calm. I shouldn't have let people push me to do what deep down I knew was not strategically the right thing to do. I think sometimes people have the best intentions, but they don't have to live with the result of what they're telling you to do.

How to handle an abusive ex-partner was a frequent theme in the online discussion groups. These discussions were rather nuanced. There was not a hard line about leaving an abusive ex-partner. It was common too for mothers who lost custody to their abusers to talk about how they struggled with leaving and how they felt in the aftermath. A common theme was that they felt that they had put themselves at a significant disadvantage in the custody dispute by leaving the family home. Staying meant continued stress and abuse, but if they left with the children, they risked being seen as kidnapping them even though many states allow that fleeing abuse should not be seen as abduction.

Gendered work inequality and financial abuse further complicate these mothers' decisions to leave. The gender wage gap and the motherhood wage penalty are both well documented, and we know that financial abuse is common in domestic violence contexts. Several of the noncustodial mothers I talked to had become stay-at-home mothers at the insistence of their ex-husbands. Some happily did so, while others felt coerced and later regretted leaving the labor market. Even if a noncustodial mother was employed, her lower earnings often did not facilitate carrying the cost of the family home alone while the divorce was being settled. Financial abuse that took the form of emptied bank accounts, unpaid utility bills, or repossessed cars further narrowed these mothers' living options and made them look financially unstable compared with their ex-partners.

Finances shaped the decisions of these noncustodial mothers in other ways too. As we saw earlier, not having good legal representation is a significant disadvantage. In the context of domestic violence, that disadvantage intensifies. For example, many abused mothers did not know they could seek temporary orders of child support, so they felt that their options while leaving their abuser were limited to moving out either with or without the children. They might flee to a shelter, live with family, or rent a small apartment. As was the case with other noncustodial mothers, their new housing arrangements were often interpreted negatively in their custody disputes because of the emphasis placed on maintaining a status quo, particularly where children's housing was concerned.

Part of the problem that these mothers experienced had to do with how we frame domestic violence and what we tell survivors. We know that "Why didn't they just leave?" remains a common query of battered women despite knowing that it takes multiple attempts before a woman leaves her abuser. We know that leaving an abuser is very dangerous, yet we place an emphasis on physically removing women from a domestic violence context without fully acknowledging the longer-term risks involved, including losing custody of children. Some of the mothers who left felt a lot of pressure from family, friends, and professionals to leave before they were ready. Patrice actually felt that her situation was worse after she left because the power imbalance was further encoded in the custody agreement:

Honestly, I probably wouldn't leave him, knowing what I now know. I would have sucked it up and stayed. Just because when I look back at it, he wasn't physically hurting me and I could be the buffer between him and the kids. I could have protected them from a lot of this. Yeah, I would have just, I would have waited. I wouldn't have left. I'd be in an abusive relationship is where I would be. And I still am! I still am in an abusive relationship, but now he has all the power and I don't have a leg to stand on and I can't help the kids.

Not all noncustodial mothers who had been abused believed that they should have stayed. Some indicated that they felt relieved and happy that they had left their abuser, even if their children were not in their custody. However, they remained in a constant state of worry and felt that the power dynamics greatly favored their ex-partners.

Bringing Gender Back

It is easy to say these noncustodial mothers' experiences are a matter of incompetent attorneys, biased judges, or mothers' poor judgment. While some or all of these factors may have weight in any given situation, taken together their experiences reflect the operation of gender as a system of power and social meanings (Acker 1990). It is crucial to understand the intertwined nature of the dimensions of domestic violence, custody, and gender. Gender has largely been removed in talking about both domestic violence and custody. *Domestic violence*, while still a gender-neutral term, has some remaining connotation of gender. Other terms such as *intimate partner violence*, *situational couple violence*, *mutual combat*, and *high conflict* are more gender neutral.

Two very different kinds of groups support gender-neutral language around domestic violence. I discussed the first, fathers' and men's rights groups, earlier in this chapter, and I would argue here that their cause is more about denying the recognition of the experiences of heterosexually partnered women than about being inclusive regarding gender practices. In contrast, domestic violence activists who focus on the experiences of queer people, trans people, and women of color rightly point to the troubles with terms like *violence against women* that are narrowly linked to cisgender heterosexuals and appear to mainly reflect the lived experiences of white, middle-class women (Crenshaw 1991; Goldscheid 2014).

Because heterosexual relationships are organized around differences in gender and power, the experiences of cisgender, heterosexually partnered women such as the noncustodial mothers in this chapter are centrally about gender and power. In fact, men's violence against women can be understood as a means through which "batterers reproduce a binary framework of gender" (K. Anderson and Umberson 2001, 358). We can thus recognize both that *violence against women* can be an exclusionary term and that it aptly describes the social pattern of men's violence against women in heterosexual relationships and families. Same-gender violence can still be understood in terms of gender when we understand gender as a nonbinary system of power and meaning and as a spectrum unlinked from biology (M. P. Johnson and Ferraro 2000).

Recall that to say something is gendered is much more than to say that there are gender differences in that phenomenon. Focusing on gender symmetry in broadly defined categories of violence does a disservice to what it means to say that a phenomenon is gendered. For example, women and men may appear to have an equal representation in some broad occupational categories like law; however, a closer look reveals that the practice of law is deeply gendered, from pay gaps and segregation within law specializations to how we evaluate the capabilities and efficacy of attorneys in ways that are gendered (Epstein 1981; Pierce 1996). A similar dynamic is at play in analyzing the gendered nature of domestic violence.

The effects of understanding domestic violence in gender-neutral terms can be seen in the laws of states like Arizona that hold that the rebuttable presumption against giving custody to an abuser does not apply "if both parents have committed an act of domestic violence" (Ariz. Rev. Stat. Ann. § 25-403.03(D), quoted in Legal Momentum 2005, 14). This exception to the rebuttable presumption intersects with efforts at framing domestic violence as a gender-neutral phenomenon.

Although it is outside the scope of this chapter to give a full analysis of the debate concerning equally violent genders (see, for example, Archer 2000; M. P. Johnson 1995, 2006), a general understanding of the debate is informative. The sides of that debate are characterized by extensive theoretical, empirical, and methodological differences (M. P. Johnson, Leone, and Xu 2014). When equal gender violence is defined using the "percent of women and men who have perpetrated at least one act of violence in their relationship" (M. P. Johnson and Ferraro 2000, 952), we overestimate the extent of gender symmetry. In addition, most domestic violence is not intimate terror but rather situational couple violence, which is perpetrated more equally by men and women in heterosexual relationships.

General surveys are unable to adequately capture intimate terrorism (IT), not only because it is less common but also because those who experience it tend to select out of such surveys. Much of this work uses data about current rather than former spouses and therefore also significantly underreports IT. Specialized samples are needed to tap this population of domestic violence survivors who have experienced IT. In contrast to these kinds of general survey data, agency data reveal much more IT, as well as violent resistance (women's responses to IT), and demonstrate that these are not gender-symmetric phenomena. Regardless of whether we are talking about IT, violent resistance, or situational couple violence, women experience greater physical harm, as well as other long-term effects on work and psychological functioning, because of their social location (K. Anderson 2010; Jasinski, Blumenstein, and Morgan 2014).

The more routine interpersonal violence, which is characterized as gender symmetrical, seldom ends in the involvement of the courts or a domestic violence shelter. Therefore, in the context of child custody, we are more likely dealing with IT. To the extent that violence appears on both sides, it is likely to be violent resistance and not situational couple violence. These gendered phenomena also intersect with other social locations like race, class, and sexual orientation that shape the effects of domestic violence. Women of color, for instance, are more likely to be seen by law enforcement as mutual combatants or less susceptible to harm (Gruber 2012). Gay and lesbian partners reporting domestic violence risk being outed in the process (K. Anderson 2010). Against the backdrop of gender-neutral language and domestic violence, women of color potentially face even greater hurdles in court.

If we encode the mistaken idea of equally violent genders in custody determinations without the deeper understanding of how gender interacts with different forms of violence, we remove the burden from domestic violence perpetrators to prove that it is in the best interests of a child for them to have the custodial rights and responsibilities for that child. We therefore fail to protect the target of abuse and any children involved.

In addition to the question of equal gender violence is the issue of harm. What constitutes harm and to whom? What harms are serious enough to change a custody outcome? While it is well beyond the scope of this chapter to detail the vast legal analysis of gender and domestic violence law, Michael El-Zein (2014) pinpoints several central troubles with the law, specifically that by degendering domestic violence, we fundamentally misconstrue how it differs from other forms of violence:

> The lack of successful prosecutions and repeated exposure to reluctant survivors has taken a toll on those within the criminal justice system. This is due in part to the way our criminal justice system typically deals with domestic violence, equating it with "paradigmatic nondomestic violence," as "discrete" and "episodic," when it is in fact "an ongoing pattern of conduct defined by both *physical and non-physical manifestations of power*." By treating one specific act of domestic violence like

any other isolated crime of violence—for example, a battery of one stranger by another—the *episodic and cyclical nature of the violence is often overlooked, as is its function as a part of a greater system of control.* As a result, both prosecutors and judges have expressed frustration with survivors and the trial process. (192; emphasis mine)

Emotional, psychological, and other nonphysical harm is an awkward fit with criminal domestic violence law (Kuennen 2010) in general; therefore, it is unsurprising that harm other than *immediate physical harm* is not always mentioned with regard to an abused parent. If states have a difficult time conceptualizing nonphysical harm in the context of domestic violence (El-Zein 2014; Kuennen 2010), adding a child custody dispute to the mix makes that all the more difficult. For example, Delaware defines domestic violence as "physical or sexual abuse, or threats of physical or sexual abuse, and any other offense against the person committed by one parent against the other parent, against any child living in either parent's home, or against any other adult living in the child's home" (Legal Momentum 2005, 15).

In Idaho's language concerning what constitutes interfering with child custody, there is a similar emphasis on the physical. Parents can defend removing their children from another parent only if they were fleeing immanent physical harm to themselves or their child. Sometimes, domestic violence must also be habitual to be relevant to custody determination: "There is a presumption that joint custody is not in the child's best interests if one of the parents is a *habitual* perpetrator of domestic violence" (Idaho Code § 32-717B, quoted in Legal Momentum 2005, 17; emphasis mine).

Perhaps one of the most difficult hurdles for survivors of domestic abuse is the need for a conviction. For example, in Montana, "the court may consider physical abuse or the threat of physical abuse against a child or one parent against another when determining the best interest of the child" (Montana Code § 40-4-212(1)(f) (2005), quoted in Legal Momentum 2005, 20).

We know that domestic violence is underprosecuted and that convictions are difficult to secure. Therefore, the preference for having a documented conviction strongly tilts the balance of power in favor of the abuser when it comes to child custody.[2]

In summary, the degendering of the language of domestic violence fundamentally misconstrues the nature of domestic violence that does not match paradigmatic nondomestic violence because harm may be immediate as well as ongoing, physical as well as nonphysical, and difficult to document via a conviction. In addition, when child custody is framed as both gender neutral and child centered, it results in institutions elevating the needs of abusers above those of both mothers and children. Some states do explicitly recognize that domestic violence perpetrated against one parent is, by definition, not in the best interest of the child. In Hawaii, "the court shall consider as the *primary factor* the safety and well-being of the child and of the parent who is the victim of family violence" (Hawaii Rev. Stat. Ann. § 571-46; emphasis mine), and in Colorado, "it is assumed that joint custody is not in the best interest of the child if there is a history of spouse abuse" (Colo. Rev. Stat. § 14-10-124(1.5)(b)–(v), quoted in Legal Momentum 2005). Domestic violence does not, however, preclude an abuser from contact with their child even in these states. It simply places the onus on the abuser to justify their access to the child. Zoe Garvin (2016, 173) explains, "In California, the presumption triggered by a finding of domestic violence does not change the 'best interest' test, nor do the rebuttal factors supplant other Family Code provisions governing custody proceedings; it merely shifts the burden of persuasion to the abusive parent to demonstrate parental fitness instead of the victimized parent having the burden to prove the abuser is unfit." In an era when the refrain "children need both parents" has been elevated to the status of common sense, the burden on the abuser to justify access may be lighter than it should be.

In states like Delaware, domestic violence is considered just one of many factors that constitute the broader criteria of the best interests of the child. While some states explicitly include harm to the abused adult, other states seem to value that harm only when it is understood as directly harming the child. Illinois provides a good example: "If the behavior of a parent is believed not to affect the relationship with the child, it will not be a consideration when the court is determining custody" (750 Ill. Comp. Stat. Ann. 5/607.1(a), quoted in Legal Momentum 2005, 17). Kentucky goes further: "However, unless the behavior of the alleged perpetrator of violence affects the child, or the child's relationship to both parents, that behavior will not impact the custody decision" (Ky. Rev. Stat. Ann. §§ 403.270(2)(f), 403.270(3) (2004), quoted in Legal Momentum 2005, 18). In other words, domestic violence is relevant only insofar as harm done to the parent then harms the child. One wonders how abuse of one parent by another *would not* harm a child. Research on polyvictimization demonstrates that domestic violence is rarely limited to one type or to one target (K. Anderson 2010). In addition, children who live in households where there is domestic violence are more likely to be abused themselves (Edelson 1999; Herrenkohl et al. 2008).

In states like Indiana, whether the child witnessed domestic violence is key, but only insofar as requiring supervised visitation. If a parent "has been convicted of a crime involving domestic or family violence that was witnessed or heard by the noncustodial parent's child," that parent will receive supervised visitation "for at least one year, but not more than two years, following the crime" (Indiana Code § 31-17-2-8.3, quoted in Legal Momentum 2005, 17). In California, the completion of a batterer's treatment program, counseling, or a parenting class can mitigate the history of domestic violence (Cal. Fam. Code § 3044(b)). Similar provisions are very common in other states.

What do these framings of the best interests of the child tell us about gender? For one, they tell us that a father's presence in a child's life outweighs domestic violence in all but the worst cases, and even then, only temporarily so. Domestic violence becomes just one among many factors to consider, such as having adequate financial resources, staying within the same school district, or working a job that enables the parent to be home at the end of the school day. Treating domestic violence as only one factor among many reproduces the gender hierarchy in heterosexual families and implicitly relies on and reproduces some aspects of intensive motherhood. In an extreme manifestation of the imperative for mothers to be selfless, mothers must sacrifice their own safety to secure their child's relationship with a violent father. The question is not whether violence is acceptable to the system, but rather *how much* violence is acceptable. How much must a mother endure in the name of being child focused? These laws construct an abstract and undefined harm that domestic violence does to children as less important than a father's access to his children. In doing so, they normalize violence against women, but they also reinforce a hollow definition of fatherhood that emphasizes the biological aspects of fatherhood rather than acknowledging the importance of what fathers actually do for and with their children.

Why do mothers lose custody to abusers when there has been so much activism around domestic violence that many states have changed their laws and advised their judges on some of the very dynamics I just outlined? It is too facile an answer to simply say that there are bad judges, there is corruption, or that money talks. All of these hypotheses may hold some truth; however, understanding them as a deviation does a disservice to the extent to which these outcomes should be expected given our social arrangements across institutions as varying as work, family, law, health, and so forth. There is a long tradition of feminist criticism of legal institutions that does precisely this. Feminist legal analyses unpack ostensibly gender-neutral laws and legal systems, revealing how power and gender are enacted through the law. In my close analysis of noncustodial mothers who lost custody to their abusers, gendered institutions, particularly when they believe they are gender neutral, rely on and reproduce gender inequality.

A lack of resources may press noncustodial mothers into alternative dispute resolution practices like mediation, which are not recommended in a domestic violence context. Poorly handled mediations and custody evaluations, forced contact with their abusers, friendly parent provisions, and pressure to drop restraining orders shape noncustodial mothers' exits from the system even when they have documented evidence of abuse to themselves or their children. They withdraw, reduce their demands, or find that other factors loom larger than domestic abuse. The failure of third parties, including courts, evaluators, and mediators, to take seriously economic inequality and nonphysical forms of abuse, particularly financial abuse, sets up survivors to look unstable or incompetent as parents. Gender-neutral legal systems that treat domestic violence the same as any other crime of assault are ill equipped to adjudicate the best interests of any child who has lived in a household with domestic violence.

Our cultural beliefs about motherhood lead us to a place where mothers must endure violence in order to be good mothers. Although courts, judges, and laws acknowledge in one way or another that custody disputes often involve domestic violence, they do so without understanding the centrality of gender to the many realms that intersect in the context before them. As a result, gendered legal, work, and economic contexts and gendered beliefs about mothers limit noncustodial mothers' ability to protect themselves and their children from a violent ex-partner.

LESSONS LEARNED

At the beginning of the twenty-first century, societal aspirations for families as postfeminist, gender-neutral spaces have outpaced the actual rate of social change, particularly in heterosexual families. We so badly want to see men's fully equal participation in the private sphere that we have skipped ahead and have proceeded as though the changes have already manifested. This is not to say that some men in some sectors of society have not practiced or increased their involvement in children's lives. Indeed, many fathers have increased their relational time with their children when compared with past generations. It is to say, however, that gendered patterns in the division of household labor and workplace disadvantage remain stubbornly entrenched. At the same time, *parenting* has increasingly become the preferred gender-neutral label for the multifaceted work of providing care to children. As a result, navigating contemporary motherhood means navigating a discursively gender-neutral space as a person whose lived experience and interactions with social institutions are in fact quite gendered. This tension between gender-neutral aspirations and discourse and gendered institutions shapes the experiences of mothers without primary custody of their children, including how they came to be noncustodial and how they experience that status.

Noncustodial mothers, whether voluntarily so or not, experience a gendered stigma because of their status. Despite the language of parenting, noncustodial mothers are judged *as mothers*, a gendered position. Noncustodial mothers may work to redefine and reframe motherhood in ways that are more expansive, but on their uncertain terrain, they may also reinscribe ideas about gender difference, intensive motherhood, heterosexual families, monomaternalism, and hegemonic family forms, all of which are further complicated by other hierarchies such as race and social class.

Three deeply gendered domains of central importance to noncustodial mothers' experiences—employment, psychology, and the legal system—each sport claims to gender neutrality. The United States has parental leave on the books rather than maternity leave. Psychology has replaced language referencing hysterical women and castrating mothers with bipolar and personality disorders. Gender-neutral understandings of domestic violence fail to acknowledge power, and formal equality before the courts stands in contrast to a gendered, classed, and raced distribution of the resources needed to engage those courts on equal footing with those in more privileged positions. This is not to argue for regendering parenthood or caregiving as women's sole terrain; rather, it is to illustrate how gender-neutral language obfuscates the gap between discourse and reality. It is in this gap that noncustodial mothers, and perhaps most contemporary mothers and some fathers, reside.

Families dissolve or change form. When children are part of those families, custody decisions must be made or adjudicated. What is required for equality in and following that process? For voluntarily noncustodial mothers, cultural shifts in ideas about motherhood and the care of children are important, and organizations and institutions must operate to acknowledge and accommodate many kinds of families. Mothers who reluctantly cede custody and those who outright lose custody benefit from these shifts as well. These mothers, however, need a more comprehensive approach that acknowledges that gender and other dimensions of social inequality, such as class, race, and sexual orientation, are important social forces that affect families and individuals in families when those families form, persist, change, or dissolve. We might begin developing such an approach by unpacking what underlies the best-interests-of-the-child standard, which seems to represent a nearly universal language deployed by noncustodial mothers and the social institutions they encounter.

The Best Interests of the Child

The best interests of the child emerged as a problematic construct that affected noncustodial mothers in many ways. Significant cultural, political, and economic baggage is packed into the concept, which, rather than serving as an objective standard, acts like an ideological Rorschach test where we project our ideas about gender, class, race, sexuality, parenting, and other ideologies onto the case at hand. All parties to a custody dispute, such as judges, mediators, attorneys, and custody evaluators, employ the vague construct subject to their own conscious and unconscious biases. Mothers themselves are not immune to the moral weight of the best-interests standard even when they are voluntarily noncustodial.

Recall that the historical shift to the seemingly gender-neutral best-interests standard unraveled custody claims based on the tender years doctrine or any primary caregiver status. Both of these standards were understood to be gender biased because they resulted in custody primarily falling with mothers even though in most cases custody decisions are made between former partners without the court's interference. The gender-neutral language of custody echoes a liberal feminist framework that identifies sameness as the route to equality. Social policies arising out of a liberal feminist framework rely on the mantra of equal treatment to further social change, but liberal feminism has been critiqued as neglecting bodily differences or needs—for example, of those who give birth or breastfeed when it comes to parental leave. While the equal treatment approach has led to many important social changes often undergirded by legislation, its language has been ripe for co-optation. Similarly, a feminism heavily reliant on formal legal equality has opened the door for claims that we have achieved a postfeminist world. Postfeminism, the idea that feminism has completed its mission, is positioned as the natural outgrowth of the successes of feminism (collapsed into a unitary, liberal feminism) that make the movement now obsolete. Indeed, in a postfeminist world, clinging to feminist ideas is seen as regressive. Gendered social patterns such as wage inequality are conceptualized as artifacts of individual choices rather than products of complex social and institutional inequalities.

Thus, in a postfeminist context, men's rights groups have been able to launch assaults on ladies' nights as well as organizations designed for women's mutual support, such as campus women's centers and women's business alliances. If gender equality has been achieved, then the logic holds that any acknowledgment of gender constitutes special treatment of women, discrimination toward men. While it is hard to imagine defending ladies' nights on the basis of claims to gender justice, other manifestations of postfeminism have had more impact. In the realm of child custody, fathers' rights organizations have set the terms of debate (see Crowley 2008). These groups' claims about problems with the child support system, a system that noncustodial mothers also identified as highly problematic, rest on ideas of sameness and choice. Women are *able* to earn the same as men, the argument goes, but *choose* not to, so why should men pay child support? Some groups extend this logic to its extreme, arguing for a "financial abortion," which releases a man from child support obligations if the person carrying the fetus chooses not to abort a pregnancy he participated in conceiving and does not want (Goldscheider and Lawton 1998). This warped inverse of abortion rights rests on an argument of equal treatment for men on the right to choose. If women have the right to choose, so do men.

In addition to being gender neutral, the best-interests standard reflects a child-centric position that aligns easily with the tenets of intensive motherhood. Pat Breton (2014) identifies child centricity in national and global contexts beginning with the elevation of children's rights as a principle by the United Nations. Arguing against children's rights is for sure a sticky wicket, but as Breton makes clear, it is the protection of "children as individual rights-holders" (318) rather than the protection of children per se that is problematic. Feminist theorists have long grappled with the incorporation of children into feminist frameworks. For some feminists, childbearing may be framed as the origin of oppression, but for many feminists, children's liberation is intertwined with women's liberation, just not in a straightforward manner within an individual rights framework (Firestone 1970; Rubin 1984). Feminists have recognized children's subjectivities (Helleiner 1999; Thorne 1987, 1993) and that children's well-being is socially and structurally linked with women's well-being (Alanen 1994; Oakley 1994; Polatnick 1996).

In contrast, a children's rights framework potentially sets children's interests at odds with those of mothers, who are simply other individual rights holders. Coupled with the demands of intensive mothering and romanticized notions of childhood innocence, a children's rights framework is one in which "mothers' issues are eclipsed in child-centric policy agendas that benefit *neither mothers nor children*" (Breton 2014, 316; emphasis mine). In Canada, this erasure of mothers is seen in the shift from the language of family well-being to child well-being in policy discourses. The rights-holding child of the United Nations Convention on the Rights of the Child reflects and reifies Western, heterosexual, white, middle-class, nuclear families based on a clear gender division of labor, but it also rests on a gender-neutral child (Breton 2014). In the United States, welfare reform in the 1990s promoted heterosexual, nuclear marriage as the solution to child poverty (Winkler 2014), neglecting complex structural causes of child poverty that are both feminized and racialized. When children's well-being is conceived of as simultaneously separate from and wholly dependent on their caregivers, enforcing children's rights amounts to increased surveillance of mothers, particularly poor mothers and mothers of color. Rather than aiming resources at the root causes of childhood poverty and neglect, child welfare approaches increasingly targeted risky mothers as the social safety net that might have supported them continued to shrink (Breton 2014). Because the discursive gender neutrality of children's rights fails to acknowledge that in heterosexual families the bulk of childcare responsibility falls on mothers, mothers are erased and devalued even as society continues to firmly embrace intensive motherhood and the mother blame that comes along with it.

A children's rights framework thus can be understood as a neoliberal project where the focus on the child displaces claims to gender equality: "Operating from the 'best interests of the child,' these protectionist policies present the rights of the child in conflict with the mother's maternal rights to care for her child" (Breton 2014, 321). It is important to fully understand how the ascendancy of the neoliberal paradigm operates alongside a powerful combination of postfeminist, childcentric, and gender-neutral discourses that work to the detriment of all. The reduction in state supports for families under neoliberalism has deflected this contraction of public support into a privatized conflict between parents who are divorcing. With the favorability of shared custody encoded into law, the resources of parents are spread thin trying to maintain two households suitable for equally shared custody of children. At the same time, government programs that provide important economic supports for families have been eroded. For example, as of this writing the current administration is seeking to reduce access to the Supplemental Nutrition Assistance Program (formerly known as food stamps). We also see increased child support enforcement, along with draconian penalties for noncompliance that can place a caregiver's livelihood at risk. With child support, the "privatization of income redistribution" (Winkler 2014, 267) becomes about apportioning finite resources between two parties, both of whom may be impoverished. Both the deadbeat dad and the single mother are social problems constructed by neoliberalism, leaving the state absolved of responsibility for adequate education, living wages, affordable housing, gender and racial equality, and good-quality, affordable childcare, among other things.

As we have seen, the complex set of problems encountered by noncustodial mothers rests at the nexus of neoliberalism and postfeminism. Judges, attorneys, psychologists, mediators, and evaluators follow the neoliberal criteria of the best interests of the child in a contest between two genderless, unconstrained individuals while denying social realities like gendered and racial wage inequality, gendered patterns of caregiving, and domestic violence. In this way, despite claims that custody decisions are not based on earning power, the neoliberal context renders economic power central although invisible. Without social supports for caregiving, the costs are borne by those who do the bulk of the caregiving. This privatization of caregiving occurs through inadequate maternity and family leave and a lack affordable childcare.[1] When it comes to determining custody, excluding claims to caregiving based on the tender years or primary caregiver criteria thus advantages whoever best approximates a breadwinner, especially if he or she has a substitute caregiver handy. Thus, the powerful nexus of gender-neutral and childcentric best interests means that the privatization of caregiving in the heterosexual gender-complementary nuclear family remains an unwritten standard.

Increasingly, states' presumptions of child custody arrangements favor more equally shared time between households. In many states, child support allocations vary to some degree with the amount of time spent with each parent. Combined, these two tendencies promote custody disputes. An otherwise marginally involved parent finds it in their financial interest to pursue a greater share of custody at the outset when child support is set. Research suggests, however, that many custody arrangements that begin as shared end up drifting toward primary mother custody over time (Emery, Otto, and O'Donohue 2005), a kind of *regression to the mom*. While there are mechanisms for enforcing the payment of child support, and perhaps minimal recourse to a parent who is denied rightful parenting time, there is no corresponding mechanism to ensure that parents use the parenting time they are allocated. At best, a parent can ask for a child support modification in line with the actual use of parenting time, but if courts are loath to take parenting time away from a parent who does not use it, they perpetuate the unequal and gendered division of caregiving and its associated costs.

There is another barrier to child support modifications in these circumstances. Assumptions and discourses embedded in the system press us to interpret regression to the mom as a by-product of maternal control or interference (maternal gatekeeping). However, it is more likely that the parents have simply reconstituted their preseparation division of labor. Absent any mechanism to ensure that parents take their allocated parenting time, the best-interests standard becomes more about ensuring fathers' access to their children and promoting the "feminisation of responsibility and obligation" (Chant 2008, 176) than about promoting fathers' caregiving. This dynamic where gender is forbidden discursively but ever present structurally in ways that advantage men, particularly white, middle-class, heterosexual men, demonstrates the "embedded masculinity politics in the neoliberal project" (Connell 2010, 33). Noncustodial mothers find themselves on the losing end of those politics.

To summarize, the construct of the best interests of the child represents a postfeminist, gender-neutral, childcentric, neoliberal paradigm that simultaneously celebrates and erases mothering in order to ensure fathers' access to children. It has little to do with encouraging parents of all genders to share equally in the care their children need. The dwindling of the social safety net and the assumption that gender and other forms of equality have been achieved render economic positions as products of the individual choices of homogenized neoliberal actors. When we reject gender as an organizing component of power while it remains embedded, albeit less discursively explicit, in our conceptualizations of family and psychology, we set up conditions for mothers to lose custody to uninvolved and even abusive ex-partners. The alignment of contemporary psychotherapy and intensive motherhood with neoliberal imperatives means that mothers suffer from their noncustodial status in economic, cultural, and interpersonal ways. They are expected uphold impossible standards of intensive mothering while pulling their own economic weight, but they must also do so without workplace equality or having primary custody of their children. And they shoulder the blame when things do not turn out right, whether the problem is poverty, domestic violence, or children's poor grades. Given this potent nexus of social forces, what kind of framework would improve how we think about child custody determination? What lies beyond the best interests of the child?

Reproductive Justice

Reproductive justice is a critique of and an antidote to the neoliberal paradigm. As a concept and a social movement, it is reflected in recent decades in the work of SisterSong, a nonprofit organization devoted to improving "institutional policies and systems that impact the reproductive lives of marginalized communities" (SisterSong, n.d.). Reproductive justice is inclusive of reproductive choices concerning rights to birth control and abortion, but it is more expansive because of the ways in which the concept acknowledges the complexity obscured by the term *choice* (Price 2010; A. Smith 2005). What does the right to an abortion mean if the closest county where abortion is available is in the next state and one lacks the means of transportation, public or private, to get there? What does the right to have children mean if public assistance, jobs that pay a living wage, and affordable childcare are increasingly scarce? Reproductive justice has as its terrain the larger social organization of inequalities exacerbated or ameliorated through social movements as well as state action. Thus, the right to raise one's children in healthy, safe, and constructive environments is as important as the right to control one's reproduction, whether it be to have or not to have children.

Many forms of social inequality have seen increasing disparity since the 1980s. Wage, income, and wealth inequalities have all increased, with larger shares of national and international wealth accruing to a shrinking proportion of the population. The gender wage gap has inched lower but remains relatively stagnant. White women have seen the greatest gains, while gender wage gaps for Latinx and Black women remain quite large. Even so, some of the apparent gains are a mere by-product of structural changes in work and employment, such as declines in unionization and increases in part-time and contingent employment, that have eroded wages in men's traditionally good jobs. The Affordable Care Act sought to close some of the gaps in access to affordable, quality health care in the United States, but it is a far cry from positioning health care as a human right rather than a privilege often attached to good jobs. Even so, the modest gains of the act are at risk, as every Congress since the act's inception has seen efforts to undo or undermine the legislation. At the federal level and in most states, there is no statutory provision of paid sick time or paid maternity and parental leave. Across schools and school districts, there remain large disparities in educational resources, which are reproduced by methods of educational funding tied to residential wealth, increasingly stratified by race and class. Awareness of sexual harassment, sexual assault, and domestic violence may have increased in the Me Too era, but we remain a culture that questions victims more harshly and more readily than perpetrators.

Reproductive justice poses the fundamental question, What is required for equality? Equality in this sense is framed as a social state rather than a contest between two abstract, homogeneous, rights-bearing individuals. Such a shift in perception may require us to gain some distance from the best-interests standard and find ways to optimize well-being among individuals in a web of relationships that extends beyond Western, nuclear, monomaternal conceptualizations of family. It will require understanding that children's well-being is intertwined but not synonymous with the well-being of those who care for them. Optimizing well-being among those in a web of relationships does not mean, however, that power recedes as a concern. To the contrary, reproductive justice rests on understanding the complex interworking of power at individual, familial, community, and societal levels.

In the context of child custody, reproductive justice means first recognizing that social supports for parenting are inadequate and unequally distributed along expected axes of inequality like race, class, sexual orientation, disability, and gender. Although discourses and policies may be gender neutral and that gender neutrality is formally encoded into laws, the care of children remains a largely gendered terrain. In a dispute between parents, we do not have a conflict between two genderless, legal-rational individuals who are interchangeable and on equal footing. We have gendered people operating in gendered social institutions in which the standards used to evaluate questions of custody have deeply gendered roots, even if those roots have been discursively severed.

Reproductive justice is thus not a framework of mothers' rights, but rather one that can address the needs of children while addressing the needs of people of all genders who do the work of caring for children. In fact, some of these recommendations may seem to echo ideas promoted by fathers' rights organizations. However similar on the surface, recommendations based on a reproductive justice framework do not rest on rights and are attentive to the multiple, intersectional operations of power in and through social institutions. Thus, we must examine the social organization of and supports for caregiving, as well as the criteria and processes employed for determining child custody.

The Social Organization of Caregiving

The first and most broadly conceived approach to child custody through a reproductive justice lens begins long before any questions of child custody arise and rests on the herculean task of promoting justice in the distribution of caregiving in society. First, mothering, and more broadly caregiving, must be detached from binary conceptualizations of gender. People of all genders can and do take on caregiving work. Fathers who take on an equal share or more of this caregiving work are operating well beyond what we know as an involved father, an expression involving a marked category that indicates that fathers are, as a rule, uninvolved. That is to say, if we must denote *involved* fathers, fathers are then, by definition, not involved. Fathers must share fully in caregiving and must do so before divorce and as a matter of course. We must not overreward fathers' caregiving, nor should it be framed as an exercise in self-actualization. For certain, there are many obstacles to equal sharing of caregiving, particularly in heterosexual unions. Wage inequalities and a lack of paid leave or even sick time often make a gendered division of labor a seemingly logical choice in a given household.

While it is important to acknowledge that historical gender divisions of labor have meant that many men have missed out on watching their kids grow, framing fathering in a narrow and sentimental fashion around nurturance rather than equitable sharing of responsibility between partners erases much of the work of caregiving. Parents are rendered solely as receivers of affective rewards from children rather than purveyors of emotional and physical labor. Caregiving should be understood to include all of the unseemly, exasperating, and boring aspects as well as the butterfly kisses and Kodak moments. This is why Mignon Duffy (2007) centers the term *reproductive labor* rather than *nurturing*. Nonnurturant reproductive labor remains the terrain of white women and women of color when it is unpaid in the home. When paid, nonnurturant reproductive labor, such as housecleaning in private settings, is the province of women of color, while in institutional settings, such as cleaning and food service jobs, men of color are overrepresented (Duffy 2007). While these jobs are notoriously low paid and precarious, women of color are underrepresented relative to white women in the paid nurturant reproductive labor jobs such as nursing and teaching that offer better pay and benefits. All of this is to say that sentimentalizing caregiving narrowly *as nurturing* fails to acknowledge the ways in which the scut work of caregiving is divided among racial and gender lines.

In addition to nonnurturant reproductive labor is the mental burden of caregiving. Parents who are caregivers clutter their heads with knowing which children's medicines are in the cabinet, who likes which cereal, how much toilet paper is in the house, when vaccines are due, when that rash started, and what day Halloween is celebrated at school this year. They should come to learn how to squeeze in the rest of life in the time confetti produced by caregiving, that is, the minute blocks of time interspersed among myriad pressing tasks and interruptions from other household members (Schulte 2014). Perhaps time confetti, as well as all the rewards and costs of caregiving, would be more evenly distributed throughout society. Most of the work of social reproduction in the world has fallen on the shoulders of women, particularly poor women and women of color. If people of all genders shared in care work, it would become more visible as work. Care work is undervalued whether it is paid or unpaid, and the time and energy spent in care work shape opportunities and rewards in other realms.

In addition, we should interrogate the construct of motherhood and the ways that it aligns with particular class- and race-based notions that demand sacrifice and place blame on mothers. Social science literatures demonstrate a complex host of factors beyond mothers or nuclear families that shape child outcomes in various arenas of their lives. Child poverty and widening social inequalities that affect things like health, education, housing, and exposure to environmental toxins have far greater influence on child well-being than whether one breastfeeds or works outside the home. Interrogating constructions of motherhood should involve paying better attention to and deepening feminist interrogations of children and childhood (Qvortrup et al. 1994), whether it is in the realm of developmental psychology or in the language of international children's rights.

Closely related to decoupling mothering from binary gender and disrupting intensive motherhood is the importance of recognizing and valuing polymaternalism wherever it may be found, whether it be in different family formations, fathers' caregiving, othermothering, stepmothering, paid mothering, or multigenerational mothering. To be sure, this is a cultural shift, but to recognize polymaternalism is to rework social institutions to be more inclusive. What would a family leave policy look like if we recognized aunts, uncles, neighbors, friends, and siblings who were caregivers? Birthing rooms and parent-teacher nights would certainly be more crowded. However, incorporating polymaternalism narrowly through a rights framework would likely further complicate family court and exacerbate some of the problematic dynamics identified in this book. Can polymaternalism be recognized without mimicking third-party rights to children (such as grandparents' rights) that disproportionately put poor mothers and mothers of color at risk of losing parental rights? If our search for better ways to make difficult determinations about children's living arrangements when their families face substantial change clings to the desire for elusive objective standards, we risk reproducing all manner of social inequalities. Employing more psychological intervention, whether through custody evaluations or psychological testing, is tempting but will continue to produce outcomes reflective of the historical biases on which their theories and practices are founded.

Setting out a precise plan for changing the social organization of caregiving is beyond the scope of this or perhaps any book; however, there are practical changes that can be made in light of what we can learn from noncustodial mothers' challenges and how they intersect with existing social inequalities.

Criteria for Custody

Compared with shifting the social organization of caregiving, rethinking the criteria used for custody is low-hanging fruit. It is not without its own challenges, however. The unwritten and sometimes written standards that value maintaining the status quo or stability for children are problematic for what they ignore and what they obscure. Sometimes state laws are explicit that no preference should be given to a primary caregiver in matters of child custody, and because *primary caregiving* is seen as gendered language, the concept largely has been ruled out as an important factor in establishing the status quo that must be maintained. If not caregiving arrangements, what, then, is supposed to remain unchanged for a child? The status quo in schools, housing, neighborhoods, and jobs is elevated in importance above the maintenance of arrangements of caregiving and affective relations in a child's life. This eclipsing of the importance of caregiving can happen because a father and a mother are conceptualized as interchangeable and generic parents without regard for actual gendered patterns of caregiving, particularly in heterosexual, nuclear families. Fetishizing the status quo in each of these areas disproportionately constrains the ability of caregivers to exist in a healthy, safe, and constructive space. For example, we saw that when mothers pursue their and their children's well-being in ways that disrupt the status quo or give the appearance of instability (for example, a residential move for a better job), they risk losing custody because we conflate child well-being with a lack of certain kinds of change, an idea for which there is scant empirical support.

Outside the context of a child custody dispute, we do not constrain or penalize parents, particularly fathers, for making an economically beneficial career move that requires significant changes in their children's lives. In fact, military children experience frequent moves, as the average military family makes a permanent change-of-station move every two to three years (General Accounting Office 2001). While not deemed wholly unproblematic, moves by military families are normalized and supports for those moves are in place. Rather than lament military children's futures, government publications frame military children as resilient and as part of a whole-family sacrifice for the country. Our children-heroes are celebrated each April in the Month of the Military Child. The Department of Defense, through the Office of Military Family Readiness Policy, provides multifaceted support for the moves made by military families, including but not limited to religious and psychological counseling, child development expertise, teen centers, access to childcare, and extra educational supports. Family courts might adopt the message from the military family context that their focus should be on support for families and their children undergoing changes rather than merely maintaining the status quo.

Another proposed alternative to the best-interests standard is called the approximation rule, a concept put forth by the American Law Institute. Under the approximation rule, when a disagreement over custody arises, a child's caregiving arrangements postdivorce would default to closely resemble what they were before the divorce (Emery, Otto, and O'Donohue 2005). This standard prioritizes continuity in relations of care and affect. People of any gender who provide substantial care to children before the dissolution of a relationship or a family should continue to do so. The dissolution of a marriage or family is not the time to determine anew arrangements that had been created in the context of that family. In terms of gender, the approximation rule raises the bar on fathers' participation in caregiving before divorce, and it makes visible and acknowledges who has been doing the work of social reproduction, inclusive of nonnurturant as well as nurturant labor.

Advocates of the approximation rule cite its clarity and predictability, both of which should lead to a decrease in long, expensive conflicts brought before the courts. Such conflicts pose a disadvantage to the partner with fewer resources, a problem cited by a majority of the noncustodial mothers who were interviewed. The approximation rule also negates the need for in-depth, costly evaluations of each parent's capacity to parent and instead relies on arrangements that had been in place in the relationship before its dissolution. The approximation rule thus sidesteps consideration of many factors that are imbued with gender bias. The costs of maintaining two households may necessitate seeking employment, but stay-at-home mothers' prior employment status will not hamper them in terms of child custody. They will not be constructed as inferior economic beings, lazy and sponging off their former spouses. Taking a lower-paid labor market reentry job will not mark them with instability, nor will they be penalized during child support calculations with imputed income based on what they would have been earning had they not been at home full time. Employed mothers of any economic status who shouldered the bulk of caregiving would not be prevented from making a job move that would enhance their economic well-being if it happened to be outside their current school district. The approximation rule constrains the mobilization of other biases such as a physical disability, mental illness, or past sexual behavior that noncustodial mothers noted worked against them. For example, if a mother who had a history of depression had been the primary caregiver in a marriage, there is no reason to suspect that she would suddenly become incapable of caregiving upon divorce. Also underlying the approximation rule is the notion that some measure of the best interests of the child, and in fact of the whole family, was embedded in existing arrangements before the dissolution of the relationship.[2] There is no need to exogenously determine the best interests, a concept shown to be tremendously problematic. In cases of domestic violence, the approximation rule takes the wind out of the sails of the friendly parent principle. It could no longer undermine a mother's ability to live free from the control of an abusive partner by elevating an abuser's access to a child over their primary caregiver's safety.

Eliminating opportunities for these biases to manifest is in line with the broad goals of reproductive justice. Keep in mind that the approximation rule only comes into effect when there is a dispute over custody, which only happens in a clear minority of cases. Parents may agree voluntarily to arrangements that vastly differ from prior caregiving arrangements, as we saw with some of the voluntarily noncustodial mothers. In cases where there is disagreement, the approximation rule sets an expectation to discourage additional conflict. Reducing conflict for children is one practice that we know produces better outcomes for children, and it is empirically supported. Using an approximation rule serves a reproductive justice rather than a rights-based agenda.

If the approximation rule were to successfully reduce the likelihood of custody disputes, we would expect any remaining disputes to be of the highest conflict. Attorneys, judges, mediators, and anyone else involved in these disputes must be thoroughly educated about the dynamic of the custody dispute as an extension of preexisting abuse. That education should include expanding understandings of abuse to include nonphysical forms such as emotional and financial abuse. It must also deconstruct false gender narratives around domestic violence, as well as false gender narratives in psychology that create powerful discourses of equally violent genders, gatekeeping mothers, and parental alienation syndrome that set up survivors of domestic violence for failure.

What of the caregiving father who truly shared equally in the nurturing, the scut work, and support of a child before the dissolution of the relationship? It is no accident that families like Olive's and Virginia's did not go through the court system. Families with truly more egalitarian gender divisions of labor were not the ones with lengthy, rancorous custody battles. Mothers whose children's fathers had always been caregivers appeared in the data as the more voluntarily noncustodial mothers and seemed most accepting of their unconventional social location. The mothers who felt best about their noncustodial status, even if not completely voluntary, shared in common that the ex-partner was already significantly involved with all aspects of caregiving before the dissolution of the relationship. These fathers were caregivers in every sense. They remained involved and practiced good communication and collaboration with the noncustodial mother. They continued to co-parent. When these unconventional families bumped up against people or gendered institutions that were stubbornly resistant to change, they handled them together and asserted the legitimacy of their arrangement. They might begin to undo gender.

The Child Custody Determination Process

In the child custody determination process itself, we find another vehicle for increasing reproductive justice. One of the most common troubles cited in online support communities was the lack of money to access legal counsel, resulting in unequal access to representation, which is stratified by gender, class, race, and other dimensions of inequality. Unlike in criminal courts, litigants in family court in most states do not have a right to legal counsel. While the approximation rule would reduce the need for expensive and extended legal proceedings, it would not eliminate the need altogether. Providing low-cost legal assistance or publicly funded attorneys would go a long way toward creating equality of representation, which is a matter of reproductive justice. Lower-income fathers and mothers would be able to face a daunting system of custody and child support with competent legal advice. Providing greater and equitable access to legal counsel would not preclude more collaborative legal approaches like mediation. In fact, legal representation used in concert with mediation could help to undermine some of the problematic power dynamics that play out in mediation, particularly in higher-conflict cases. With greater access to legal support in some form, families might begin to work proactively to determine what child custody arrangements would be best in the event of a relationship dissolution. However, any increase in the utilization of collaborative law should be undertaken only when all participants are knowledgeable about the gendered power dynamics that can manifest in collaborative law (Wiegers and Keet 2008). Cases where domestic violence is present require additional safeguards before, during, and after custody determination.

Some noncustodial mother participants recommended increased support for and acceptance of pro se litigants. Formally educated or not, some noncustodial mothers I came across had extensive working knowledge of the law. Some represented themselves in court with varying degrees of success, but nearly all who went pro se noted feeling some level of antagonism from the judges and opposing attorneys in their case. Community legal education would help those who want to represent themselves and could begin to level the playing field even in the absence of increased legal representation. Many noncustodial mothers became noncustodial because they lacked funds to engage in litigation or because they felt the system itself was too daunting. Some of these mothers agreed to terrible arrangements that they likely would not have had they had a better understanding of the law and some form of legal counsel. Increased community legal education in family law would be broadly beneficial. At the same time, the aim is to decrease the involvement of the legal apparatus through clarity and predictability of criteria for child custody and the elimination of biases embedded in current standards.

Psychological custody evaluations should not be used as disqualifier or a tiebreaker. They should be circumscribed to situations in which there are good reasons to believe that a child faces physical or emotional danger. Evaluations of this sort should require evaluators to have demonstrated expertise in domestic violence. Nonvalidated and unreliable psychological tests should be prohibited. Use of any psychological instrument should be justified and limited to the scope for which the instrument was developed and validated. Mental health professionals' main role should be to provide therapy to parents or children who are struggling with family changes. Access to our current mental health system is at least as stratified as the rest of the health care system. Destigmatizing mental illness and prioritizing mental health *as health care* would improve access. In the absence of large-scale institutional changes to access in mental health care, psychologists would do better to make their expertise available in the form of low-cost or free counseling than as custody evaluators. Increasing access to mental health support is certainly in line with the goals of reproductive justice.

In custody cases where there is a history of domestic violence, great care needs to be taken to ensure that the custody dispute does not itself become a form of continued abuse. There should be better buffers between perpetrators and targets of abuse at all times, even beyond the custody dispute. These buffers should not be dependent on the ability to pay. If custody is shared to any extent, safeguards should be in place for abused partners and children. The National Council of Juvenile and Family Court Judges (Dalton, Drozd, and Wong 2006) offers a judicial guide about custody evaluations in the context of domestic violence. There are some helpful caveats for judges contained in the guide; however, the gender-neutral framing of domestic violence in it does a disservice to empirically based scholarship on gender and family violence. All references to gender in the context of domestic violence are limited to the footnotes and bibliography. For example, the fact that most abuse is perpetrated by men against women is mentioned only in a footnote ten pages into the document, and citations of important work on the problematic interpretation of the Minnesota Multiphasic Personality Inventory in cases of domestic violence do not appear until twenty pages into the document. Gender should frame rather than annotate this guide. Finally, judges must be aware of and take seriously research that demonstrates the co-occurrence of child abuse with domestic violence. Any shared custody with an abuser should be seen as a significant potential danger to the child and their well-being. In the context of reproductive justice, children should be free from growing up in homes where they witness violence or experience its aftermath in any form, including its detrimental effects on their targeted parent. Those who care for children should be free from violence. If we take seriously the link between freedom from domestic violence and reproductive justice, mothers would not lose custody to their abusers because, by definition, residing with a parent who abused the child's other parent is harmful to that child.

While certainly not unique to them, many noncustodial mothers noted problems with enforcement of child custody agreements. A typical issue is the custodial parent's refusal to allow a child to see or talk on the phone to the noncustodial mother. Also at issue is the phenomenon that custody drifts back toward a mother over time. Some noncustodial mothers found themselves with more parenting time than initially agreed on. They welcomed the additional time, but even in cases where they regained primary custody, noncustodial mothers were hesitant to seek a corresponding change in child support. In cases where abuse had been present, it was not unusual for a noncustodial mother to say that she would forgo child support altogether if primary custody were returned to her. The more that states use child support formulas that account for shared custody, the more important the consequences for not exercising parenting time, particularly for the parent with fewer resources. The only recourse to enforcement issues for most seemed to be to go to court. However, a reproductive justice approach would hesitate at greater involvement of law enforcement in these instances.

Nobody enjoys paying child support. But child support systems should be informed by the extensive existing body of knowledge pertaining to gender, race, and class inequalities. The neoliberal dismantling of the social safety net means that the conflict over resources is shifted from a public debate of the use of public funds and privatized to a conflict between parents, neither of whom may have adequate resources, in the form of child support. When both parents are impoverished, in the absence of the social safety net, child support does not promote reproductive justice. We must also reexamine the punitive nature of child-support arrears policies. Taking away a driver's license or occupational license only serves to make everyone's situation worse when the parties are not upper-middle class. The loss of a driver's license can mean the loss of a job, which can quickly snowball financial decline.

Parents should not be punished for time taken out of the labor force for caregiving. Most of the time it is women who have taken on a stay-at-home parent role. Labor market reentry can be difficult and take time. In addition, the increasingly contingent nature of work means that those with less education and those in female-dominated fields may be more subject to disruptions in their work histories. It is time to reconsider what is meant by the term *willfully underemployed* when jobs that pay a living wage are in decline, particularly if one is female, working class, of color, or has a disability.

Some fathers' rights groups have called for custodial parents to account for how they spend all child support monies. This is not unlike calls to require more work or greater accounting of funds from welfare recipients. From a reproductive justice approach, it is important to resist calls for further oversight of those who depend on child support or public monies to provide a safe, healthy home for their family. The problem of child support cannot be solved within the child support or child custody arena; rather, the solution lies in addressing the ever-declining state of employment and the social welfare system. The state of social support brings us to the last piece of the reproductive justice framework, increasing social supports for caregiving.

Social Supports for Caregiving

If one thing is clear from speaking with noncustodial mothers for over a decade, it is that although we give lip service to the importance of mothers, we do not support the activities that constitute mothering or the people who undertake caregiving activities. What things do caregivers need? In the context of reproductive justice, the health and well-being of the whole family is on the table. When we support eliminating workplace discrimination or ending police violence against communities of color, these are matters of reproductive justice. When we support universal health care or programs to promote food security or clean drinking water, these are matters of reproductive justice. When we bring families of whatever form out of poverty, it is a matter of reproductive justice.

Caregivers also need their work to be recognized as including labor that requires some measure of skill. That labor, as we have established, is also quite gendered. There are a host of invisible forms of labor within caregiving that are unevenly distributed among genders. At the same time, we should be careful not to resurrect intensive mothering and the surveillance it brings, whether formal or informal. The standards of intensive mothering, by definition, are impossible to meet no matter one's social location. For some mothers, freedom from intensive mothering means that there might be fewer sports and after-school enrichment activities for children to attend. For others, particularly poor women and women of color, it means freedom from state surveillance and intervention for perceived failures to demonstrate intensive mothering.

Caregivers need time. There is no federal entitlement of workers to paid time off, whether it be sick time, vacation days, maternity leave, or family leave. Higher-status jobs come not only with better health insurance but also with more paid time off. Domestic violence survivors need workplace protections that acknowledge that the effects of domestic violence are felt beyond the home. They need a living wage with access to quality health care for themselves and for their children. Ideally, health care access would be uncoupled from the insurance that comes with some employment. Caregivers, particularly women, are less likely to occupy jobs that come with workplace benefits like paid time off and health insurance. If caregiving is as important as our cultural myths around motherhood would have us believe, there would be some form of universal minimal income support for caregivers. Caregivers also need time away from caregiving, whether it is to go to work or to do something else. Affordable, high-quality daycare is elusive even for those who make a living wage. But day care workers should make a living wage as well. Doing the math that provides a living wage to day care workers means that privatization of caregiving is not the answer. Respite for some is merely maintained on the backs of paid caregivers.

Caregivers need greater social support for their children. Recall the array of supports identified for military children and families because they are frequently required to move. Imagine if all families had access to mental health counseling, safe recreational and social opportunities, job counseling, support groups, relocation assistance, and help with school transitions. Imagine if these supports were easily engaged in times of crisis or family change. Restringing the social safety net would mean that caregivers need not "take on the Herculean task of being everything to their children because *no one else is doing anything to help them*" (Hallstein 2014, 304, emphasis in the original).

Toward Gender Equality?

Is noncustodial motherhood feminist? Does it challenge the gender order? One could hypothesize that disrupting patterns of mother custody postdivorce is feminist. Potentially, it is. But as it exists, noncustodial motherhood rests on a vast terrain of inequalities that affect all mothers, noncustodial or not. The individual-level gender bias one might experience at the hands of a custody evaluator is one thing. Deeply gendered social institutions that disadvantage women in ways that intersect with class and race when custody is contested is another. The experiences of noncustodial mothers and their trajectories into noncustodial motherhood take place in a largely discursively gender-neutral social space. Courts fear demonstrating gender bias by recognizing the importance of primary caregivers because that work is still primarily done by women. Psychologists may have revised the language of family discord or decoupled mental disorders from the gendered origins of hysteria and the like, but gender is built into the theoretical foundations, the seemingly objective tests, and the diagnoses themselves. Economic gender inequality puts women at a disadvantage in the face of an adversarial family court system that requires money to make it work in one's favor. This is how a mother, employed or not, who has been a primary caregiver can lose custody to a former partner who has never taken a child to the doctor. This is how survivors of domestic violence can lose custody to someone with a documented record of abusing them.

One of the conundrums of contemporary feminism is the unidirectional nature of some social changes. Women have moved into formerly male-dominated spheres (albeit not on equal footing) and have taken on responsibilities traditionally associated with men with little corresponding movement of men to shoulder the responsibilities that have fallen to women, employed or not. Mothers not having primary custody of their children potentially disrupts gender, although as we see in other arenas such as transnational motherhood, ideas about gender and motherhood reaccommodate to such disruptions in ways that often uphold the current gender order. The stigma that surrounds noncustodial mothers is an indication of this unidirectionality. A father with primary custody of his children sounds like social progress to embrace, but a mother without custody is, at best, suspect. Only when fathers participate in all aspects of caregiving inside families and before divorce can noncustodial motherhood be a sign of gender equality. Families that share caregiving before separation would more readily continue to share caregiving afterward, and regardless of the custodial arrangements, a mother without primary custody would still be a mother.

Notes

1. A CONTRADICTION IN TERMS

1. I use the convention of capitalizing Black but not white as an anti-racist practice that acknowledges the power and historicity of language that decenters whiteness. When capitalized, white as an identity is an intentional practice of white supremacists. Capitalizing Black is the recognition of a historically constructed racial identity that because of slavery cannot be traced via the continental geography of Africa (as white Americans can do with their European roots).

2. THE MOTHERS

1. Counting noncustodial parents and obtaining demographic data on them is quite difficult. For some discussion, see Meyer, Cancian, and Cook (2017).

2. Some were extreme to the point of physical and emotional abuse. These are discussed in greater detail in chapter 7.

3. SHE MUST HAVE DONE SOMETHING

1. Race, class, and other hierarchies among women will be addressed further in chapters 4 and 8.

2. A fuller discussion of how noncustodial mothers undo gender follows in the next chapter.

3. Biocentric ideas of motherhood emphasize the importance of genetic and physical aspects of motherhood.

4. STILL A MOTHER

1. Most often participants spoke with the assumption of a heterosexual, nuclear family, but some did not.

2. The concept of the friendly parent is taken up in greater detail in chapter 7 with regard to how it operates in the context of domestic violence.

3. Transnational motherhood—that is, when mothers migrate across national borders to work while their children stay home—is a form of noncustodial motherhood that the participants did not reference.

4. It is difficult to tell in every situation what prompts someone to enact gatekeeping against a noncustodial mother. There were two common scenarios. Sometimes the school was acting on directions from an ex-partner without proper documentation. Other times, the child and the mother having different addresses or last names seemed to invite scrutiny.

5. FATHER OF THE YEAR

1. Scholarship on LGBT families' household divisions of labor has increased in recent decades. For a review, see Brewster (2017), Goldberg (2013), or Patterson (2000). Generally, there is more egalitarian sharing in same-sex couples than in heterosexual couples. For some discussion of the household division of labor in families with trans men, see Pfeffer (2010).

2. The idyllic nuclear family with a breadwinning husband and stay-at-home wife has always been overestimated in our cultural imagination. The specialization model represents

a family form limited both in terms of historical time frame and by its class and race blindness. Poor men and women and men and women of color were much less likely to meet this cultural ideal.

3. This overrecognition of men's parenting is taken up in greater detail in the next section.

4. In Eva Feder Kittay and Ellen Feder's (2002) discussion of dependency and gender, they note that the illusion of independence rests on privatizing dependency through the nuclear family such that "the dependent is pathologized, feminized, and racialized" (4).

5. This is taken up in chapter 7. In Carla's situation, her ex-husband accused her new husband of sexually abusing her young daughters. He was eventually cleared of any wrongdoing.

6. It should be no surprise that in many cases of split-time joint custody, the bulk of the parenting time reverts to the mother over time (Emery 2005).

7. Many groups of women have always participated in paid work; the greatest changes in paid work for middle-class white women occurred after World War II, and today their employment patterns more closely resemble those of working-class women and women of color.

8. Available research has shown that men of color are more likely than white men to be active in day-to-day care of children (Jones and Mosher 2013).

6. MANUFACTURING BAD MOTHERS

1. Disability has actually been identified as a discriminatory issue in family court. See Lanci (2018) for an extensive overview and recommendations.

2. Lamb (2019) documents the daunting task she faces as a psychologist evaluating parental fitness in family court on behalf of the state. She raises a host of concerns about the process, ranging from legal coercion of parents to participate to reliance on dubious psychological assessment tools.

3. In 2018, the APA issued a revision of its 2007 *Guidelines for Psychological Practice with Girls and Women*. Among its recommendations is the idea that psychologists must recognize and acknowledge very real structurally based discriminatory and other experiences of women, people of color, and sexual minorities. The document includes a sizable bibliography. Nevertheless, considerable work on gender in psychology remains.

4. There exists a more general reproducibility crisis in psychology (Open Science Collaboration 2015), which further calls into question the heavy involvement of psychological paradigms in the context of child custody.

7. STILL IN AN ABUSIVE RELATIONSHIP

1. To be sure, noncustodial fathers may share the experience of unenforceable court orders where law enforcement declines to intervene. The concern here is the context of domestic violence.

2. Further complicating matters is the possibility that mothers could be prosecuted for a "failure to protect" a child from abuse, including by living in an environment where the child witnesses abuse of another (Kopels and Sheridan 2002).

8. LESSONS LEARNED

1. Making childcare affordable is going to require greater social support if it is not to be done on the backs of those who do perform caregiving. Currently, childcare jobs are very low paid, offer few benefits, and can fall outside the protections of the Fair Labor Standards Act.

2. This is not to say that the arrangements before the relationship's dissolution were arrived at unproblematically and through completely egalitarian means, just that we cannot assume that exogenous determination is any better in determining the best interests of the child.

Bibliography

Acker, Joan. 1990. "Hierarchies, Jobs, Bodies: A Theory of Gendered Organizations." *Gender and Society* 4 (2): 139–158.

Ackerman, Mark J., and Melissa C. Ackerman. 1997. "Custody Evaluation Practices: A Survey of Experienced Professionals (Revisited)." *Professional Psychology: Research and Practice* 28 (2): 137–145.

Adams, Michele A. 2006. "Framing Contests in Child Custody Disputes: Parental Alienation Syndrome, Child Abuse, Gender, and Fathers' Rights." *Family Law Quarterly* 40 (2): 315–338.

Addis, Michael E., and James R. Mahalik. 2003. "Men, Masculinity, and the Contexts of Help Seeking." *American Psychologist* 58 (1): 5–14.

Alanen, Leena. 1994. "Gender and Generation: Feminism and the 'Child Question.'" In *Childhood Matters: Social Theory, Practice, and Politics*, edited by Jens Qvortrup, Marjatta Bardy, Giovanni Sgritta, and Helmut Wintersberger, 27–42. Aldershot, UK: Avebury.

Albelda, Randy. 2001. "Fallacies of Welfare-to-Work Policies." *Annals of the American Academy of Political and Social Science* 577 (1): 66–78.

Ali, Alisha. 2004. "The Intersection of Racism and Sexism in Psychiatric Diagnosis." In *Bias in Psychiatric Diagnosis*, edited by Paula J. Caplan and Lisa Cosgrove, 71–75. Lanham, MD: Jason Aronson.

American Association of University Women. 2018. *The Simple Truth about the Gender Pay Gap*. Washington, DC: AAUW.

American Bar Association. 2008. *A Judge's Guide: Making Child-Centered Decisions in Custody Cases*. [Washington, DC]: ABA Center on Children and the Law.

American Psychiatric Association. 2013. *Diagnostic and Statistical Manual of Mental Disorders*. 5th ed. Arlington, VA: American Psychiatric Publishing.

American Psychological Association. 2010. "Guidelines for Child Custody Evaluations in Family Law Proceedings." *American Psychologist* 65 (9): 863–867.

Anderson, Julie. 2016. *Breadwinner Mothers by Race/Ethnicity and State*. Quick Figures, IWPR #Q054. Washington, DC: Institute for Women's Policy Research. https://iwpr.org/publications/breadwinner-mothers-by-raceethnicity-and-state/.

Anderson, Kristin L. 2010. "Conflict, Power, and Violence in Families." *Journal of Marriage and Family* 72 (3): 726–742.

Anderson, Kristin L., and Debra Umberson. 2001. "Gendering Violence: Masculinity and Power in Men's Accounts of Domestic Violence." *Gender and Society* 15 (3): 358–380.

Appel, Anne E., and George W. Holden. 1998. "The Co-occurrence of Spouse and Physical Child Abuse: A Review and Appraisal." *Journal of Family Psychology* 12 (4): 578–599.

Appleton, Susan Frelich. 2014. "Leaving Home? Domicile, Family, and Gender." *UC Davis Law Review* 47 (5): 1453–1519.

Archer, John. 2000. "Sex Differences in Aggression between Heterosexual Partners: A Meta-analytic Review." *Psychological Bulletin* 126 (5): 651–680.

Armstrong, Louise. 2004. "The Psychiatric Policing of Children." In *Bias in Psychiatric Diagnosis*, edited by Paula J. Caplan and Lisa Cosgrove, 99–107. Lanham, MD: Jason Aronson.

Arrighi, Barbara A., and David J. Maume. 2000. "Workplace Subordination and Men's Avoidance of Housework." *Journal of Family Issues* 21 (4): 464–487.

Arrigo, Bruce A. 2003. "Psychology and the Law: The Critical Agenda for Citizen Justice and Radical Social Change." *Justice Quarterly* 20 (2): 399–444.

Ashley, Wendy. 2014. "The Angry Black Woman: The Impact of Pejorative Stereotypes on Psychotherapy with Black Women." *Social Work in Public Health* 29 (1): 27–34.

Athan, Aurelie, and Heather L. Reel. 2015. "Maternal Psychology: Reflections on the 20th Anniversary of Deconstructing Developmental Psychology." *Feminism and Psychology* 25 (3): 311–325.

Atwood, Margaret. 1986. *The Handmaid's Tale*. Toronto: Mcclelland and Stewart.

Ault-Riche, Marianne. 1986. *Women and Family Therapy*. Rockville, MD: Aspen.

Barak, Azy, Meyran Boniel-Nissim, and John Suler. 2008. "Fostering Empowerment in Online Support Groups." *Computers in Human Behavior* 24 (5): 1867–1883.

Battered Mothers Custody Conference. n.d. Homepage. Accessed April 21, 2020. http://www.batteredmotherscustodyconference.org.

Berns, Sandra. 2005. "Mothers-in-Law: Lying Down for the Father Again." *Hecate* 31 (2): 78–89.

Bertoia, Carl, and Janice Drakich. 1993. "The Fathers' Rights Movement: Contradictions in Rhetoric and Practice." *Journal of Family Issues* 4 (4): 592–615.

Best Interests of the Child; Visitation, Va. Code Ann. § 20-124.3. (Current through the 2019 Regular Session of the General Assembly and Acts 2020, cc. 1, 198, 201, 202, 249, 255, 278, 356.)

Blair, Peter Q., and Bobby W. Chung. 2017. "Occupational Licensing Reduces Racial and Gender Wage Gap: Evidence from the Survey of Income and Program Participation." HCEO Working Group Paper Series 2017-050, Human Capital and Economic Opportunity Working Group, University of Chicago.

Blum, Linda M. 2007. "Mother-Blame in the Prozac Nation: Raising Kids with Invisible Disabilities." *Gender and Society* 21 (2): 202–226.

Bowles, Jerry J., Kaye K. Christian, Margaret B. Drew, and Katheryn L. Yetter. 2008. *A Judicial Guide to Child Safety in Custody Cases*. Reno, NV. National Council of Juvenile and Family Court Judges.

Boyd, Elizabeth R. 2002. "'Being There': Mothers Who Stay at Home, Gender, and Time." *Women's Studies International Forum* 25 (4): 463–470.

Boyd, Susan B. 2003. *Child Custody, Law, and Women's Work*. Ontario: Oxford University Press.

Bradbury, Katherine, and Jane Katz. 2002. "Women's Labor Market Involvement and Family Income Mobility When Marriages End." *New England Economic Review* Q4:41–74.

Braver, Sanford L., Marnie Whitely, and Christine Ng. 1994. "Who Divorced Whom? Methodological and Theoretical Issues." *Journal of Divorce and Remarriage* 20 (1–2): 1–20.

Breton, Pat. 2014. "Deserving Children and 'Risky Mothers': Situating Public Policy and Maternal/Child Welfare in the Canadian Context." In *Mothering in the Age of Neoliberalism*, edited by Melinda Vandenbeld Giles, 315–326. Butler, ON: Demeter.

Brewster, Melanie E. 2017. "Lesbian Women and Household Labor Division: A Systematic Review of Scholarly Research from 2000 to 2015." *Journal of Lesbian Studies* 21 (1): 47–69.

Bruch, Carol S. 2002. "Parental Alienation Syndrome and Parental Alienation: Getting It Wrong in Child Custody Cases." *Family Law Quarterly* 35 (3): 557–552.

Budig, Michelle J., and Paula England. 2001. "The Wage Penalty for Motherhood." *American Sociological Review* 66 (2): 204–225.

Bullock, Heather E. 2004. "Diagnosis of Low-Income Women." In *Bias in Psychiatric Diagnosis*, edited by Paula J. Caplan and Lisa Cosgrove, 115–120. Lanham, MD: Jason Aronson.

Burman, Erica. 2017. *Deconstructing Developmental Psychology.* 3rd ed. New York: Routledge.

Butler, D. H. 2014. "Other Mothers in Motion: Conceptualizing African American Stepmothers." In *Patricia Hill Collins: Reconceiving Motherhood*, edited by Kalia A. Story, 78–96. Bradford, ON: Demeter.

Cancian, Maria, Daniel R. Meyer, Patricia R. Brown, and Steven T. Cook. 2014. "Who Gets Custody Now? Dramatic Changes in Children's Living Arrangements after Divorce." *Demography* 51 (4): 1381–1396.

Caplan, Paula J. 2002. *The New Don't Blame Mother: Mending the Mother-Daughter Relationship.* New York: Harper-Collins.

——. 2004. "The Psychological Is Political." *PsycCRITIQUES* 9 (6): 794–797.

Caplan, Paula J., and Lisa Cosgrove, eds. 2004. *Bias in Psychiatric Diagnosis.* Lanham, MD: Jason Aronson.

Chalabi, Mona. 2015. "Are Moms Less Likely Than Dads to Pay Child Support?" FiveThirtyEight, February 26, 2015. https://fivethirtyeight.com/features/are-moms-less-likely-than-dads-to-pay-child-support/.

Chant, Sylvia. 2008. "The 'Feminisation of Poverty' and the 'Feminisation' of Anti-Poverty Programmes: Room for Revision?" *The Journal of Development Studies* 44 (2): 165–197.

Chapin, Angelina. 2016. "Dad's Rights: The Rise of Firms for Fathers Going through Divorce." *Guardian*, October 15, 2016. https://www.theguardian.com/lifeandstyle/2016/oct/15/fathers-rights-divorce-lawyers.

Chernin, Jeffrey, Janice Miner Holden, and Cynthia Chandler. 1997. "Bias in Psychological Assessment: Heterosexism." *Measurement and Evaluation in Counseling and Development* 30 (2): 68–76.

Chesler, Phyllis. 1972. *Women and Madness.* New York: Doubleday.

——. 1984. *Mothers on Trial.* Chicago: Lawrence Hill Books.

——. 2005. *Women and Madness.* New York: Palgrave Macmillan.

——. 2011. *Mothers on Trial.* Chicago: Lawrence Hill Books.

Chodorow, Nancy. 1978. *The Reproduction of Mothering.* Berkeley: University of California Press.

Clatterbaugh, Kenneth. 2000. "Literature of the U.S. Men's Movements." *Signs* 25 (3): 883–894.

Clumpus, Lynne. 1996. "No-Woman's Land: The Story of Noncustodial Mothers." *Feminism and Psychology* 6 (2): 237–244.

Cohn, D'Vera, Gretchen Livingston, and Wendy Wang. 2014. "After Decades of Decline, a Rise in Stay-at-Home Mothers." Pew Research Center, April 8, 2014. https://www.pewsocialtrends.org/2014/04/08/after-decades-of-decline-a-rise-in-stay-at-home-mothers/.

Collins, Patricia H. 1991a. *Black Feminist Thought: Knowledge, Consciousness, and the Politics of Empowerment.* New York: Routledge.

——. 1991b. "The Meaning of Motherhood in Black Culture and Black Mother-Daughter Relationships." In *Double Stitch: Black Women Write about Mothers and Daughters*, edited by Patricia Bell-Scott, 41–60. Boston: Beacon.

Coltrane, Scott, and Neal Hickman. 1992. "The Rhetoric of Rights and Needs: Moral Discourse in the Reform of Child Custody and Child Support Laws." *Social Problems* 39 (4): 400–420.

Connell, Raewyn. 1987. *Gender and Power: Society, the Person, and Sexual Politics.* Stanford, CA: Stanford University Press.

Connell, Raewyn. 2010. "Understanding Neoliberalism." In *Neoliberalism and Everyday Life*, edited by Susan Braedley and Meg Luxton, 22–36. Montreal: McGill-Queen's University Press.

Contratto, Susan, and Jessica Rossier. 2005. "Early Trends in Feminist Therapy and Practice." *Women and Therapy* 28 (3/4): 7–26.

Cosgrove, Lisa, and Bethany Riddle. 2004. "Gender Bias and Sex Distribution of Mental Disorders in the DSM-IV-TR." In *Bias in Psychiatric Diagnosis*, edited by Paula J. Caplan and Lisa Cosgrove, 127–140. Lanham, MD: Jason Aronson.

Cozzolino, Elizabeth, and Christine L. Williams. 2017. "Child Support Queens and Disappointing Dads: Gender and Child Support Compliance." *Social Currents* 4 (3): 228–245.

Crenshaw, Kimberle. 1991. "Mapping the Margins: Intersectionality, Identity Politics, and Violence against Women of Color." *Stanford Law Review* 43 (6): 1241–1299.

Criteria and Procedure in Awarding Custody and Visitation; Best Interest of the Child, HRS § 571-46. (This document is current through Ch. 1 of the 2020 Legislative Session. Subject to changes by Revisor pursuant to HRS 23G-15.)

Crowley, Jocelyn Elise. 2008. *Defiant Dads: Fathers' Rights Activists in America*. Ithaca, NY: Cornell University Press.

Dallam, Stephanie J. 1999. "Parental Alienation Syndrome: Is It Scientific?" Leadership Council on Child Abuse and Interpersonal Violence. http://leadershipcouncil.org/1/res/dallam/3.html.

Dalton, Clare, Leslie M. Drozd, and Frances Q. F. Wong. 2006. *Navigating Custody and Visitation Evaluations in Cases with Domestic Violence: A Judge's Guide*. Reno, NV: National Council of Juvenile and Family Court Judges.

Deleuze, Gilles, and Felix Guattari. 1988. *A Thousand Plateaus: Capitalism and Schizophrenia*. Minneapolis: University of Minnesota Press.

Deutsch, Francine. 2007. "Undoing Gender." *Gender and Society* 21 (1): 106–127.

DiFonzo, J. Herbie. 2014. "From the Rule of One to Shared Parenting: Custody Presumptions in Law and Policy." *Family Court Review* 52 (2): 213–239.

DiMaggio, Paul J., and Walter Powell. 1983. "The Iron Cage Revisited: Institutional Isomorphism and Collective Rationality in Organizational Fields." *American Sociological Review* 48 (2): 147–160.

Dore, Margaret K. 2004. "The 'Friendly Parent' Concept: A Flawed Factor for Child Custody." *Loyola Journal of Public Interest Law* 6:41–56.

Douglas, Susan, and Meredith Michaels. 2004. *The Mommy Myth: The Idealization of Motherhood and How It Has Undermined Women*. New York: Free Press.

Downey, Douglas B. 1994. "The School Performance of Children from Single-Mother and Single-Father Families: Economic or Interpersonal Deprivation?" *Journal of Family Issues* 15 (1): 129–147.

Duffy, Mignon. 2007. "Doing the Dirty Work: Gender, Race, and Reproductive Labor in Historical Perspective." *Gender and Society* 21 (3): 313–336.

Dutton, Mary Ann, Lisa A. Goodman, and Lauren Bennett. 1999. "Court-Involved Battered Women's Responses to Violence: The Role of Psychological, Physical, and Sexual Abuse." *Violence and Victims* 14 (1): 89–104.

Edelson, Jeffrey L. 1999. "The Overlap between Child Maltreatment and Women Battering." *Violence against Women* 5 (2): 134–154.

Edin, Kathryn, Laura Tach, and Ronald Mincy. 2009. "Claiming Fatherhood: Race and the Dynamics of Paternal Involvement among Unmarried Men." *Annals of the American Academy of Political and Social Science* 621 (1): 149–177.

Ellis, Jonathan. 2014. "Shared Parenting Could Be New Divorce Outcome." *USA Today*, January 27, 2014. https://www.usatoday.com/story/news/nation/2014/01/27/shared-parenting-could-be-new-divorce-outcome/4950111/.

El-Zein, Michael. 2014. "Gender-Conscious Confrontation: The Accuser-Obligation Approach Revisited." *Michigan Journal of Gender and Law* 21 (1): 177–215.

Emery, Robert E. 1995. "Divorce Mediation: Negotiating Agreements and Renegotiating Relationships." *Family Relations* 44 (4): 377–383.

——. 2005. "Parental Alienation Syndrome: Proponents Bear the Burden of Proof." *Family Court Review* 43 (1): 8–13.

Emery, Robert E., Lisa Laumann-Billings, Mary C. Waldron, David A. Sbarra, and Peter Dillon. 2001. "Child Custody Mediation and Litigation: Custody, Contact, and Co-parenting 12 Years after Initial Dispute Resolution." *Journal of Consulting and Clinical Psychology* 69 (2): 323–332.

Emery, Robert E., Randy K. Otto, and William T. O'Donohue. 2005. "A Critical Assessment of Child Custody Evaluations: Limited Science and a Flawed System." *Psychological Science in the Public Interest* 6 (1): 1–29.

Ennis, Linda R., ed. 2014. *Intensive Mothering: The Cultural Contradictions of Modern Motherhood.* Butler, ON: Demeter.

Epstein, Cynthia F. 1981. *Women in Law.* New York: Basic Books.

Erickson, Steven K., Scott O. Lilienfeld, and Michael J. Vitacco. 2007. "Psychological Testing and Child Custody Evaluations in Family Court: A Dialogue." *Family Court Review* 45 (2): 157–174.

Factors to Consider When Awarding Custody, 23 Pa.C.S. § 5328. (Pa.C.S. documents are current through 2020 Regular Session Act 34; P.S. documents are current through 2020 Regular Session Act 34.)

Firestone, Shulamith. 1970. *The Dialectic of Sex: The Case for Feminist Revolution.* New York: Bantam.

Foucault, Michel. 1988. *Madness and Civilization: A History of Insanity in the Age of Reason.* New York: Vintage Books.

Fox, John. 2004. "How Men's Movement Participants View Each Other." *Journal of Men's Studies* 12 (2): 103–118.

Frantz, Carolyn J. 2000. "Eliminating Consideration of Parental Wealth in Post-divorce Child Custody Disputes." *Michigan Law Review* 99 (1): 216–237.

Friedan, Betty. 1963. *The Feminine Mystique.* New York: Norton.

Friend of the Court Bureau. 2016. *Custody and Parenting Time Investigation Manual.* Lansing, MI: Friend of the Court Bureau.

Fondas, Nanette. 2013. "The Many Myths about Mothers Who Opt Out." *Atlantic*, March 25, 2013. https://www.theatlantic.com/sexes/archive/2013/03/the-many-myths-about-mothers-who-opt-out/274354/.

Gardner, Richard A. 1985. "Recent Trends in Divorce and Custody Litigation." *Academy Forum* 29 (2): 3–7.

Garner, Terri. 1989. "Child Custody Mediation: A Proposed Alternative to Litigation." *Journal of Dispute Resolution* 1989 (8): 139–155.

Garvin, Zoe. 2016. "The Unintended Consequences of Rebuttable Presumptions on Child Custody in Domestic Violence Cases." *Family Law Quarterly* 50 (1): 173–192.

General Accounting Office. 2001. *Military Personnel: Longer Time between Moves Related to Higher Satisfaction and Retention.* Washington, DC: US General Accounting Office.

Gibson, Pamela Reed. 2004. "Histrionic Personality." In *Bias in Psychiatric Diagnosis*, edited by Paula J. Caplan and Lisa Cosgrove, 201–206. Lanham, MD: Jason Aronson.

Giles, Melinda Vandenbeld, ed. 2014. *Mothering in the Age of Neoliberalism.* Butler, ON: Demeter.

Gilligan, Carol. 1982. *In a Different Voice: Psychological Theory and Women's Development.* Cambridge, MA: Harvard University Press.

Glauber, Rebecca. 2011. "Limited Access: Gender, Occupational Composition, and Flexible Work Scheduling." *Sociological Quarterly* 52 (3): 472–494.

Goffman, Erving. 1959. *The Presentation of Self in Everyday Life*. Garden City, NY: Dou-
    bleday.
———. 1961. *Asylums: Essays on the Social Situation of Mental Patients and Other Inmates*.
    Garden City, NY: Anchor Books.
———. 1963. *Stigma: Notes on the Management of Spoiled Identity*. Englewood Cliffs, NJ:
    Prentice-Hall.
Golan, Limor, and Usa Kerdnunvong. 2016. "Home Economics: The Changing Work Roles
    of Wives and Husbands." *Regional Economist*. October 2016.
Goldberg, Abbie E. 2013. "'Doing' and 'Undoing' Gender: The Meaning and Division of
    Housework in Same-Sex Couples." *Journal of Family Theory and Review* 5 (2): 85–104.
Goldner, Virginia. 1985. "Feminism and Family Therapy." *Family Process* 24 (1): 31–47.
Goldscheid, Julie. 2014. "Gender Neutrality and the 'Violence against Women' Frame."
    University of Miami Race and Social Justice Law Review 5 (2): 307–324.
Goldscheider, Frances K., and Leora Lawton. 1998. "Family Experiences and the Erosion
    of Support for Intergenerational Coresidence." *Journal of Marriage and the Family*
    60 (3): 623–632.
Grall, Timothy. 2016. *Custodial Mothers and Fathers and Their Child Support: 2013*. Cur-
    rent Population Reports. Washington, DC: US Census Bureau.
———. 2018. *Custodial Mothers and Fathers and Their Child Support: 2015*. Current Popu-
    lation Reports. Washington, DC: US Census Bureau.
Grams, Mary. 2004. "Guardians Ad Litem and the Cycle of Domestic Violence: How the
    Recommendations Turn." *Law and Inequality* 22 (1): 105–139.
Greenspan, Miriam. 1983. *A New Approach to Women and Therapy*. New York: McGraw-Hill.
Gross, Christi L., Brianna Turgeon, Tiffany Taylor, and Kasey Lansberry. 2014. "State In-
    terviention in Intensive Mothering: Neo-liberalism, New Paternalism, and Poor
    Mothers in Ohio." In *Intensive Mothering: The Cultural Contradictions of Modern
    Motherhood*, edited by Linda Rose Ennis, 163–179. Bradford, ON: Demeter.
Gruber, Aya. 2012. "A 'Neo-feminist' Assessment of Rape and Domestic Violence Law Re-
    form." *Journal of Gender, Race and Justice* 15 (3): 583–615.
Gupta, Sanjiv. 2007. "Autonomy, Dependence, or Display? The Relationship between Mar-
    ried Women's Earnings and Housework." *Journal of Marriage and Family* 69 (2):
    399–417.
Gustafson, Diana L. 2005. *Unbecoming Mothers*. New York: Routledge.
Hall, Elaine J., and Marnie Salupo Rodriguez. 2003. "The Myth of Postfeminism." *Gender
    and Society* 17 (6): 878–902.
Hallstein, Lynn O'Brien. 2014. "When Neoliberalism Intersects with Post-Second Wave
    Mothering: Reinforcing Neo-traditional American Family Configurations and Exac-
    erbating the Post-Second Wave Crisis in Femininity." In *Mothering in the Age of Neo-
    liberalism*, edited by Melinda Vandenbeld Giles, 297–314. Bradford, ON: Demeter.
Hart, Barbara J. 1990. "Gentle Jeopardy: The Further Endangerment of Battered Women
    and Children in Custody Mediation." *Mediation Quarterly* 7 (4): 326–327.
Haselschwerdt, Megan L., Jennifer L. Hardesty, and Jason D. Hans. 2011. "Custody Evalu-
    ators' Beliefs about Domestic Violence Allegations during Divorce: Feminist and
    Family Violence Perspectives." *Journal of Interpersonal Violence* 26 (8): 1694–1719.
Hays, Sharon H. 1996. *The Cultural Contradictions of Motherhood*. New Haven, CT: Yale
    University Press.
Heilbrun, Kirk. 1992. "The Role of Psychological Testing in Forensic Assessment." *Law and
    Human Behavior* 16 (3): 257–272.
Heilman, Madeline E. 2001. "Description and Prescription: How Gender Stereotypes Pre-
    vent Women's Ascent up the Organizational Ladder." *Journal of Social Issues* 57 (4):
    657–674.

Heim, Sheila, Helen Grieco, Sue Dipaola, and Rachel Allen. 2002. *Family Court Report*. Sacramento: California National Organization for Women.

Helleiner, Jane. 1999. "Toward a Feminist Anthropology of Childhood." *Atlantis* 24 (1): 27–38.

Herek, Gregory M., Keith F. Widaman, and John P. Capitanio. 2005. "When Sex Equals AIDS: Symbolic Stigma and Heterosexual Adults' Inaccurate Beliefs about Sexual Transmission of AIDS." *Social Problems* 52 (1): 15–37.

Herrenkohl, Todd I., Cynthia Sousa, Emiko A. Tajima, Roy C. Herrenkohl, and Carrie A. Moylan. 2008. "Intersection of Child Abuse and Children's Exposure to Domestic Violence." *Trauma, Violence, and Abuse* 9 (2): 84–99.

Hochschild, Arlie R. 1989. *The Second Shift: Working Parents and the Revolution at Home*. New York: Penguin Books.

——. 2000. "Global Care Chains and Emotional Surplus Value." In *On the Edge: Living with Global Capitalism*, edited by Will Hutton and Anthony Giddens, 130–146. London: Jonathan Cape.

Hondagneu-Sotelo, Pierette, and Ernestine Avila. 1997. "'I'm Here, but I'm There': The Meanings of Latina Transnational Motherhood." *Gender and Society* 11 (5): 548–571.

Horney, Karen. 1967. *Feminine Psychology*. New York: Norton.

Hundley, Heather L., and Sara E. Hayden. 2016. *Mediated Moms: Contemporary Challenges to the Motherhood Myth*. New York: Peter Lang.

Huntington, Clare. 2018. "The Empirical Turn in Family Law." *Columbia Law Review* 118 (1): 227–312.

Hyde, Janet S. 2007. "New Directions in the Study of Gender Similarities and Differences." *Current Directions in Psychological Science* 16 (5): 259–263.

——. 2014. "Gender Differences and Similarities." *Annual Review of Psychology* 65:373–398.

Jaffe, Peter G., Claire V. Crooks, and Samantha E. Poisson. 2003. "Common Misconceptions in Addressing Domestic Violence in Child Custody Disputes." *Juvenile and Family Court Journal* 54 (4): 57–67.

Jasinski, Jana, Lindsey Blumenstein, and Rachel Morgan. 2014. "Testing Johnson's Typology: Is There Gender Symmetry in Intimate Terrorism?" *Violence and Victims* 29 (1): 73–88.

Jimenez, Mary Ann. 1997. "Gender and Psychiatry: Psychiatric Conceptions of Mental Disorders in Women, 1960–1994." *Affilia* 12 (2): 154–175.

Johnson, Margaret E. 2008. "Redefining Harm, Reimagining Remedies, and Reclaiming Domestic Violence Law." *UC Davis Law Review* 42 (4): 1107–1164.

Johnson, Michael E. 1995. "Patriarchal Terrorism and Common Couple Violence: Two Forms of Violence against Women." *Journal of Marriage and Family* 57 (2): 283–294.

——. 2006. "Conflict and Control Gender Symmetry and Asymmetry in Domestic Violence." *Violence against Women* 12 (11): 1003–1018.

Johnson, Michael P., and Kathleen J. Ferraro. 2000. "Research on Domestic Violence in the 1990s: Making Distinctions." *Journal of Marriage and the Family* 64 (2): 948–963.

Johnson, Michael P., Janele M. Leone, and Yili Xu. 2014. "Intimate Terrorism and Situational Couple Violence in General Surveys: Ex-Spouses Required." *Violence against Women* 20 (2): 186–207.

Johnson, Nancy E., Dennis P. Saccuzzo, and Wendy J. Koen. 2005. "Child Custody Mediation in Cases of Domestic Violence: Empirical Evidence of a Failure to Protect." *Violence against Women* 11 (8): 1022–1053.

Jones, Jo, and William D. Mosher. 2013. "Fathers' Involvement with Their Children: United States, 2006–2010." *National Health Statistics Reports* 71.

Jordan, Ana. 2018. "Masculinizing Care? Gender, Ethics of Care, and Fathers' Rights Groups." *Men and Masculinities*. Published ahead of print, May 22, 2018. https://doi.org/10.1177/1097184X18776364.

Kanner, Leo. 1943. "Autistic Disturbances of Affective Contact." *Nervous Child* 2:217–250.

Kelly, Joan B. 2007. "Children's Living Arrangements Following Separation and Divorce: Insights from Empirical and Clinical Research." *Family Process* 46 (1): 35–52.

Kelly, Joan B., and Janet R. Johnson. 2001. "The Alienated Child: A Reformulation of Parental Alienation Syndrome." *Family Court Review* 39 (3): 249–266.

Kelly, Robert F., Laura Redenbach, and William C. Rinaman. 2005. "Determinants of Sole and Joint Physical Custody Arrangements in a National Sample of Divorces." *American Journal of Family Law* 19 (1): 25–43.

Kittay, Eva Feder, and Ellen K. Feder. 2002. *The Subject of Care: Feminist Perspectives on Dependency.* Lanham, MD: Rowman and Littlefield.

Klaff, Ramsay Laing. 1982. "The Tender Years Doctrine: A Defense." *California Law Review* 70 (2): 335–372.

Knudson-Martin, Carmen. 1994. "The Female Voice: Applications to Bowen's Family Systems Theory." *Journal of Marital and Family Therapy* 20 (1): 35–44.

Kochhar, Rakesh, Kim Parker, and Molly Rohal. 2015. *Three in Ten U.S. Jobs Are Held by the Self-Employed and the Workers They Hire: Hiring More Prevalent among Self-Employed Asians, Whites, and Men.* Washington, DC: Pew Research Center, October.

Kopels, Sandra, and Marcie Chesnut Sheridan. 2002. "Adding Legal Insult to Injury: Battered Women, Their Children, and the Failure to Protect." *Affilia* 17 (1): 9–29.

Kuennen, Tamara L. 2010. "Private Relationships and Public Problems: Applying Principles of Relational Contract Theory to Domestic Violence." *Brigham Young University Law Review* 2010 (2): 515–595.

Kuperberg, Arielle, and Pamela Stone. 2008. "The Media Depiction of Women Who Opt Out." *Gender and Society* 22 (4): 497–517.

Lachance-Grzela, Mylene, and Genevieve Bouchard. 2010. "Why Do Women Do the Lion's Share of Housework? A Decade of Research." *Sex Roles* 63 (11–12): 767–780.

Ladd-Taylor, Molly, and Lauri Umansky, eds. 1998. *"Bad" Mothers: The Politics of Blame in Twentieth-Century America.* New York: New York University Press.

Lamb, Sharon. 2019. *The Not Good Enough Mother.* Boston: Beacon.

Lanci, Michael. 2018. "In the Child's Best Interests? Rethinking Consideration of Physical Disability in Child Custody Disputes." *Columbia Law Review* 118 (3): 875–914.

Land, Stephanie. 2016. "Free-Range Parenting Is a Privilege for the Rich and White." *The Establishment*, August 9, 2016. https://medium.com/the-establishment/free-range -parenting-is-a-privilege-for-the-white-and-affluent-1ac7ce8a4b8c.

Landrine, Hope, Elizabeth A. Klonoff, and Alice Brown-Collins. 1992. "Cultural Diversity and Methodology in Feminist Psychology: Critique, Proposal, Empirical Example." *Psychology of Women Quarterly* 16 (2): 145–163.

Lee, M., and M. S. Rendalli. 2001. "Self-Employment Disadvantage in the Working Lives of Blacks and Females." *Population Research and Policy Review* 20 (4): 291–320.

Legal Momentum. 2005. *Legal Resource Kit: Domestic Violence and Child Custody.* New York: Legal Momentum. https://www.legalmomentum.org/sites/default/files/kits /dv11resources-1.pdf.

Leslie, Leigh A. 1995. "Psychotherapy: The Evolving Treatment of Gender, Ethnicity, and Sexual Orientation in Marital and Family Therapy." *Family Relations* 44 (4): 359–381.

Levin, Amy, and Linda G. Mills. 2003. "Fighting for Child Custody When Domestic Violence Is at Issue: Survey of State Laws." *Social Work* 48 (4): 463–470.

Lin, Luona, Andrew Nigrinis, Peggy Christidis, and Karen Stam. 2015. *Demographics of the U.S. Psychology Workforce: Findings from the American Community Survey.* Washington, DC: American Psychological Association, Center for Workforce Studies.

Linder, Meadow. 2004. "The Construction of Illness." In *Bias in Psychiatric Diagnosis*, edited by Paula J. Caplan and Lisa Cosgrove, 3–7. Lanham, MD: Jason Aronson.

Lindsay, K. A., and T. A. Widiger. 1995. "Sex and Gender Bias in Self-Report Personality Disorder Inventories: Item Analysis of the MCMI-II, MMPI, and PDQ-R." *Journal of Personality Assessment* 65 (1): 1–20.

Lorber, Judith. 1997. *Gender and the Social Construction of Illness*. Thousand Oaks, CA: Sage.

Lorde, Audre. 1984. *Sister Outsider*. Freedom, CA: Crossing.

Love, David A. 2008. "On the Criminalization of Black Motherhood." *Black Commentator*, May 8, 2008. http://blackcommentator.com/276/276_col_criminalization_of_black_motherhood.html.

Ludwig, Doreen. 2015. *Motherless America: Confronting Welfare's Fatherhood Custody Program*. CreateSpace Independent Publishing Platform.

Mantovani, Nadia, and Hilary Thomas. 2014. "Stigma, Intersectionality, and Motherhood: Exploring the Relations of Stigma in the Accounts of Black Teenage Mothers 'Looked After' by the State." *Social Theory and Health* 12 (1): 45–62.

Maryland General Assembly, Commission on Child-Custody Decision-Making. 2014. *Final Report*. HB 687/CH 633, 2013 (MSAR #9554).

Mason, Mary Ann. 1994. *From Father's Property to Children's Rights: The History of Child Custody in the United States*. New York: Columbia University Press.

Mattingly, Marybeth J., and Suzanne M. Bianchi. 2003. "Gender Differences in the Quantity and Quality of Free Time: The U.S. Experience." *Social Forces* 81 (3): 999–1030.

Maume, David J. 2011. "Reconsidering the Temporal Increase in Fathers' Time with Children." *Journal of Family Economic Issues* 32 (3): 411–423.

Maume, David J., Rachel A. Sebastian, and Anthony R. Bardo. 2009. "Gender Differences in Sleep Disruption among Retail Food Workers." *American Sociological Review* 74 (6): 898–1007.

McHenry, Kristen Abatsis and Denise L. Schultz. 2014. "Skinny Jeans: Perfection and Competition in Motherhood." In *Intensive Mothering: The Cultural Contradictions of Modern Motherhood*, edited by Linda Rose Ennis, 299–312. Bradford, ON: Demeter.

McLellan, Betty. 1999. "The Prostitution of Psychotherapy: A Feminist Critique." *British Journal of Guidance and Counseling* 27 (3): 325–337.

Meier, Joan S. 2009. "A Historical Perspective on Parental Alienation Syndrome and Parental Alienation." *Journal of Child Custody* 6 (3): 232–257.

Mercer, Jean. 2009. "Child Custody Evaluations, Attachment Theory, and an Attachment Measure: The Science Remains Limited." *Scientific Review of Mental Health Practice* 7 (1): 37–54.

Metzl, Jonathan. 2014. "The New Science of Blaming Moms." MSNBC, July 16, 2014. Last updated July 21, 2014. http://www.msnbc.com/melissa-harris-perry/the-new-science-blaming-moms.

Meyer, Daniel R., Maria Cancian, and Steven T. Cook. 2017. "The Growth in Shared Custody in the United States: Patterns and Implications." *Family Court Review* 55 (4): 500–512.

Mills, C. Wright. 1959. *The Sociological Imagination*. New York: Oxford University Press.

Minaker, Joanne, and Brian Hogeveen, eds. 2015. *Criminalized Mothers, Criminalizing Mothering*. Bradford, ON: Demeter.

Mink, Gwendolyn. 1998. *Welfare's End*. Ithaca, NY: Cornell University Press.

Monaghan, Lee F. 2017. "Re-framing Weight-Related Stigma: From Spoiled Identity to Macro-social Structures." *Social Theory and Health* 15 (2): 182–205.

Mulder, Clara H., and Michael Wagner. 2010. "Union Dissolution and Mobility: Who Moves from the Family Home after Separation?" *Journal of Marriage and Family* 72 (5): 1263–1273.

Nagel, Thomas. 1986. *The View from Nowhere*. New York: Oxford University Press.

National Conference of State Legislatures. 2002. *Child Support 101: An Introductory Course for Legislators*. Washington, DC: National Conference of State Legislatures.

——. 2014. "License Restrictions for Failure to Pay Child Support." https://www.ncsl.org/Research/Human-Services/License-Restrictions-For-Failure-To-Pay-Child-Support.Aspx.

Neustein, Amy, and Michael Lesher. 2005. *From Madness to Mutiny: Why Mothers Are Running from the Family Courts—and What Can Be Done about It*. Boston: Northeastern University Press.

Nicholson, Robert A., and Steve Norwood. 2000. "The Quality of Forensic Psychological Assessments, Reports, and Testimony: Acknowledging the Gap between Promise and Practice." *Law and Human Behavior* 24 (1): 9–44.

Oakley, Ann. 1981. "Interviewing Women: A Contradiction in Terms." In *Doing Feminist Research*, edited by H. Roberts, 30–61. London: Routledge and Kegan Paul.

——. 1994. "Women and Children First and Last: Parallels and Differences between Children's and Women's Studies." In *Children's Childhoods: Observed and Experienced*, edited by Berry Mayall, 13–32. London: Falmer.

Ogloff, James R. 2000. "Two Steps Forward and One Step Backward: The Law and Psychology Movement(s) in the 20th Century." *Law and Human Behavior* 24 (4): 457–483.

Open Science Collaboration. 2015. "Estimating the Reproducibility of Psychological Science." *Science* 349 (6251): Aac4716.

Palladino, Hallie. 2014. "The Cultural Contradictions of Fatherhood: Is There an Ideology of Intensive Fathering?" In *Intensive Mothering: The Cultural Contradictions of Modern Motherhood*, edited by Linda Rose Ennis, 280–298. Bradford, ON: Demeter.

Park, Shelley M. 2013. *Mothering Queerly, Queering Motherhood: Resisting Monomaternalism in Adoptive, Lesbian, Blended, and Polygamous Families*. Albany: State University of New York Press.

Parrenas, Rhacel S. 2015. *Servants of Globalization: Migration and Domestic Work*. Palo Alto, CA: Stanford University Press.

Patterson, Charlotte J. 2000. "Family Relationships of Lesbians and Gay Men." *Journal of Marriage and the Family* 62 (4): 1052–1069.

Pearson, Kim H. 2012. "Sexuality in Child Custody Decisions." *Family Court Review* 50 (2): 280–288.

Pepiton, M. Brianna, Lindsey J. Alvis, Kenneth Allen, and Gregory Logid. 2012. "Is Parental Alienation Disorder a Valid Concept? Not according to Scientific Evidence." *Journal of Child Sexual Abuse* 21 (2): 244–253.

Pescosolido, Bernice A. 2013. "The Public Stigma of Mental Illness: What Do We Think; What Do We Know; What Can We Prove?" *Journal of Health and Social Behavior* 54 (1): 1–21.

Pescosolido, Bernice A., and Jack K. Martin 2015. "The Stigma Complex." *Annual Review of Sociology* 41:87–116.

Pew Charitable Trust. 2018. "American Families Face a Growing Rent Burden." April 19, 2018. https://www.pewtrusts.org/en/research-and-analysis/reports/2018/04/american-families-face-a-growing-rent-burden.

Pfeffer, Carla A. 2010. "Women's Work? Women Partners of Transgender Men Doing Housework and Emotion Work." *Journal of Marriage and Family* 72 (1): 165–183.

Pierce, Jennifer L. 1996. *Gender Trials: Emotional Lives in Contemporary Law Firms*. Berkeley: University of California Press.

Polatnick, M. Rivka. 1996. "Diversity in Women's Liberation Ideology: How a Black and White Group of the 1960s Viewed Motherhood." *Signs* 21 (3): 679–706.

Press, Sharon. 2013. "Family Court Services: A Reflection on 50 Years of Contributions." *Family Court Review* 51 (1): 48–55.

Price, Kimala. 2010. "What Is Reproductive Justice? How Women of Color Activists Are Redefining the Pro-choice Paradigm." *Meridians* 10 (2): 42–65.

Qvortrup, Jens, Mariata Bardy, Giovanni Sgritta, and Helmut Wintersberger. 1994. *Childhood Matters: Social Theory, Practice, and Politics*. Aldershot, UK: Avebury.

Rich, Adrienne. 1976. *Of Woman Born: Motherhood as Experience and Institution*. New York: Norton.

Rivera, Echo A., April M. Zeoli, and Cris M. Sullivan. 2012. "Abused Mothers' Safety Concerns and Court Mediators' Custody Recommendations." *Family Violence* 27 (4): 321–332.

Rogers, Jackie Krasas. 2000. *Temps: The Many Faces of the Changing Workplace*. Ithaca, NY: Cornell University Press.

Rose, Elizabeth. 1998. "Taking on a Mother's Job: Day Care in the 1920s and 1930s." In *"Bad" Mothers: The Politics of Blame in Twentieth-Century America*, edited by Molly Ladd-Taylor and Lauri Umansky, 67–98. New York: New York University Press.

Rosewater, Lynne B. 1985. "Schizophrenic, Borderline or Battered?" In *Handbook of Feminist Therapy: Women's Issues in Psychotherapy*, edited by Lynne B. Rosewater and Lenore E. A. Walker. New York: Springer.

Rothman, Barbara Katz. 1989. *Recreating Motherhood: Ideology and Technology in a Patriarchal Society*. New York: Norton.

Rowlingson, Karen, and Stephen McKay. 2005. "Lone Motherhood and Socio-economic Disadvantage: Insights from Quantitative and Qualitative Evidence." *Sociological Review* 53 (1): 30–49.

Rubin, Gayle. 1984. "Thinking Sex: Notes for a Radical Theory of the Politics of Sexuality." In *Pleasure and Danger: Exploring Female Sexuality*, edited by Carol Vance. London: Routledge and Kegan Paul.

Ruddick, Sara. 1980. "Maternal Thinking." *Feminist Studies* 6 (2): 342–367.

Rustin, Michael. 2015. "Psychotherapy in a Neoliberal World." *European Journal of Psychotherapy and Counselling* 17 (3): 225–239.

Saccuzzo, Dennis P., Nancy E. Johnson, and Wendy J. Koen. 2003. *Mandatory Custody Mediation: Empirical Evidence of Increased Risk for Domestic Violence Victims and Their Children*. Washington, DC: US Department of Justice.

Saunders, Daniel G., Kathleen C. Faller, and Richard M. Tolman. 2012. *Child Custody Evaluators' Beliefs about Domestic Abuse Allegations: Their Relationship to Evaluator Demographics, Background, Domestic Violence Knowledge and Custody-Visitation Recommendations*. Final technical report submitted to the National Institute of Justice. Washington, DC: US Department of Justice.

Schepard, Andrew. 2004. "The Model Standards of Practice for Family and Divorce Mediation" in *Divorce and Family Mediation: Models, Techniques, and Applications* edited by Jay Folberg, Ann L. Milne, and Peter Salem, 516–543. New York: The Guilford Press.

Schulte, Brigid. 2014. *Overwhelmed: How to Work, Love, and Play When No One Has the Time*. New York: Sarah Crichton Books, Farrar, Straus, and Giroux.

Shafer, Kevin, and Spencer L. James. 2013. "Gender Gap in Remarriage: Gender and Socioeconomic Status Differences in First and Second Marriage Formation." *Journal of Marriage and Family* 75 (3): 544–564.

Singh, Ilina. 2004. "Doing Their Jobs: Mothering with Ritalin in a Culture of Mother-Blame." *Social Science and Medicine* 59 (6): 1193–1205.

SisterSong. n.d. Homepage. Accessed April 22, 2020. https://www.sistersong.net/mission/.

Smith, Andrea. 2005. "Beyond Pro-choice versus Pro-life: Women of Color and Reproductive Justice." *NWSA Journal* 17 (1): 119–140.

Smith, Dorothy. 2005. *Institutional Ethnography: A Sociology for People.* Lanham, MD: Altamira.

Smith, Holly. 2016. "Parental Alienation Syndrome: Fact or Fiction? The Problem with Its Use in Child Custody Cases." *University of Massachusetts Law Review* 11 (1): 64–99.

Smith, Morag. 1997. "Psychology's Undervaluation of Single Motherhood." *Feminism and Psychology* 7 (4): 529–532.

Solinger, Rickie. 1998. "Poisonous Choice." In *"Bad" Mothers: The Politics of Blame in Twentieth-Century America*, edited by Molly Ladd-Taylor and Lauri Umansky, 381–402. New York: New York University Press.

Starnes, Cynthia Lee. 2007. "Mothers, Myths, and the Law of Divorce: One More Feminist Case for Partnership." *William & Mary Journal of Women and the Law* 13 (1): 203–233.

Stelloh, Tim. 2014. "Do Courts Use a Controversial Theory to Punish Mothers Who Allege Abuse." Al Jazeera, January 24, 2014. http://america.aljazeera.com/articles/2014/1/24/does-a-controversialdiagnosishelpfathersdodgeabusecharges.html.

Stewart, Susan D. 1999. "Disneyland Dads, Disneyland Moms?: How Nonresident Parents Spend Time With Absent Children." *Journal of Family Issues* 20 (4): 539–556.

Stewart, Abigail J., and Andrea L. Dottolo. 2006. "Feminist Psychology." *Signs* 31 (2): 493–509.

Swift, Karen. 1995. *Manufacturing "Bad Mothers": A Critical Perspective on Child Neglect.* Toronto: University of Toronto Press.

"Tender Years Doctrine" Abolished, S.C. Code Ann. § 63-15-10. (This document is current through chapters 113-140 of the Second Regular Session.)

Thompson, Derek. 2011. "Women Are More Responsible with Money, Studies Show." *Atlantic*, January 31, 2011. https://www.theatlantic.com/business/archive/2011/01/women-are-more-responsible-with-money-studies-show/70539/.

Thorne, Barrie. 1987. "Re-visioning Women and Social Change: Where Are the Children?" *Gender and Society* 1 (1): 85–109.

——. 1993. *Gender Play: Girls and Boys in School.* New Brunswick, NJ: Rutgers University Press.

Tiefer, Leonore. 1991. "A Brief History of the Association for Women in Psychology." *Psychology of Women Quarterly* 15 (4): 635–649.

——. 2009. *A Brief History of the Association for Women in Psychology, Part II.* Association for Women in Psychology. https://www.awpsych.org/docs/AWP-Herstory-Part-2-1991-2008.pdf.

Tilly, Chris. 1990. *Short Hours, Short Shrift.* Washington, DC: Economic Policy Institute.

Tippins and Wittmann. 2005. Empirical and Ethical Problems with Custody Recommendations: A Call for Clinical Humility and Judicial Vigilance. *Family Court Review*, 43: 193–222.

Turner, Kimberly J., and Maureen R. Waller. 2017. "Indebted Relationships: Child Support Arrears and Nonresident Fathers' Involvement with Children." *Journal of Marriage and Family* 79 (1): 24–43.

Uhlmann, Eric Luis, and Geoffrey L. Cohen. 2005. "Constructed Criteria: Redefining Merit to Justify Discrimination." *Psychological Science* 16 (6): 474–480.

US Bureau of the Census. 2015. "Wives' Earnings Make Gains Relative to Husbands', Census Bureau Reports." Release Number CB15-199, November 23, 2015. https://www.census.gov/newsroom/press-releases/2015/cb15-199.html.

——. 2018. *Quarterly Residential Vacancies and Homeownership, Second Quarter 2018.* Release Number CB18-107. https://www.census.gov/housing/hvs/files/qtr218/Q218press.pdf.

US Department of Justice. n.d. "Domestic Violence." Accessed April 22, 2020. https://www.justice.gov/ovw/domestic-violence.

Venn, Susan, Sara Arber, Robert Meadows, and Jenny Hislop. 2008. "The Fourth Shift: Exploring the Gendered Nature of Sleep Disruption among Couples with Children." *British Journal of Sociology* 59 (1): 79–97.

Vissing, Helena. 2014. "The Ideal Mother Fantasy and Its Protective Function." In *Intensive Mothering: The Cultural Contradictions of Modern Motherhood*, edited by Linda Rose Ennis, 104–119. Bradford, ON: Demeter.

Waldfogel, Jane. 1997. "The Effect of Children on Women's Wages." *American Sociological Review* 62 (2): 209–217.

Walzer, Susan. 1996. "Thinking about the Baby: Gender and Divisions of Infant Care." *Social Problems* 43 (2): 219–234.

West, Candace, and Don Zimmerman. 1987. "Doing Gender." *Gender and Society* 1 (2): 125–151.

Wiegers, Wanda Anne, and Michaela Keet. 2008. "Collaborative Family Law and Gender Inequalities: Balancing Risks and Opportunities." *Osgoode Hall Law Journal* 46 (4): 733–772.

Wigginton, Britta, and Michelle N. Lafrance. 2016. "How Do Women Manage the Spoiled Identity of a 'Pregnant Smoker'? An Analysis of Discursive Silencing in Women's Accounts." *Feminism and Psychology* 26 (1): 30–51.

Williams, Joan. 2000. *Unbending Gender: Why Family and Work Conflict and What to Do about It.* Oxford: Oxford University Press.

Winkler, Celia. 2014. "Redefining Single Motherhood: The 1990s Child Support Discourse and the Dismantling of the U.S. Welfare State." In *Mothering in the Age of Neoliberalism*, edited by Melinda Vandenbeld Giles, 255–277. Butler, ON: Demeter.

Winnicott, Donald W. 1960. "The Theory of the Parent-Infant Relationship." *International Journal of Psycho-analysis* 41:585–595.

Worell, Judith. 2000. "Feminism in Psychology: Revolution or Evolution?" *Annals of the American Academy of Political and Social Science* 571 (1): 183–196.

Yavorsky, Jill E., Claire M. Kamp Dush, and Sara J. Schoppe-Sullivan. 2015. "The Production of Inequality: The Gender Division of Labor across the Transition to Parenthood." *Journal of Marriage and Family* 77 (3): 662–679.

Index

CPSIA information can be obtained
at www.ICGtesting.com
Printed in the USA
LVHW030331110321
681111LV00006B/251

9 781501 754302